T0245731

JAMES LONGMAN

THE INHERITED MIND

A STORY OF FAMILY, HOPE, AND THE GENETICS OF MENTAL ILLNESS

HYPERION AVENUE
LOS ANGELES NEW YORK

First Edition, January 2025
10 9 8 7 6 5 4 3 2 1
FAC-004510-24297
Printed in the United States of America

This book is set in Chronicle and Gotham
Designed by Amy C. King

All photographs courtesy of James Longman, except the following: Page 70 (middle): Photograph by Drew Pulley/ABC; Page 70 (bottom): Photograph courtesy of BBC News; Pages 133 (middle and bottom), 182 (top), 252 (top left): Photographs by Andrew Leo; Page 104 (bottom): Photograph courtesy of ABC News; Page 133 (top left): Photograph by Angus Hines/ABC; Page 252 (top right): Photograph by Nicky de Blois/ABC; Page 252 (middle center): Photograph by Scott Munro/ABC; Page 252 (bottom right): Photograph by Sohel Uddin/ABC; Page 252 (middle left): Photograph by Juan Renteria/ABC; Page 252 (bottom left): Photograph by Jasmine Brown/ABC

Library of Congress Control Number: 2024935487
ISBN 978-1-368-09947-9
Reinforced binding

www.HyperionAvenueBooks.com

Logo Applies to Text Stock Only

CONTENTS

INTRODUCTION

"ISIS is coming!"

Not exactly the words you want to be woken up with at four in the morning in the Syrian Desert. I often prefer something like "We've got some Turkish coffee going" or, better yet, "Don't worry, just go back to sleep." But on this occasion, I was roused by my news team's military escort banging frantically on the windows of our news van. I use the term "military escort" loosely—he had been hired by the Kurdish and Arab forces fighting ISIS to look after journalists on the front line, but it was safe to assume he had no formal training whatsoever. I guessed he was about seventeen or eighteen, only because I couldn't imagine someone younger would have been supplied a weapon. Actually, thinking about it now, he was probably a preteen. Clad in his too-baggy uniform, he continued screaming, hitting our windows with a dilapidated AK-47. The team was up in seconds.

I should probably rewind a couple of days. It was March 2019, and I was with my ABC colleagues—producer Sohel Uddin and cameraman Jamie Baker—in southeastern Syria. We had been assigned to report on what was being dubbed "the fall of ISIS." Down near the Euphrates, toward the Iraq border, life in these rural areas had been relatively simple during peacetime. But the ISIS cancer had embedded itself deeply here, and coalition forces had almost entirely obliterated the place in their attempts to regain this last bastion of terrorist territory. Day after day, we'd drive through towns that had been reduced to rubble and mud. We'd rush past the blurred faces of damp and dirty children playing with discarded bits of metal, wearing clothes that likely hadn't been changed in months. Bleak doesn't even begin to describe it.

Finally, we arrived in Baghouz, the so-called "last ISIS town," where the endgame between the terrorists and the West would play out. This was the middle of nowhere, an endless barren landscape peppered with strips of the same types of squat, gray, and unfinished concrete buildings you often see in this part of the world. We found a spot behind a shelled-out building about a mile from the front line, where we hoped our van would be safe from gunfire. We needed a spot high enough for *Good Morning America* and *World News Tonight* viewers to see what was going on behind us, but safe enough to avoid becoming targets ourselves. The boy in uniform posted there for our protection waved vaguely at the building and said, "Don't go in buildings, because bombs. Stairs okay." His warnings were spot-on: Two weeks after we left the area, a member of another news team went into one of the rooms of that same building in search of a bathroom, and stepped on an IED.

The bombing campaign would start not long after nightfall. For hours we watched what looked like giant orange and yellow fireflies streaking through the air, then disappearing above us. We'd turn to each other, our faces unsure and purple in the silent gloom. Seconds later, a faint wind would kick dust into our eyes, and through it we'd see the massive, white-hot explosion in the distance.

In moments like this, the rivalry that exists between competing news networks melts away. Even though the CNN team had the best position, we all huddled together to take in the spectacle like it was some twisted, deadly fireworks display. We'd catch a couple of hours of sleep in our van, then go back up on the roof of the shelled-out building as daylight broke to watch for movement.

"Here, take a look through these." The CNN cameraman passed me his binoculars, and, sure enough, I could see ISIS fighters standing on rooftops and walking around between buildings. I watched one clean his teeth. He was very thorough.

"If we can see them, surely they can see us?" I asked, a little surprised they were so close.

"They don't want to waste their bullets" came the chilling reply.

At this point in my career, I was thirty-three years old, and I'd been at ABC for nearly two years. I'd reported from all kinds of places—many of them pretty dodgy—and I'd got into my share of scrapes. In Syria, as a naïve twenty-four-year-old covering the protest movement of 2011 for British newspapers, I'd almost been caught at a government checkpoint. I'd been at the scenes of terror attacks across Europe where gunmen had been on the loose. I'd been at far-right rallies with skinheads brandishing swastikas and other deeply disturbing symbols. But this was perhaps the most immediate danger I'd faced. I don't think it's danger itself that drives me to do this work, although there's certainly an adrenaline rush. I do have colleagues for whom that is an essential thrill. For me, it's more about being in a place where something truly consequential is happening. The world is watching remotely, but I'm *actually there*. I'm seeing it, breathing it, living it.

And in these moments, you see what humans are capable of. Yes, the harm and the malice. But also the extraordinary bravery and goodness and grace. I will never forget the story of one man I met in Paris, whose wife was killed in the 2015 Bataclan terror attacks. He wrote a letter to her murderers, forgiving them. We asked him to read his words to our cameras, and the video became one of the most-watched videos the BBC has ever produced. Or the story of Alina and Andriy, a young couple I met in Ukraine in the spring of 2023. When the war with Russia broke out, twenty-seven-year-old Andriy answered the call to serve. Not long after signing up as a drone operator, a mortar round hit him almost directly. He lost both arms, his sight, and part of his hearing. A tragic story. But his young wife, Alina, was the focus of our piece: her immediate rush to his side, hundreds of miles away in the muddy trenches; her decision to live with him in the hospital during his recovery, becoming his eyes, ears, and hands; her complete commitment to the man she loved. These are stories of immense courage in the face of profound anguish, and they taught me something important about my work: People want hope, not despair. And being part of that—bringing moments of hope to what would otherwise be completely hopeless situations—is what motivates me.

But back to our frosty desert morning, and the hysterical shouting from outside the news van. Through our escort's hyperventilating, we managed to establish that fighters had been seen escaping the nearby town and heading into the field in front of our position. Like rats being smoked out of their holes, they'd scattered, and now they were coming right for us. We had minutes to get away. In a rather surreal series of events, we soon discovered that the rope securing our huge satellite in place was stuck, and I found myself trying to convince the driver, who hadn't really clocked the seriousness of the situation, that we might in fact have to leave the satellite behind and *get in the van!* Before we made our escape, a member of our team rushed up to the roof of the building to tell CNN what we'd heard. They decided to stay.

Now, years later, it is still not clear to me whether or not ISIS did in fact arrive. If they did, they thankfully didn't trouble anyone on that roof. I was hugely relieved to see Ben Wedeman, CNN's correspondent, on television the next day. I would later learn that their team remained on that broken-down roof for a total of fifty days, surviving on canned tuna, crackers, and adrenaline. An incredible feat, and a testament to their bravery.

Without the demands of continuous news coverage, my own team's work there was done, and so we headed back north. The lack of cell service in Syria is rivaled perhaps only by that of my living room, and it was only once we got back to our accommodations near the northern border with Iraq that my phone buzzed back to life with messages. Colleagues and friends imploring me to stay safe. Viewers sharing our work on social media. Messages from people I'd long lost touch with who'd just seen us on the news.

But then I saw the messages from my mother. *I don't want to live anymore. You've inherited the Longman curse. You're sick like your father.*

The "sickness" she was referring to is my father's schizophrenia, which caused him to end his life when I was nine years old. The "curse" she was talking about refers to his brother, my uncle, who also had schizophrenia, and their father, my grandfather, who also ended his life.

And the message—which I'm sure has shocked you—is a refrain I've heard for most of my life. My relationship with my mother broke down after my father's death, and attacks like these have become a feature of our relationship, spat at me in fits of rage or cried through great gulping tears. I'm used to it by now. It's part of an ongoing pattern that means I'm more at home in a news van, with literal bombs exploding nearby, than I am in a family in which every day is war.

The comments always hurt, not just because they come from a parent, but because I do have depression. I first had deeply depressive thoughts when I was in my mid-twenties, although I didn't understand what was happening to me at the time. I had been working in journalism for a few years and was still unsure if it was something I really wanted to do. With hindsight, I know this lack of direction is something many of us feel at that juncture in life. But I felt very lost. I started to lose energy and dis-associate with friends. I felt that my life was slowly unraveling, and that whatever potential I might have had was not being realized.

Things came to a head one day at work, when I had a panic attack and found myself on the curb of a London sidewalk wondering whether I should walk out into traffic. I didn't discover the details of my father's suicide until later, when I was twenty-six, but I knew about his mental illness. It made the feelings of inevitability, the sense that I was destined to follow his lead, even more profound.

Ten years later, the same deep sadness returned, and I found myself thinking about suicide again. All the milestones I thought would make me happy in those intervening years—professional success, a meaningful relationship—somehow had lost their power. It was as though they had only been a distraction from the path I was meant to walk all along. And observing my mother's own battles with depression only further reinforced the idea of genetic inevitability. While I mostly attribute the notion of the "Longman curse" to my mother's flair for hyperbolic drama, at times like this, I can't help but wonder: Could my mother be right? Does sadness run in families? Have I *inherited* mental illness?

So much of my early life has been about escaping my unconventional family and the neuroses of my childhood but never truly succeeding. My mother is part Lebanese, and I grew up surrounded by Arab culture. I decided I wanted to live in the Middle East, so I opted for a degree in Arabic. During my studies I developed a love affair with Syria, and when the war there started, my knowledge of the country became an asset. At twenty-four, I started reporting undercover for British newspapers and providing access for TV news networks. I did consider other routes, like diplomacy and further academic study. But there was something freeing about journalism. I wanted to make my own decisions and be my own person. It felt to me that a great injustice was happening in President Assad's war on his own people, and my instinct told me that the quickest way to "help"—in that incredibly naïve sense you have when you're starting out in journalism—was to meet people who were suffering, and to tell their stories.

When it became too dangerous to continue on my own, I took a job at Sky News and then at the BBC, where I stayed for five years, eventually becoming the corporation's correspondent in Beirut. I then joined ABC News as a foreign correspondent with a much wider brief, and I've since traveled to more than sixty countries to report on all kinds of stories: everything from wars in Syria, Ukraine, and Gaza, to LGBTQ+ abuses in Uganda, to helicopter rides to the Mount Everest base camp. For one rather strange year I tracked the coronavirus across Europe and farther afield while much of the rest of the world was on lockdown. The unpredictable nature of my work means I'm often just sitting down for dinner in London when I get a last-minute call to head to the airport.

Mania seems to work for me; I've long been attracted to chaos. But I've also come to realize that chaos seems to be inside me all the time. I wonder how much of that feeling is actually burnt into my DNA. Was this chaos instilled in me as a child, or does it go further back than that? Are there generations of chaos that are not just family eccentricities, but scientific inevitabilities? We all obsess over our physical health, and what we may or may not have inherited from our parents. History of heart disease? Stroke? Any cancer in the family? We hear these questions every time we get routine checkups. But I have only once been asked about my family's mental health history during a doctor's visit.

Before we go any further, I want to make something clear. There is absolutely nothing uncontroversial about the study of mental illness. Every term, every area of research, every corner of this field is hotly debated and has been since the earliest days of psychiatric discovery. Even the word *schizophrenia* itself is a label that not everyone agrees on. It's been defined, redefined, and subcategorized over and over again. It is a condition that, in some ways, lies at the heart of the study of human psychology. A lot of people who know much more than I do have been trying to understand it for decades, and I realize that my effort to understand how we might "inherit" a mental illness like this may, to some people, sound misguided. There are many researchers who feel that focusing on outcomes and treatments is a better use of time and resources than continuing an endless debate about the reasons we feel the way we do. They want, rightly, to find ways to help people live happier and healthier lives.

Well, I want to do that, too. I want to contribute to a better understanding of these illnesses, and I'm putting my dad at the heart of it, as well as many other people with their own unique experiences. This book is intended, in part, to humanize the word *schizophrenia*. It's a heavy word, isn't it? It's come to mean so much in our society. It connotes insanity, unpredictability, multiple personalities, and hallucinations. We think if someone has schizophrenia, they are beyond help: broken, unfixable, dangerous. I hope to show you that none of that is true.

This book will focus on three specific mental illnesses: schizophrenia and related psychotic illness, bipolar disorder, and clinical depression. It is tempting to see them as existing on some kind of spectrum that starts with depression and ends in schizophrenia. That is not true. They are separate conditions, and one does not "become" one of the others. But I'll be speaking to people with each of these conditions, because they can manifest in similar ways, and because the nascent genetic studies this book will explore show that there is some overlap between them.

In his book *The Heartland,* Nathan Filer writes, "There is another part of the thing we call 'mental illness' that will forever exist beyond the reach of statistical analysis, probabilities and distribution curves, or otherworldly pictures of neurochemical imaging. It is the person. It is their story." I agree wholeheartedly. But I also think finding biological patterns, and how they interact with our experiences, is more than worthwhile.

Filer also points out that medical definitions of mental illness are extremely unreliable and have changed repeatedly over time. The *Diagnostic and Statistical Manual of Mental Disorders* (*DSM*) is considered a bible of sorts for the diagnosis of mental illness. It's intended as a kind of handbook for doctors in the United States and the United Kingdom so that treatment of these conditions can be as consistent as possible. But its first edition—published in the 1970s—listed homosexuality as a mental illness. Incidentally, I am gay. According to that manual, I would have been considered mentally unstable and likely recommended for treatment. That edition was clearly a product of its time, but it makes clear that we should approach any conclusions that are drawn today with healthy skepticism. Current research into the genetics of mental health is *also* a product of our time; it reflects a focus on new brain-mapping technologies, neuroscientific breakthroughs, and the endless possibilities that seemed to emerge with the discovery of the genome.

Even with all these caveats, I think the study of mental illness is fascinating, and I want you to discover some of its most exciting advancements alongside me. I'm going to share my family's story with you, and along the way try to translate the often-complicated medical and scientific jargon into something more digestible.

We all know, at least on an anecdotal level, that our family histories and experiences shape the people we become. But I want to better understand what might be happening on a *biological* level. As I set out to do research for this book, I decided on four broad issues to investigate.

FIRST: Is there something in our DNA that affects our mental health? If so, what exactly is it? How does it work?

SECOND: Do environmental factors impact these genetic traits? If so, how and how much?

THIRD: Can the experiences and traumas of our parents be passed down genetically?

And finally, and perhaps most importantly: Can we find ways to thrive through all of this, and if so, how?

Because they affect the brain, these mental illnesses are often presented as purely thought conditions, as issues that exist purely in the mind. But they are so much more than that. The genetics of depression, bipolar disorder, and schizophrenia is a complex field, and epigenetics—the study of how our genes can be impacted by our environment and trauma specifically—is a relatively new one. But I'm going to have a go at explaining it anyway, with the help of psychiatrists and geneticists doing extraordinary work. And you'll hear from all kinds of people who are living with some of these conditions, too.

Among the many people in my dad's life who I've been able to track down for this book are some of his art school friends. They paint a vivid picture of his student days, during which he became heavily involved in the Transcendental Meditation movement of the 1960s. After his studies, he went to live in Switzerland to join its founder, Maharishi Mahesh Yogi. There is an emerging body of science that is starting to explore links between intense meditation and psychosis. In writing this book not only have I discovered how closely linked my dad was to the origins of this spiritual movement—which remains hugely popular today—I have also discovered how his first psychotic episode may have been triggered in some way by some of the extreme meditation practices at the time. Experts in this area will explain what happens in the brain when the push to access the subconscious goes too far.

I have also had some incredibly emotional reunions with some of the people who helped my father through his illness. His medical notes were released to me, and I was able to track down his support worker and clinical nurse—two people who not only helped him, but demonstrate in a wider sense how important compassion and kindness are in the treatment of these conditions. Through sharing moments in my life, and in my father's life, and by speaking to others who have had similar experiences, I hope to show in this book how much our bodies can empower and inform us about our own personal mental health histories. We carry so much in our genetics and biology, and science has only recently begun to understand their connection to the complexities of mental well-being.

It's worth nothing that there is a trend at the moment that seems to conflate mental health with mental illness. They are not the same. We all have mental health needs, because we all have brains. But we will not all develop clinical depression, bipolar disorder, schizophrenia, or any of the related conditions that can provoke psychosis, delusions, or hallucinations. The blurring of these lines seems to me to depathologize mental illness as a whole, which conversely has allowed us to marginalize those with the kinds of conditions that a walk in the park or a mental health day are not going to solve. Establishing that reality is a foundational truth of this book.

Another preoccupation of the book is that we may have genetic histories that our behaviors can unlock. In much the same way as a history of heart disease may make you more predisposed to illness but does not definitively predict it, the development of a mental illness is not inevitable, if you change your habits. So I'd like to really know—as much as it's possible right now—what may be going on in my body, and how it affects how I feel. Because we humans *do* have an extraordinary capacity to heal. As one doctor told me for this book, "The brain is where psychology and biology meet." There are things we are born with, and there are things we learn. Which means we might also *un*learn bad habits and behaviors, wherever they originated. And that gives me hope.

I know this will be difficult, not least because I'm practically innumerate and was absolutely useless at science and math in school. So I'll be doing my best to work this science out on the page, asking experts to explain difficult concepts at a glacial pace, and showing you that perhaps you don't have to be a molecular biologist to find all of this useful, too. What this book will *not* do is provide an exhaustive summary of mental illness statistics from every corner of the earth. Instead, you will note occasional references to mental illness in the United Kingdom and in the United States. The reason for this focus is simple: I live in the UK, I work in American television, and much of the research I highlight in this book is being developed in these two countries.

For some people, knowing they've "inherited" depression or some other mental illness might not be particularly useful. But I've always wanted answers. Perhaps that's why I became a journalist. Making sense of my own brain, and what my life experiences may have done to it, is helpful because it means I can treat these issues with the kind of logic that depression can often take away from you. It's also exciting to think about what a better medical understanding of mental illness might mean for how we treat it in the future. If my dad were alive today, I'd like to think he'd have a wider range of options for treatment. Perhaps someday soon, with better scientific knowledge of the brain and its genetic patterns, someone with his condition will be far better understood—and accepted—by society.

This book is also the story of how I rediscovered my father—what he left me, what I'm still missing. What I need to hold on to and what I don't. My journey of coming to terms with his loss.

This book is for anyone who's felt down and wondered why. It's for anyone who has a tricky relationship with their family, but perhaps feels torn between anger and loyalty. It's for anyone who has been in a dark place, or knows someone who has, and wants a better understanding of how our brains are wired. And if you're someone who just thinks from time to time about life and death and our place in all of it, then this book is for you, too.

My hope is that you'll come away with an appreciation of how mental health patterns work in families, and what the very latest science is telling us about them. You're going to hear from specialists and experts, but also regular people who've perhaps had experiences similar to your own. Researching the exciting new world of mental health genetics has really helped me feel better about my life. Put simply, I don't feel so alone anymore, and I hope reading this book will do the same for you.

Ann and John Longman at their wedding in 1985. (top)

Ann and John on vacation in 1987. (middle)

John with newborn James. (bottom)

CHAPTER 1

A SUICIDE IN THE FAMILY

We all carry, inside us, people who came before us.

—LIAM CALLANAN, *THE CLOUD ATLAS*

I have few memories that are more vivid. I was nine years old, and it was a cold autumn evening at school. The dayroom was deserted aside from me and a friend, rolling around on the floor. I wasn't a fat child, but I've always liked to eat, and I was definitely bigger than the other kids my age. I had blond hair parted down the middle and a round little face, cheeks red from the excitement of our play-fight. From the corner of my eye, I saw my housemaster appear, looking rather solemn-faced.

"James, can you come here, please?"

My heart sank. I hated getting into trouble and thought for sure I was in for it. I remember immediately pretending we hadn't been doing anything wrong. I got up quickly and followed Mr. Owers to his office so I could explain myself.

He sat on his swivel chair, and as it sank beneath his weight with a soft hissing sound, he looked at me with his big gray eyes. “There’s been an accident,” he said.

Instant confusion. I realized he wasn’t talking about me.

Mr. Owers was a large man who moved slowly. I regarded him as a kind of friendly giant. He radiated kindness, and when I think of my early school days, I picture my friends and me as small woodland creatures, while he was a kind of large magical bear who’d vowed to protect us. With his big worker’s hands, he reached across his desk for a tissue for the tears he thought would come.

“I’m afraid it’s your dad, son. I’m so sorry.” His voice was a soft rumble, like a distant train. “There was nothing they could do.”

I stared at him, unsure of what he meant. He proffered the tissue, but I didn’t need it. “What do you mean?”

There was a silence. And then: “He’s died, James.”

I don’t know if I voiced it or just felt it, but I remember utter disbelief. I’d seen my father only the weekend before. How was that possible? How could a person be here one day and gone forever the next? It was completely inconceivable to my young mind. “Mum’s here,” Mr. Owers said, trying to sound cheerful. “She’s with Matron. Come with me?”

He got up and ushered me out of his office. The dayroom felt strangely busy now, bright and hot in a way it hadn’t been before. My winter sweater felt way too thick. I could feel tears in my eyes. As I walked behind Mr. Owers, I concentrated on his feet. His brown shoes against the blue carpet. Stopping at a door, a corridor. Another corridor. The fluorescent lights were too vivid. I avoided eye contact with anyone we passed. I didn’t want them to see me cry.

Matron's flat was just off the main dormitory wing. My mother was waiting there in a dimly lit sitting room, on a cream sofa. She'd been crying. She pulled me toward her instantly. I could smell alcohol on her breath. There are some things you will never forget—I think my mother being drunk the night I was told my father had died is among my most powerful memories. She started crying hysterically, asking if I was okay, hugging me tight. I sat on her lap, my feet not quite touching the floor. "I'm okay," I kept repeating, more worried about her than myself. I was all at once confused and embarrassed and desperate for the moment to pass quickly.

I don't remember the rest of that evening. It was decided that I would stay at school. Anyone I've told that to since says it sounds cruel—to leave your only son at school after he's been given news like this. But I think it was the right decision. I wanted to stay, if only so I wouldn't have to deal with my mother. It must have been heartbreaking for her to leave me behind that evening, but I think she also knew it was the best place for me in that moment. Life at home had been unpredictable at best—the whole reason I was at boarding school was to give me some stability. So, in this most destabilizing moment, it was the obvious place to be. And I loved school. I'd always felt comfortable there. No one told me how my father had died, just that there'd been a fire. And again, that "there was nothing they could do."

The next few days were a strange blur. Everyone went out of their way to be kind to me, but there was a definite sense of walking on eggshells. I shared a room with five other boys—two single beds sat in the middle of the room, with bunk beds at each end. My bed was one of the top bunks, and I had virtually covered it in stuffed animals. I had a monkey from one of my grandmothers and a bear from the other. And I had a long green snake from my dad that I called Jake. Up in the safety of my top bunk, it was only at night that I would allow myself to cry, with Jake wrapped around my arm.

I remember the morning of the funeral most clearly. It was to be held on a weekday, and so I was to be taken out of lessons and to the country, to my grandmother's house, where the wake would be. That morning, I put on my blazer and went down to breakfast.

Children are funny—they forget some things almost instantly. All through the morning, friends bounded up to me asking, "Why are you in Sunday best, James?" Anything remotely out of the ordinary at a school like ours was of deep interest to everyone, and wearing a blazer on a weekday was headline stuff. "It's my father's funeral today," I quietly replied. Silence.

I shuffled through my first few periods, trying to avoid any difficult stares. And then it was double art, from which I would have to leave early. In came Mr. Owers, trying to look cheerful in his black suit and tie. He spoke quietly to my art teacher, and they gestured kindly for me to come forward. The room was silent as I took off my overall and replaced it with the blazer. I could feel my classmates' eyes on me as I signaled that I was ready to go.

The car was parked across the road, and when we were halfway to it, Mr. Owers's hand gripped my shoulder. I stopped to look up at him; he pointed back to the art block. I remember it being a bright sunny day, and I had to squint to see through its two large windows. I could see the whole class waving at me. "Good luck, James!" I heard them shout, climbing over one another to make sure I could see them all. Individually, my classmates had been understandably unable to find the words to comfort me. But as a group, they could. I'll always remember their smiling faces in that window.

At the funeral, I felt very small. There were lots of people there, and

I remember wondering who they all were, huddled in the musty, damp air of this English country church. I wondered why I hadn't seen any of them when my father was alive. I sat on a pew at the front and listened as my aunt read a poem, her voice an echo against the ancient stone. It was something about my father finally being free, and I thought it seemed odd to be saying something like that at a funeral. Still, no one told me that my father had started the fire himself.

The nine-year-old in that church didn't know this at the time, but my dad was diagnosed at various times in his life with schizophrenia, schizoaffective disorder, and psychotic personality disorder. By the time I was three years old, his illness was so bad that my parents separated. My mother says she was scared to leave him on his own with me, and that he would often disappear for days at a time.

Because of these absences, my memories of him are patchy. Perhaps it's natural to romanticize someone you love who has died. Kurt Gray and Daniel Wegner's book *The Mind Club* describes the phenomenon: "Not only do people's moral characters freeze at death, but we also tend to exaggerate who they were—the good becoming truly heroic, and the bad becoming truly evil."

For me, my father has become a hero, however unheroic he might have been during his life. When I was a kid, the scraps of memory were woven into an almost completely imaginary person—universally good, and beyond reproach. As I grew older, my memory of him weakened, and as my own battles with mental illness appeared, it became diluted and compromised. What remains is a far murkier picture than the one I held on to in my childhood. But his fundamental goodness still shines through to me, decades after his death.

John Longman was an artist, and he had that slightly unkempt bohemian look, which I always thought was so cool. He had an effortless charm:

denim jeans and Doc Martens, hands jammed firmly in his pockets, one leg crossed under the other as he leaned against a wall or doorway. I remember his shock of silver hair (which I haven't yet inherited) and his smirk (which my friends tell me I have). I remember long walks around London on his shoulders, and the patch of yellow between his fingers from his endless roll-up cigarettes. I remember the math homework he'd take great pleasure in doing for me, and I remember the scratchy touch of his stubbly chin as I sat close to him while he did it. I remember huge bowls of cereal with lots of milk, and his massive homemade bed, which I would hide under when we played hide-and-seek in his flat. I remember his bare feet, and his utter disregard for material things. I remember full ashtrays and old brushes in dried-out jam jars caked with oil paint. I remember his quiet moments and I remember his humor—dark and eccentric, occasionally slapstick, and always self-deprecating. The laugh that would change his whole face, so you could see the shiny silver fillings at the back of his mouth. I remember his love of making things—he was so good with his hands. He had a particular gift for making paper airplanes, and in some of my last moments with him, I remember folding them on the roof of the house, sitting together and watching the planes dip and bob their way down to the pavement below.

I don't remember precisely when I was told he had ended his life, but I think it was probably said in anger at some point in my teens, in the midst of one of the fights that came to characterize my relationship with my mother. And it wasn't until I was twenty-six that I learned the full story. After a depressive episode, and thinking properly for the first time about my family's history, I pitched an idea to my BBC editor for a program about my father. As part of the research, I went to our local library to look for newspaper articles, and, sure enough, I found a few. "Blaze Room Death Leap" read the front page of the October 3, 1996, edition of the *Kensington News*. I discovered that he had not just set fire to his flat but thrown himself from the window.

In the article, an unnamed neighbor explains how angry they are that my dad seems to have been abandoned by social services. They say they had tried to get my father help repeatedly, but it had never been possible. They explain that he was hallucinating and had complained of hearing voices. He'd been to a hospital, but they didn't have space for him and so he was sent home. In the days before his death, he'd been seen in a robe out in the street.

As a journalist, I find something rather odd about seeing my own family's tragedy sensationalized in this way. I'm usually the person reporting on tragic events, rather than being reported on. It makes me wonder how everyone I've ever spoken to has responded to the TV story or written article about their lives. Seeing my father described as "a schizophrenic," rather than "a father of one" or simply "a man," highlights to me how important it is to report on people with these conditions with more compassion. I hope things have changed in the intervening years. I think they have. The *Kensington & Chelsea Mail* chose instead to focus on the failures that led to my father's death, and I am eternally grateful to his neighbor, Nicholas Hennessy—quoted in the article—who seemed genuinely angry that my father was not better looked after.

The impact of my father's death, and his absence from my life, has obviously been profound. For much of my life I simply told people he'd died in a fire, avoiding any further questions that I would find difficult. But there was always secrecy around the incident. I grew up in the top-floor flat of one of the stucco-fronted houses in Notting Hill, and I lived on Colville Road with both parents until they separated. My mother says she decided it had become too much of a liability to have my dad around the house. She says she would come home and ask where I was,

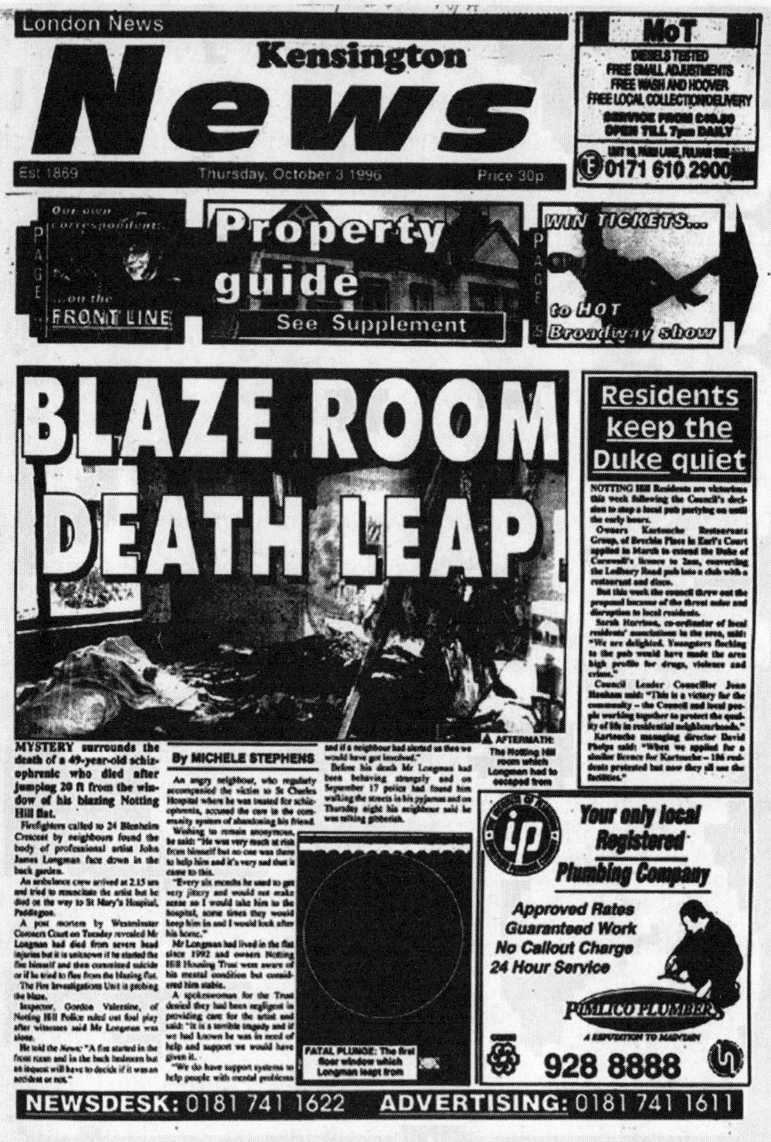

London News

Kensington News

Est 1869 Thursday, October 3 1996 Price 30p

PAGE Our own correspondent: ...on the FRONT LINE

Property guide See Supplement

PAGE WIN TICKETS... to HOT Broadway show

BLAZE ROOM DEATH LEAP

MYSTERY surrounds the death of a 49-year-old schizophrenic who died after jumping 20 ft from the window of his blazing Notting Hill flat.

Firefighters called to 24 Blenheim Crescent by neighbours found the body of professional artist John James Longman face down in the back garden.

An ambulance crew arrived at 2.15 am and tried to resuscitate the artist but he died on the way to St Mary's Hospital, Paddington.

A post mortem by Westminster Coroners Court on Tuesday revealed Mr Longman had died from severe head injuries but it is unknown if he started the fire himself and then committed suicide or if he tried to flee from the blazing flat.

The Fire Investigations Unit is probing the blaze.

Inspector, Gordon Valentine, of Notting Hill Police ruled out foul play after witnesses said Mr Longman was alone.

He told the *News*: "A fire started in the front room and in the back bedroom but an inquest will have to decide if it was an accident or not."

By MICHELE STEPHENS

An angry neighbour, who regularly accompanied the victim to St Charles Hospital where he was treated for schizophrenia, accused the care in the community system of abandoning his friend.

Wishing to remain anonymous, he said: "He was very much at risk from himself but no one was there to help him and it's very sad that it came to this.

"Every six months he used to get very jittery and would not make sense so I would take him to the hospital, some times they would keep him in and I would look after his home."

Mr Longman had lived in the flat since 1992 and owners Notting Hill Housing Trust were aware of his mental condition but considered him stable.

A spokeswoman for the Trust denied they had been negligent in providing care for the artist and said: "It is a terrible tragedy and if we had known he was in need of help and support we would have given it.

"We do have support systems to help people with mental problems and if a neighbour had alerted us then we would have got involved."

Before his death Mr Longman had been behaving strangely and on September 17 police had found him walking the streets in his pyjamas and on Thursday night his neighbour said he was talking gibberish.

▲ AFTERMATH: The Notting Hill room which Longman had to escaped from

FATAL PLUNGE: The first floor window which Longman leapt from

Residents keep the Duke quiet

NOTTING Hill Residents are victorious this week following the Council's decision to stop a local pub partying on until the early hours.

Owners Kartouche Restaurants Group, of Brechin Place in Earl's Court applied in March to extend the Duke of Cornwall's licence to 2am, converting the Ledbury Road pub into a club with a restaurant and disco.

But this week the council threw out the proposal because of the threat noise and disruption to local residents.

Sarah Harrison, co-ordinator of local residents' associations in the area, said: "We are delighted. Youngsters flocking to the pub would have made the area high profile for drugs, violence and crime."

Council Leader Councillor Joan Hanham said: "This is a victory for the community – the Council and local people working together to protect the quality of life in residential neighbourhoods."

Kartouche managing director David Phelps said: "When we applied for a similar licence for Kartouche – 186 residents protested but now they all use the facilities."

NEWSDESK: 0181 741 1622 ADVERTISING: 0181 741 1611

The front page of our local newspaper

and sometimes he wouldn't know. He would have not thought to feed me or bathe me or change my diaper.

Eventually she was too worried to leave me alone with him. So he

KENSINGTON & CHELSEA MAIL

THE ROYAL BOROUGH'S QUALITY LOCAL PAPER

'75 October 4, 1996 Tel: 0171 381 6262 Classified: 0181 579 6969 Fax: 0181 566 5525/1201 25p

INSIDE THIS WEEK – A SUPERB BARGAIN BREAK

PLEASE TURN TO PAGE 5

IS THIS REALLY CARE?

By SIMON PRITCHETT

DISTURBED man who set re to his Notting Hill flat nd plunged to his death om a window was a vic- m of the failure of care in e community, a neighbour as claimed.

ohn Longman, 49, of Blenheim escent, was a former patient of St aarles' Hospital in North nsington.

He had a long history of psychi- ric illness dating back to the 70s.

Police believe he deliberately set e to a makeshift bed, locked him- f in his flat, and jumped out of his cond floor window on Friday last week. Next door neighbour Nicholas Hennessy claimed the dead man was a schizophrenic who needed full time care.

He branded community care "a disgrace".

He said: "I took him to St Charles' Hospital a couple of times, and he's returned home before me.

"They didn't have any beds for him. He was in a bad way. He should have been in hospital full-time.

"On Tuesday last week the police found him wandering the streets wearing only a bath robe.

"I have lost a good neighbour. He was a properly trained artist and had plenty of talent. I feel very sorry for him."

Fire crews from North Kensington attended the fire at 2.15am and called police to the terraced house's back garden where Mr Longman was found.

He suffered serious injuries in his fall and was taken to St Mary's Hospital, Praed Street, Paddington, where he was pronounced dead at 3.35am.

Detective Inspector Gordon Valentine of Notting Hill police said: "The fire appears to have been started deliberately.

"He set fire to a makeshift bed. He locked himself in and jumped out of the window."

A spokeswoman for the dead man's landlords, the Notting Hill Housing Trust, said that the man had been living there since 1992.

She said: "We were aware that he had had certain mental health problems in the past, but at the time he was stable.

"Had we been made aware that this man was in need of help and support we would have been there for him."

A spokeswoman for Parkside Health NHS Trust, which manages St Charles' Hospital, said Mr Longman was an outpatient of the Exmoor Street hospital's mental health unit at the time of his death.

He was last admitted to a hospital bed in April last year.

She said: "He came to see a senior consultant on a regular basis for treatment.

"We are confident that the senior consultant would have admitted Mr Longman had he felt he needed re-admitting.

"Ninety-nine per cent of our patients at the mental health unit are actually outpatients admitted as and when it's felt necessary."

She added: "Since the inquest into his death has not yet taken place, there's no clear evidence to suggest that Mr Longman took his own life."

The dead man lived alone. He was a divorced father. No-one else is being sought in connection with his death. Anyone with information can call Det Insp Valentine on 0181 246 0191.

INSIDE

OLICE chiefs warn residents of ew terrorism threat ....page 3

re we at risk from the food at we eat? Readers' opinions ....page 4

hat sight made the dinosaurs ush? ....page 5

ctagon owner consults his wyers – *Grapevine* ....page 7

Help! It's the laddy in red!

STICK 'em up! Four-year-old Kensington Kindergarten pupil Thomas Evans got his marksman's eye in at the harvest festival carnival in Elizabeth Street, Belgravia. Organised by The Belgravia Traders Association, it raised £11,000 for Greycoat Hospital School, Eaton Square School and The Renton Foundation, a charity for the mentally handicapped, whose patron Norma Major judged the fancy dress. The event attracted 1,500 people. Local restaurants provided food and drink.

PO pledge

POST office bosses have told residents their Kensington Church Street branch will not move. More than 30 customers were at a public meeting at Kensington Town Hall on Monday to hear from Post Office Counters. Despite the pledge, neighbours still have doubts. Retired singer Stella Wright, who has lived in Linden Gardens for 40 years, said: "I'm not 100 per cent convinced."

Carnival noise

BOOMING sound systems drove residents to despair and trapped them in their homes during this year's Notting Hill carnival.

And a council helpline set up to tell residents the location of sound systems was frequently unmanned and unhelpful over the August Bank Holiday, neighbours have claimed.

Complaints about noise topped a long list of grievances voiced by residents at a rowdy post-carnival meeting at Kensington Town Hall on Tuesday.

The most extreme opponents wanted it moved to Hyde Park.

Carnival organisers were also urged to extend the processional route as far as Holland Park, to employ more environmental health officers to crack down on illegal street traders, and to provide more loos.

Royal Borough environmental health officer Peter Ramage told residents the number of sound systems had been reduced from more than 150 in 1989 to 45 this year.

Another local paper asked how the death could have happened

moved to a small apartment around the corner. He was a bit of a recluse, and the Notting Hill apartment had been his haven for more than ten years. Moving around the corner to a new flat on Blenheim Crescent—this one supplied by the government—must have been a massive shock to his mental well-being.

Now that I know about him jumping from the window, the building has a sinister feel about it. If I'm going by in a car, I always crane my neck to see the spot from the window. If walking nearby, I'll change my route to make sure I can walk along the pavement immediately outside, and I'll try to picture the scene. It's almost like visiting a cemetery. But this is the place where he died, and there is nothing sacred about it for anyone else. Dogs are walked, buses are run for, children are chased by their friends. Each paving stone as inconsequential as the next. But for me it's the place where my father's life ended, and mine changed immeasurably.

Matt Haig's *How to Stop Time* is one of my favorite books. It's a historical fantasy about a group of people who live for centuries but must grapple with the same questions of love and loss that all regular people must deal with. Like so much of Haig's work, it is a creative take on mortality and the human condition, and his words sum up my father's last day for me: "That's the thing with time, isn't it? It's not all the same. Some days—some years—some decades—are empty. There is nothing to them. It's just flat water. And then you come across a year, or even a day, or an afternoon. And it is everything. It is the whole thing."

That single moment on Blenheim Crescent has become "the whole thing" for me. There is not a day I don't think about him, or it. Not a doubt or sadness I have that I don't wonder is linked to him in some way. Not a person I come across I don't imagine what he would make of, nor a place I go I don't imagine him in. Sometimes when I'm in the kitchen, I glance over toward the sitting room and imagine him lying on the sofa, cigarette hanging from one side of his mouth, squinting through the smoke at some book or other.

I wonder what he would make of my life. Of my job and my friends. I think about him meeting my husband, Alex, and spending time in our house. He was a total hippie and a definite rebel, so I know he would have been accepting of me as a gay man. Before he met my mother, he had spent ten years living in Europe following the practices of Maharishi Mahesh Yogi, the founder of Transcendental Meditation. He was interested in science, in philosophy, and in spirituality. He was a deep thinker with an open soul, and I found not having him around when I was struggling with my sexuality very hard. I've already said how much we romanticize the dead, and the truth is I have no idea what it would have been like. But in my heart, I feel he would have been a loving ally even while my mother took her time to accept how she felt about having a gay son.

I worry my life is too shiny for him. I don't know if he'd be proud. In *The Mind Club*, Wegner and Gray explain how humans have a hard time believing the mind can die when the body is no longer here. My father's mind is still here, still thinking, still judging... although I know, really, he was not a judgmental person. But I do worry he'd think I have too much stuff, too much time for material things. When dating my mother, he would take all the belongings from his apartment every few months and just leave them on the street below, she said. Was that part of his illness? Or a lesson in modesty and restraint I badly need? If he were here, would I be better?

Because of the fire, much of what he did own is lost. When his mother died, she left me my favorite painting of his. It's a simple scene in oil: a living room in light greens and blues with a large window and open shutters. He captures the light so beautifully. One solitary chair sits to the right of center, its faint shadow cast across the floor. There is a stillness and serenity to it that he clearly missed for much of his life. It sits above my fireplace to remind me of his simplicity. It's made all the more remarkable because he would have painted it when he was only about twenty.

I have a handful of other paintings. And I have the note he wrote to my mother on their wedding day. It's the only example of his handwriting I own. He called her the Sea, and she called him the Rock. I still don't fully understand the reasons for these nicknames, but I imagine it's because my mother's natural affinity for histrionics made her unpredictable, like the sea. And my father's often quiet and withdrawn nature made him a rock. The script is not dissimilar to my own, which again makes me happy.

It reads:

To A, Love J, From the Rock, to the Sea. See you at 3 x

The last piece of him I have is his dinner suit. I don't wear it anymore because it's almost threadbare, but it hangs in my closet, and it makes me happy to know it's there. Maybe it's silly, but in my head it's kind of an old grandfather of the wardrobe, greeting my clothes as they come and bidding them farewell as they go. Animated, as though in *Beauty and the Beast,* the Dinner Suit talks to all the young shirts and trousers, and they tell him stories of what I did with my day. His name is stitched on the inside collar: *John J Longman.* The *J* was for *James.*

In *The Year of Magical Thinking,* Joan Didion explores her grief in the year following her husband's death. She is able to detach herself from the emotion of his passing in order to ask herself: "Why did I remain so unable to accept the fact that he had died? Was it because I was failing to understand it as something that had happened to him? Was it because I was still understanding it as something that had happened to me?"

This has been one of the most useful perspectives for coming to terms with my father's death. I don't think I have found it difficult to accept. But I have found it hard to separate his death from what it means for my life.

And I've felt the depressive episodes I've experienced are linked in no small part to him. In an odd way, because of his illness, he might not have been very present in my life had he lived. But because he has died—and because of the manner of his death—he has become more present. It's as though his death reanimated the genetic traits I worry he left me. Like turning on a switch from beyond the grave. Didion's words have helped me try to untangle myself from his death. But they alone haven't been enough.

In her book *Life after Suicide*, my colleague and friend Dr. Jen Ashton explains, in an extraordinarily profound way, how she found meaning after her ex-husband, Rob, ended his life. Her words spoke to me very deeply: "Grief is love. You grieve because you loved. Grief work helps you move away from the trauma of how they died to remembering how they lived, and then helps you develop a new relationship with the deceased—the death of a loved one doesn't mean the death of a relationship after all."

My father remains my father even though he has died. I am still a son. He means as much to me now as he did when he lived. He will go on being my father. His death has not stopped him from being that person. I have had occasional pangs of anger at him over the years. Some of the people Jen spoke to for her book described the same feelings. It's a natural reaction, to feel angry at someone you love for deserting you.

But I believe my father's suicide was not a choice he made in hate. It was a way out of a clinical illness over which sadly he had little control. I guess grief work, as Jen calls it, is different for everyone. My grief work has been to ensure he didn't die for no reason: to try to understand what might have caused his illness, and how I might escape it.

Berwick "Jimmy" Longman in his Naval uniform, 1930s. (top left)

Nancy Craig-Barr in Scotland, 1930s. (middle right)

Gabrielle Sawaya in her twenties in Cairo. (bottom left)

CHAPTER 2

FINDING THE TRUTH

We are braver and wiser because they existed, those strong women and strong men. . . . We are who we are because they were who they were. It's wise to know where you come from, who called your name.

—MAYA ANGELOU, *EBONY* MAGAZINE

Whenever I go into a church, I light a candle for my grandmother. My mother's mother, Gabrielle.

Gabrielle Sawaya was a young Lebanese woman in wartime Cairo when she met my New Zealander grandfather Harold Claridge at a ball for King Fuad of Egypt's birthday. She spoke French, Arabic, Greek, and Italian, but not much English. He was in Egypt fighting for the British and had been invited to represent his regiment, the Royal Engineers. But he was not a linguist. After a giggly encounter full of misunderstandings on a balcony that night, she wrote her address for him on a cigarette packet. He wrote her letters from the front lines at Alamein, and while he was away, she learned English for him.

When the war ended, they married in Cairo and moved around the Middle East in the years that followed, escaping the Ba'ath revolution in Iraq and the civil war in Lebanon before eventually settling in the UK, and into fifty years of marriage. They essentially became refugees many times over, and by the time they arrived in London they had little money. Their bond was extraordinary. My grandfather would often joke that the secret to their happiness was not being totally sure what the other was saying.

As I write this now, I realize I loved Gabrielle as perhaps the only stable, constant figure in my early life. She lived with us and was always full of love and grace. A Lebanese Christian woman, she was supremely glamorous and deeply religious. She had a huge swathe of snow-white hair and a series of silk dresses with asymmetric designs. She wore blue in May for Mary and would never go anywhere without an ample supply of red lipstick and rose water. Whenever anything was lost, up went the prayers to St. Anthony in a mixture of French and Arabic. I could only speak to her in French, but I knew I was in trouble if either she or my mother started shouting at me in Arabic. She was a wonderful cook, and I remember coming home from school and immediately being hurried out of the kitchen, where every surface was covered in vine leaves drying out, before being rolled and stuffed with meat and rice. But her real love was desserts—I get my sweet tooth from her. In fact I think because of her, all my teeth are sweet! I remember her smile at my eating her delicious ma'amoul—a date-filled pastry—and no sooner had I finished one than she was pressing another into my hand. She strung the most enormous rosary beads over her bed—each bead was the size of my head—and I was convinced that if they ever fell, they'd immediately kill anyone lying on the pillow.

She died at ninety-six, in my mother's arms at a convalescence home in the south of France. She had a wicked sense of humor and would laugh with a kind of deep chuckle that betrayed her otherwise feminine habits. She was a proud woman, with a keen sense of family tradition and loyalty. My mother had me quite late in life, which as a Lebanese mother caused Gabrielle not a small amount of distress. She would buy baby gifts and other not-so-subtle trinkets for my mother well before she became pregnant. I still have a large stuffed bear from her that I think is more than two years older than me. And she spent a long time making a christening gown for her nonexistent grandchild.

When eventually my mother announced she was having a son, Gabrielle's joy was unbounded. But not long before my mother was due, a cousin, Andre, asked to borrow the christening robe for her grandchild who was to be born before me. Consequently, the gown—which presumably by this point was so long it would have needed several people to hold the train—didn't make it back to Gabrielle in time for my own christening. My grandmother held a grudge against Andre for years. And in her final moments, after the rice recipes had been explained, and the instructions over which jewels to bury her in had been given, she leaned into my mother with a message. "Tell Andre . . ." she began. (*Ah,* my mother thought, *at last, she's letting this go.*) ". . . I will never forgive her." And then she died. I still laugh at this now.

I could always count on Gabrielle—my "grand-maman"—to try to shield me from some of the drama at home. If I'd upset my mother in some way, and provoked the crying and screaming we'd all become used to, Grand-maman would go into my mother's room to try and console her, and then come back to me to offer a knowing look and a long hug. Her role was peacemaker—between my parents, and especially between my mother and her mother-in-law. After my dad died, my mum and I moved in with Gabrielle and Harold. My mum had bought them a small apartment in Eastbourne on the south coast of England, and although we didn't share bedrooms, the setup did make me feel a bit like Charlie in a kind of Franco-Arab version of *Charlie and the Chocolate Factory*.

Harold Claridge was a very old-school kind of grandfather. I knew him as "grandpus," and I remember a few occasions when he looked up at the dinner table, noticed me sitting there, and shouted out to nobody in particular, "Children at the table?! When I was his age, I'd eat in the kitchen with the dogs!" As I grew up and he grew older, he softened. My best moments with him were at bedtime, when he used to tell me the long, entertaining adventures of two old Shire horses he'd invented, Clip and Clop.

But it wasn't all whimsical family fun. As I reached my teens, my relationship with my mother began to fall apart, with Gabrielle back in her role as peacemaker. The fights became louder and more violent, and I was no longer a small child my grandmother could console. My mother worshipped her, but I could sense Gabrielle's frustration at the seemingly endless drama. All she could do was pray. Which she did. A lot. I don't know how religious I am anymore. I often call myself culturally Catholic if anyone asks, mostly in tribute to her. As part of my work, I once traveled with the pope on his plane to Myanmar and Bangladesh and took the opportunity to tell him my grandmother would have been very proud. He took my hand and smiled warmly, as popes do, and filled my heart with memories of her.

If my mother's side of the family brought histrionics and a certain amount of international glamour, my dad's side could not have been more different. My father's parents were Nancy and Jimmy Longman. She was Scottish, the daughter of a Presbyterian clergyman, and he was a stockbroker from Hampshire. The best way for you to imagine Nancy is as a Scottish version of the late Queen Elizabeth II: immaculately turned out in long pleated skirts, with matching blouses or cardigans. It was always marmalade on toast with coffee for breakfast, always tea in the afternoon. And in a classically British way, she never spoke about how she felt about anything. She rarely mentioned my dad, except when she occasionally confused me for him. "John," she'd say, glancing up from the newspaper at the breakfast table. Then she'd look at me for a moment, clench her eyes shut, and smile. "James! Argh, you look so alike sometimes!" I'd suddenly be filled with butterflies, desperate to find out more. "Really?" I wanted to shout. "In what way? How am I like him? Tell me more!" But no. A polite smile, the dragging of a coffee cup across the table. A bite of toast.

Nancy trained as an artist at the Slade in London and painted her whole life. When I was a young teenager on visits to her cottage in Somerset, she'd sit and draw me, commenting on how much I looked like my dad. While we sat together on winter nights in her small living room, as the blue glare of the TV flashed across her face, she'd look at me intently, biting her lip as her pencil moved across the pad on her lap. It was almost like she was looking for her son and found me. I so wanted to ask her questions about him but decided if any memories were sparked by the shape of my jaw or the point of my nose, they would remain hers, just like her private grief. These drawings were packed up into boxes after she died, and in the division of her belongings that added further strain to my already distant relationship with my uncle and his wife, I was left only with the memory.

It wasn't until after Nancy's death that I discovered my grandfather

Jimmy had also ended his life. I always knew something strange had happened, but no one had ever explained it until my mother decided to tell me. (So much of what happens in families is kept secret, but why people eventually choose to reveal those secrets can remain a mystery, too.) Jimmy had been given a cancer diagnosis, and not long afterward shot himself in the garage of their family home. My father was the one to find him.

I was told Jimmy had planned it that way so Nancy would be spared the trauma of the discovery. But planning for your son to find your body—a son who had already, by that time, been admitted to psychiatric care—is a decision I can't fully understand. My father's only sibling, my uncle Tony, was also diagnosed with schizophrenia when he was in his late teens. Like my father, he was put into psychiatric care at various times in his life. He was a jolly man, a heavier version of my father with the same gray-white hair, who I could tell was trying his best to perform the uncle-type duties he felt he should. But there was a nervousness to him. He would tell me the occasional story from their youth, but I always got the sense his own memories were a blur to him, and this uncertainty would bleed into his every movement. A shaky hand returning a teacup to its saucer. A half-remembered anecdote relayed to a suspicious nephew. Like my father, Tony explored excessive meditation in his youth, and family friends have made the connection between the brothers' meditative experimentation and their psychotic breaks. The truth has never been clear to me, although later in this book we'll take a look at the possible connections. But whether it was Tony's medication or his nature, he seemed ambivalent when it came to my life. Our only contact would come whenever I visited my grandmother, but after her death that contact ceased. He died in 2022, and in keeping with our family tradition of shame and secrecy, I was only told about it six months later.

My mother has always blamed Nancy for the tragedy that seems to have befallen her family. The two of them found it hard to be in the same room: my mother, hot-tempered and hard done by; Nancy, the hard-hearted mother-in-law. My mother could never accept that Nancy had suffered something terrible—the loss of a child. As my mother saw it, Nancy was the cause of this devastation, and so had no right to mourn its consequences. She also measures the misfortune of others against her own, and in that she cannot be beaten. But I loved my grandmother, and she loved me deeply in turn. I would not have written this book were Nancy still alive. She felt these secrets were best kept hidden, and while I don't want to perpetuate that mistake, I recognize that she lived through these moments and would not have wanted them shared. I was her only grandchild, and I think her silence about my father's death was born of her desire to protect me. But every time I visited her, the photographs of him around the house would remind me of the uncomfortable truth. I would stand, gazing at them, trying to force the memory if I was in the picture, or waiting for him to come alive in the frame, turn to me, and smile.

I love how much I look like him. It's always regarded as a gift from my father by those who knew him. When people see a photo, I'm inevitably told, "Wow, you *are* his double." A long nose—that seems unfortunately only to grow as I get older—and eyes that almost disappear when I laugh. It's always given me great comfort, and an enormous amount of pride, that anything from my father could be reflected in me. But this pride is tempered by doubt: In what other ways am I like him?

Just as when I'm in a church I light candles for Gabrielle, when I'm in my old neighborhood in London, I stand outside my old house in tribute to my dad. It's a four-story Victorian terraced house, large sash windows with bright white casing on every floor. It is currently a chic shade of gray, while its neighbors are pastel pinks and blues—the famous Notting Hill color scheme. It is still divided into apartments, but the occupants look better off now than when I lived here. Hints of their privilege are visible even from down on the pavement: the warm, low lighting; healthy potted plants; colonial blinds. Back then, there were tie-dyed sheets hanging across these same windows, men sitting on the sills smoking, loud music, and feral cats. Standing outside the building, I try to revive memories of going in and out through the front door, of heading out with my dad on his shoulders for long walks, of the friends whose parents would pick me up at the curb to take me to school, of the neighborhood in all its grubby bohemian charm. The reality is that much of it is difficult to remember. I find myself trying to be happy about whatever my life was like, simply because my father was in it. But the truth is a blur.

Much of what happened to my dad has been kept from me. There is such a stigma attached to serious mental illness—and I think anyone with a family history of it can probably relate to this—that people simply do not want to talk about it. Overwhelming feelings of shame and sadness mean the truth often remains hidden. Yet it's become clear to me that finding out what really happened to my dad will not only help me grapple with my own problems, but put an end to this intergenerational silence. Family histories are all at once objective and subjective; there is *what happened,* and then there is *what people remember or say happened.* I wanted to find the objective facts about my father. To do that, I knew I needed to find his medical records.

Easier said than done. For those of you not familiar with Britain's National Health Service, let's just say "bureaucratic nightmare" doesn't begin to explain it. The only name my mother could remember from the time was my father's doctor, a Dr. Salkeld. Google quickly became my friend. I called around the various health centers in my father's neighborhood until I discovered that Dr. Salkeld's first name was Anne, and that she wasn't practicing anymore. One receptionist did tell me that she had been married to another doctor, who *was* practicing, and if I contacted the General Medical Council, they might be able to put me in touch with him. All you are allowed to do, however, is leave your name and number. The very officious voice on the phone told me in no uncertain terms, "We cannot pass on a specific message, sir. They won't know what it's about, but they'll have your name." So, after weeks of fruitless phone calls and emails, I left a message containing only my name and number to the husband of a woman who might have treated my father thirty years before. I wasn't holding my breath.

That was my "bottom-up" approach. In parallel, I tried getting hold of my father's medical records by starting at the top. I discovered each UK hospital has someone called a Caldicott Guardian, who is responsible for protecting patient confidentiality and issuing records. In the years since my father's death, the British health system has been centralized, which means smaller hospitals or clinics gradually came under the control of larger trusts. *Good news,* I thought. *Fewer people to email.* Then it dawned on me that the one email I did find probably corresponded to one person, who had to administer health records for hundreds of thousands of people. Not such good news. Another email into the wind. Everyone I spoke to said it was likely any records that did exist would have been destroyed because NHS records are deleted seven years after a person dies. I was deflated.

Some months later, I received a response out of the blue. The Caldicott Guardian had come through. He explained that records that should have been deleted were in fact found in the archive. The attachment was a 140-page medical history for John James Longman. I've never been happier about a clerical error. Therapy notes, social workers' observations, emergency room visits. I began to look through it all. There was a summary of his psychiatric history going back to the 1960s. He had been committed to psychiatric care in 1976 for two months and received electroshock therapy while in hospital. I found this very upsetting to read—I couldn't help but imagine my father strapped down with wires stuck to his head. As we'll see later, modern electroconvulsive therapy—or ECT—has become a valuable treatment for many people, especially those for whom other treatments or medications are not working. But in this moment Hollywood visions of a Victorian asylum flooded my mind. There were also records of his medication. He was prescribed chlorpromazine, an antipsychotic drug, which he would be on and off for the rest of his life. It seems his doctors had a constant struggle in convincing him to stay on the medication, which he felt blunted his creativity and left him numb. Most of the time, he didn't accept that he had an illness and only agreed to take medication "if he needed it," though by the time he was having an episode, it was already too late.

A psychiatrist who assessed him in June 1995 described his illness as being characterized by "brief psychotic episodes, which are associated with semireligious experiences, feelings of knowing things in greater depth and making discoveries about himself." He reported "visual and olfactory hallucinations. In the 1960s and 1970s, these episodes were happening at roughly seven-year intervals, but over the last few years and particularly since the breakup of his marriage, he has had more frequent episodes. His admissions to hospital are precipitated by acute paranoia and fear."

Some of the notes on specific hospital admissions are very detailed. In one 1991 admission, for what was diagnosed as a "hypomanic episode in schizoaffective disorder," he complained of having crabs running across his skin, his garbled sentences reproduced by the doctor: "The underlying personal complexities . . . is infinite . . . so long . . . basic so complicated . . . I've invented a system of how the world works." They also paint a picture of the scenes themselves, of my mother arriving in the evening, sometimes with a friend, sometimes alone. Of my father not speaking in full sentences, of all at once realizing he needed help but not really wanting the help that was on offer.

Another assessment in 1994 goes into detail about how his illness manifested: an obsession with "highly abstract and intellectualized" notions about the world and the universe. "A common theme in his thinking is the importance he places on staying in touch with his inner experience. He places particular emphasis on the importance of 'feeling,' which he regards as the primary element of experience, and regards 'thinking' as being secondary." When he saw health professionals, they often described him as agitated, incoherent. On one occasion, he said he felt like he was underwater. "I can't breathe," he said. And then, "Oh, yes I can. What am I talking about?!" He sometimes paced up and down, talking in garbled sentences. At other times, he was calm and reflective.

He swung between "bright and cheerful today" and then, a few days later, complaining of "low mood and isolation." I feel closer to him in this respect, because that pattern—feeling okay one minute, then down the next—is something I have felt throughout my life. His whole life is mapped out in front of me: the good and the bad, the desperate and the upbeat. This journey of peaks and troughs seems exhausting. One particularly graphic trough jumps out at me. He told a doctor, "Please inject me with painless drugs [f]or the result of my death then please when I am completely unconscious cut off my head. Cutting off the head or being completely dead. Life isn't worth anything to me now." As I read this, I can only feel utter sadness for him. His desperation screams out from the words on the page.

The notes from toward the end of his life, and when I came into it, are also hurtful to read. I come across a suicide attempt, and then I see the date: April 1987. "Took near fatal dose of paracetamol [acetaminophen], 11 weeks after the birth of his son James." This is one of the few times I am mentioned in any of these notes, and it fills me with sadness to think my birth might have precipitated his attempted suicide. Later in his therapy notes, I read, "John admits that relationship was positive with his wife until the pregnancy. John admits he never wanted a child." The notes are full of descriptions of arguments between him and my mother over me. But later on, a social worker writes, "John informs me that he is meeting up with his ex-wife and son this weekend, which he is looking forward to." In August 1996—a month before his death—he told his social worker he was spending more time with his wife and son. "He feels this is quite nice, and feels unable to see me," it reads.

Reading through these notes is a strange experience. No one would normally be able to access personal information about their parents. It feels like I'm prying into details I was never meant to read. But there are things in here that fill huge gaps in the timeline of my father's life. They transform him from the two-dimensional character of my imagination into the three-dimensional person he really was. For the first time, I have objective facts about him, rather than half-remembered, emotion-laden recollections.

My most overwhelming feeling is one of gratitude. This is information compiled by professionals, people whose job it was to understand and treat my father's symptoms. I am so thankful that he seems to have received so much help. From psychiatric assessments to at-home visits to frequent therapy sessions, he seems to have been surrounded by people who cared about him. And of course, there is my mother, who features heavily in the notes—not just as the person who was with him

-2-

Re: Mr John LONGMAN.

TREATMENT AND PROGRESS:

Following admission Mr Longman remained quite agitated. He accepted Chlorpromazine 100mgs qds. After two days on the ward he became increasingly distressed and thought disordered. He had marked persecutory ideas believing people were accusing him of doing terrible things, for example of killing his father. It was suggested to him that due to his marked thought disorder he may find it easier to express himself in writing. He wrote the following note:

To Doctor

> "please inject me with painless drugs or the result of my death then please when I am completely unconscious cut off my head. Cutting of the head or being completely dead. Life isn't worth anything to me now".

It was felt that Mr Longman presented a significant suicidal risk and he was "specialled" for next few days. Medication was increased: Chlorpromazine 200mgs qds. He responded rapidly to this treatment and developed good insight and became less agitated. After a further week on the ward he had maintained the improvement in mental state. He was calm with an appropriately cheerful affect. He possibly remained mildly thought disordered with vague pseudo-philosophical abstract content of speech. It was felt this was probably usual for him.

Mr Longman did not wish to engage with occupational therapy. Hostel accommodation was suggested but Mr Longman said that he would prefer to retain his independence.

On the 5th May 1995, mental state was reviewed. Mr Longman felt "back to normal". He held no abnormal ideas and mood was bright and reactive. It was agreed to discharge him with outpatients follow-up. His rehab worker was informed. He was advised to continue with medication but chose not do so.

Mr Longman was reviewed 5 days after admission. He was maintaining his improvement. It was agreed that follow-up would be by his rehab worker.

Graham N. Smith

Dr Graham Smith.,
Clinical Assistant to Dr A Higgitt,
Consultant Psychiatrist.

GS/SB/MPI 102291/23.05.95

cc. Pat Leung
Community Rehab Team
209 Harrow Road W2

John Longman's medical notes

when he was taken to the hospital, but as the subject of much of his therapeutic treatment. In reading these notes, I'm struck by just how horrific this entire period must have been for her, as she sought to balance both bringing me up and managing his illness at the same time. It's not an easy task for a caregiver.

Another important takeaway is that these health professionals drew a line between his psychotic episodes and his low mood. My father often complained of a low mood when on the medication that prevented his psychosis. It seems that's one of the reasons he didn't want to take it. His depression and his schizophrenia were consistently assessed as different conditions that needed different treatments. Reading these notes has helped me disentangle my father's psychosis from my own feelings of sadness. At the same time, he does describe feelings of hopelessness that I can relate to. And the overlap between his experiences and my own is precisely what I am most interested in.

My father's last few days are included in these notes. In the month before his death, he seems to have been doing well, with regular check-ins with social workers. "My last meeting with John was on the 19.08.1996," wrote his caseworker. "John presented fairly stable, discussed personal issues regarding ex-wife. His son appeared to be more involved with them lately. There were no obvious signs of depression or major changes in his mental state. We discussed future plans and reassurance was given."

But his social worker went on vacation in late August of 1996, and the notes show there wasn't much contact with him from around mid-September. He'd gone quiet, which in retrospect looks like a bad sign. Efforts were made to contact him, until on September 27 a representative from the housing association where he was living called the community rehabilitation team to tell them he'd died. There is a big asterisk in the margin, with the date 27/09/96, and a brief description of

24/09/96 Seen by Dr-Niggitt. at St-Charles.

27/09/96 John Longmans mother contacted
left message for me to contact.

am. Contacted mother no-reply.
Presume concerns re John to discuss at
CPM with Dr-Niggitt.

- Rang John am no-reply.

27/09/96

- Receptionist/Admin Tracey White came
to Rehab Team- 1.pm claiming she had
received a phone call from.
Rebecca Reece 0181-563-4963 from
Notting Hill Housing Trust claiming that
the above person John Longman is
dead.
Advised could I contact urgently.

WZZ 976 PF 361

NAME John Longman Page No.

(1)

- Contacted Rebecca Reece who
informed me that John had set a light
to his flat in the early hours of the morning
2-am and then threw himself out the
window - presumed by Rebecca this is
of a suicidal nature.

John Longman's medical notes: the day his death was recorded the events. He set fire to his apartment at two a.m. that morning and then threw himself out of the window. There is a sad finality to it, especially after reading the preceding pages, in which he'd been describing to social workers how much he was looking forward to seeing my mother and me. How he'd found a part-time volunteering job and been helping a friend with some computer work. It seems things were going in the right direction, until suddenly they weren't.

Gabrielle on the beach in Alexandria. (top right)

Gabrielle and Harold Claridge in Libya, early 1950s. (bottom left)

Ann and John Longman, Gabrielle (Sawaya) Claridge, and baby James on vacation in 1987. (top)

James in his dad's clothes, eight years old. (right)

CHAPTER 3

SCHIZOPHRENIA: NOT JUST ONE THING

So many people had stopped seeing them as human beings a long time ago. Schizophrenia's inaccessibility may be the most destructive thing about it. The thing that keeps so many people from connecting to people with the illness. Mistake, temptation, especially if you're a relative, is to confuse inaccessibility, with a loss of self.

—ROBERT KOLKER, *HIDDEN VALLEY ROAD*

Going through my father's notes brought me instantly closer not only to him, but to a condition with which some twenty-four million people have been diagnosed worldwide. But I knew that to more fully

John Longman

27/10/95.

CARE PLAN SUGGESTED FORMAT

PROBLEMS	GOALS	PRIMARY (prevention)	SECONDARY (intervention)
John has a distorted perception of reality based on pseudo-philosophical ideas. John does not feel medication can help him.	John to cope with anxiety. For John to gain insight about delusions. To link with more social interventions John feels happy with. For John to look at ways he can feel good and not become isolated.	To maintain contact with reality. To make note of any changes Prevent John from becoming isolated. To look at Johns views and opinions and discuss why he feels like this at times.	To see regular and go out and involve John in reality. ie coffee bar - walks. Accept clients needs for delusion. explore with client what causes stress. Develop a relationship with John by seeing regular and maintaining contact. Discuss delusional thinking as a problem in Johns life.

mj.4/11/94

27/10/95

CARE PLAN SUGGESTED FORMAT

PROBLEMS	GOALS	PRIMARY (prevention)	SECONDARY (intervention)
Potential to relapse after recently been admitted under Sec 3. Past not complying with medication	To help John in the community as recently discharged from hospital. To advise John the importance of taking a minimal amount.	To educate John re-medication issues. To be reviewed by Dr. on our team regularly	To monitor John is happy and complying with medication. To understand and listen to how John feels espoally re medication To support and reassure John.

mj.4/11/94

John Longman's medical notes

understand the condition's genetic component, I would need to speak to more people who live with it and have family members who have been diagnosed. Luckily, my father's doctor, Dr. Anne Salkeld, finally got in touch. Her husband had returned the cryptic message I'd sent through the General Medical Council, slightly confused as to what it could be about. Once I'd explained, and he'd passed the message to Anne, he confirmed that she would be more than happy to chat. I sent over my father's medical records and waited for her response.

It came, as Murphy's Law dictates, while I was on deployment with ABC in Ukraine. And so it was over a very crackly phone connection that I heard the voice my father would hear when he was most in need of help. Dr. Salkeld had a reassuring tone and a southern English accent, and proved just how British she was by apologizing immediately. "I'm so sorry I can't remember much," she said quietly, "but these notes are helpful." Anne has treated tens of thousands of patients over the years, and she didn't know my father well. But it didn't matter so much what details she could or couldn't remember—just talking to her made me feel closer to him. I felt almost as though I had become him, her patient. We spoke for nearly an hour, Anne in her home in the English countryside, me hunched over my dad's notes in a Kyiv hotel.

Anne helped me understand how difficult it is for medical professionals to get a grip on schizophrenia, how broad a term it is, and how a lot of people, like my father, receive multiple diagnoses for related conditions. She admitted there had been no training for mental illness when she was in medical school. "We didn't know, these new diagnoses came in after we qualified," she told me. "I think it was a diagnosis where they weren't sure what was going on, to be honest, and they wanted to give him a label.

"He had quite a lot of beliefs about the mind, and he was trying to make sense of it. You do see that with people with psychosis or schizophrenia.

FAO Pat Longm

DISCHARGE SUMMARY
ST CHARLES HOSPITAL
Exmoor Street, London. W10 6DZ

GP: Dr Susan Salkeld
Colville Health Centre
51 Kensington Park Road
London
W11 1PA

CASE NO: MPI 102291
DOB: 25.01.47
SURNAME: LONGMAN
FIRST NAME: John
ADDRESS: 24F Blenheim Crescent, London. W11 1NW.

CONSULTANT: Dr Higgitt ADMITTED: 24.04.95 DISCHARGED: 05.05.95

DIAGNOSIS: SCHIZO-AFFECTIVE DISORDER - DEPRESSIVE TYPE

ICD.10 CODE: F25.1

DRUGS ON DISCHARGE: NIL

REASON FOR ADMISSION:

Mr Longman presented to the Assessment Room with his ex-wife with a history of a 3 day period of feeling unwell. He was not sleeping and his concentration was poor. His speech did not make much sense. He described things around him as seeming unreal. A diagnosis of relapse of schizo-affective disorder was made and, with some persuaSion, Mr Longman was informally admitted.

PAST PSYCHIATRIC HISTORY:

Known schizo-affective disorder. Several admissions since at least 1977. Usually responds quickly to treatment. Non-compliant with medication between relapses. Very serious Paracetamol overdose 1987. Inbetween relapses mental state characterised by probable mild thought disorder, mood disturbance - usually depression, and derealisation and depersonalisation.

PERSONAL HISTORY:

See previous summaries. Lives in his own flat. Socially isolated. Some contact with his ex-wife and 6 year old son.

MENTAL STATE EXAMINATION ON ADMISSION:

Aroused and slightly agitated. Speech pressured. Mood excitable. Subjectively impaired sleep, poor concentration, denied suicidal ideation. Thought form - formally thought disordered with Knight's move thinking. Thought content - pseudo philosophical content, difficult to follow with persecutory themes. Perceptions - auditory and visual hallucinations, poorly described. Cognitive state not tested.

contd/...

John Longman's medical notes

I would go and visit people who were badly affected, and the table would be covered either with astronomical books or log tables or things like that. It was like there was a secret somewhere that would help them to cope if only they could uncover it. And the impression I got from him, he seemed to be saying, 'I don't wanna take drugs, because I've had these insights, and they stop me from having insights.'

"I think the care that he received is better than he'd get now, to be honest. My impression is that there was much more community support then than there is now. I was really impressed, actually, reading these notes." I was immediately heartened by this—by the knowledge that Anne, too, felt my father had been well cared for. Because he ended his life, I think I assumed that he was never well cared for, that he had fallen through cracks in the system. Speaking to Anne and reading his notes helped me realize that wasn't the case.

When I set out to write this book, I was repeatedly told to read *Hidden Valley Road* by Robert Kolker, which tells the story of the Galvin family and the six brothers who were diagnosed with schizophrenia. Like this one, Kolker's book uses the Galvin family's struggles to explore medical research about mental illness. One theme persists throughout: people tormented by both their condition and its treatment. Of one of the brothers, the author writes, "One of the consequences of surviving schizophrenia for fifty years is that sooner or later, the cure becomes as damaging as the disease." I feel that same beat running through my father's notes.

The six Galvin brothers became the subject of major scientific interest because geneticists were able to compare their experience to that of the general population. By then, scientists were building on two centuries of serious academic study of schizophrenia. One of the most famous early cases in this long history of research was that of Daniel Schreber, a

DISCHARGE SUMMARY – ST CHARLES HOSPITAL

G.P: Dr Wall SANKEY
Colville Health Centre
51 Kensington Park Road
LONDON W11

CASE NO: CH063320
DOB: 25/2/47
SURNAME: LONGMAN/LANGMAN.
FIRST NAME: John
ADDRESS: 25 Colville Road
London W11

CONSULTANT: Dr Higgitt

ADMITTED: 6/11/91

DISCHARGED:

DIAGNOSIS AND DRUGS ON DISCHARGE:

DIAGNOSIS: Hypomanic episode in Schizo effective disorder

DRUGS:

REGISTRAR'S SUMMARY:

REASON FOR ADMISSION:

Referred urgently by G.P because he was felt to be suffering an acute relapse. He was not sleeping, was hyperactive, was expressing grandiose delusions on invulnerability, was insightless and felt to be in grave danger of coming to physical harm e.g believed he could walk out in a busy road and not get hurt.

PRESENTATION:

Patient was brought to hospital by ex-wife and her friend. Ambulance was ordered but situation felt so intolerable that they could not wait, and so Mrs Longman drove. Mr Longman seemed somewhat bewildered and somewhat reluctant to be seeing me, he said "I was getting very proud of myself... of what I thought I achieved.... yesterday.. it had to do with sex... the underlying personal complexities... is infinite... so long..... basic so complicated... I'v invented a system of how the world works". "This is Anne, my wife... we are the same person.... she is the body. me the mind... she is indestructible... Maharishi... we are me (pointing to both, his ex-wife Anne and wife's friend)... your (pointing to me) Maharishi.

Mrs Longman gave the following history. Her ex-husband John had apparently come to her flat which she shares with their 4 year old son James the previous night. She said he was in his "usual state of elapse". She described him as very shaky and pacing and talking rubbish, and expressing ideas of grandiosity. She said he also appeared to be imagining feeling a crab crawling on him.

1

John Longman's medical notes

German judge who in the late 1800s wrote a personal account of his own experiences, *Memoirs of My Nervous Illness.*

Schreber demonstrated many of the symptoms you might imagine when you think of someone with schizophrenia: intense paranoia, delusions, and a search for deeper meaning. In fact, his memoir details an entire cosmology in which he, like my father, sought to place his own experience in relation to the universe. Schreber's case received attention from generations of notable scientists—among them, Sigmund Freud and Carl Jung. It was Jung who went on to take schizophrenia out of the mind and place it into the body; that is, he was the first to understand the illness as a biological process, rather than simply a thought illness. But while Jung emphasized the importance of the environment over any genetic predisposition, it was another famous case—the Genain sisters—that allowed a new generation of scientists to consider the idea that both might be at play.

The Genain quadruplets were sisters born in 1930, and all of them were diagnosed with schizophrenia. The name *Genain* is a pseudonym, deriving from the Greek meaning "dire birth." David Rosenthal, a research psychologist at the National Institute of Mental Health, was the lead researcher on the sisters' case. He found that, like the Galvin brothers, they had experienced years of abuse and neglect at the hands of their father. In a 1964 study, he set out to explain that nurture, not nature, was the root cause of the condition. But he found he could not overlook biology—not necessarily in a straightforward parent-to-child inheritance, but in a more amorphous, less obvious way. Or, as he described it, "How the disease wanders and meanders through families." Crucially, his study found that schizophrenia "cannot be imposed on someone who is not genetically predisposed."

I think it's important to stress here again: You will find many people who disagree with genetic explanations for mental illness. But what the Kolker, Schreber, and Rosenthal research did find were similar symptoms in those who had been diagnosed, as well as a similar trajectory for the condition.

There are a number of stages that those with schizophrenia will go through. The first is the prodromal phase, which occurs before noticeable psychotic episodes emerge. A person undergoing this phase may become more withdrawn, anxious, or irritable, and they may also lack motivation and have difficulty concentrating. Because many of these symptoms overlap with other mental illnesses, schizophrenia can go undiagnosed in the prodromal phase. My father's first psychotic episode occurred when he was nineteen. All the boys in the Galvin family also experienced psychosis around this age. For women, the symptoms may not emerge until later, possibly not even until their thirties. It is not known why this disparity exists.

The active phase of the condition usually manifests in the later teenage years or early twenties. This is when the person may hear voices or hallucinate. They may see, hear, smell, or feel things that aren't there. They may become paranoid or delusional, and sometimes become violent as a result. My father was never violent, but often complained of animals on his skin—crabs or bugs crawling across him. On one occasion, he felt he was being burnt alive. His condition was characterized not by visions, but by a sense that there was a deeper truth that he had to uncover. And it was not so much a paranoia about people, the government, or authority out to get him—although that is common—as it was about a deeper truth about the world that was his job to uncover.

Research into schizophrenia has long depended on the brains of patients being donated for science after their deaths. But neuroimaging has revolutionized the field. Scientists can now look for changes in brain activity and structure while their subjects are alive. They have reported abnormalities within the prefrontal cortex, which is often referred to as the brain's "boss."

Among its many functions, the prefrontal cortex is involved with decision-making, risk assessment, impulse control, judgment, managing emotional reactions, coordinating complex behaviors, and more. It does all of this by communicating closely with other parts of the brain. In those with schizophrenia, connectivity between the prefrontal cortex and the rest of the brain seems to be disrupted. Specifically, researchers have found impaired relations between the parts of the brain that manage perception of the external world and the part that manages internal motivations. This is why schizophrenic symptoms can include hallucinations, and a person with the condition might experience an intense and sometimes paranoid sense of how the world might impact them.

There are three main areas in the brain between which communication is commonly interrupted or activity is too intense in people with schizophrenia. They are: the frontal lobe, the temporal lobe, and the thalamus. The frontal lobe is the largest of the brain's four regions in the cerebral cortex. The area just behind the forehead, it is associated with language production, memory, judgment, motor tasks, and creativity. It also controls our social interactions and helps us manage appropriate behaviors. The temporal lobe, just above the temple, is another of the cortex regions. It is the first area responsible for interpreting sounds and giving meaning to language. As such, it is also associated with emotion and memory, and composes a significant part of the brain's limbic system, where the amygdala and hippocampus, the areas that store and interpret different kinds of memories, are found. Finally, there's the thalamus, which is an egg-shaped structure in the middle of the brain that acts as a kind of information relay center. Modern brain-mapping technologies have shown researchers that the connections between these areas do not function as they should in people with schizophrenia.

Structural abnormalities in the brain have also been recorded in those with schizophrenia. About 60 percent of the brain is white matter—a large network of nerve fibers that enables the exchange of that information. It connects different parts of your brain's gray matter, which makes up the other 40 percent and is the brain tissue rich in neuronal cell bodies, where information is processed and sent to various parts of the body. In people with schizophrenia, reduced gray matter has been observed, specifically as a thinning of the cerebral cortex. This is also true of those with neurodegenerative diseases like Alzheimer's. The white matter in a schizophrenia patient's brain can also be impaired.

With the right medication, many people with schizophrenia can live ordinary lives—you'll meet some of them later in this chapter. My father was among these. Many others cannot function outside of dedicated care. My father also spent time in these places and lived in fear of them becoming his permanent reality. All the symptoms described in this chapter can appear very suddenly, perhaps in response to a sudden trauma or difficult life event. But just what activates schizophrenic behavior, more broadly, is at the core of modern studies into the condition.

In my research, I came across a podcast called *A Bipolar, a Schizophrenic, and a Podcast.* Its blurb reads, "Each episode looks at life through the unique lens of people living with depression, schizophrenia, and bipolar disorder." Its cohost Michelle Hammer connected the three conditions in her podcast because so many of the symptoms overlap. It sounded like the podcast for me.

Michelle calls herself a schizophrenia activist. She spoke to me from her home in New York City. She's got jet-black hair, wears a baseball cap, and speaks in a distinctive New Yorker accent at about one hundred miles per hour. It's all *cawfee* and *flawahs* and *whateva,* and I love it.

"Things started around high school," she recalls. "I was exhibiting symptoms of schizophrenia, but I didn't know that at the time. I was hearing voices telling me that I was dumb, that everything I said was stupid. And I would cry at night."

She says she gradually stopped engaging in classes. "I even had a problem in English class. I didn't want to write the essays, because I thought the teacher would know me, like get into my head. It freaked me out. It was extreme paranoia, but I didn't know that at the time." Every part of her life was being impacted, but she didn't know by what.

Michelle says she assumed everyone had a voice in their head. She had no reason to think otherwise. She describes the voice as "a kind of mean girl. It wasn't my voice, but it wasn't someone else's, either. It kept telling me, 'You're a burden on everyone, you should just die. You make everything worse.' It was an entity that had read my most vulnerable thoughts, and it was repeating them back to me."

All through high school, her mother tried to get her help, but Michelle was convinced she was trying to kill her. "I felt she was trying to sabotage my life," she says. When she eventually went to college in upstate New York, the same thoughts hit her. "This time, I thought my roommate was going to kill me. And that's when I realized: Something isn't right. So that's when I went to the health center. But they told me I was bipolar within fifteen minutes." Michelle says she was given medication that didn't work. She ended up in a psychiatric unit twice in her freshman year and once in her sophomore year.

Until this point in our conversation, Michelle is still speaking very quickly. She's funny and sharp and knows how to paint a picture. But when I ask her about her committal to psychiatric care, her answers are monosyllabic. I know not to go there. It's clearly traumatic for her.

Eventually, Michelle was referred to a psychiatrist who gave her a diagnosis of schizophrenia. "I was really upset when I received the news," she says, "but then I went out with my friends to tell them. And seriously, their reaction was 'Wasn't that what you had the whole time?! We told you that!' One friend even laughed: 'I could have told you that three years ago—you were talking to yourself the whole time!'"

It sounds like you were willing to listen to the diagnosis, I tell her. My father was not. For Michelle, it was a question of maturity. She tried to shrug it off in college and would skip taking her medication. With time, she realized that the diagnosis was going to help her. "Being diagnosed with schizophrenia is the best thing that can happen to you, because then you can get the help that you need."

Her family took some time to adjust. Her mother wanted the best for her, but it felt to Michelle that she was being judged. "She'd say things like 'I told Jan and Robert what's going on with you. And I told Margot what's going on with you, because Margot's son is a meth addict.' I was, like, 'You're comparing me to a meth addict?'"

Public perceptions of people with schizophrenia are generally negative. A 2015 survey by the UK's Office for National Statistics found that people diagnosed with a mental health problem were most likely to be seen as unpredictable, hard to talk to, and unlikely to recover, and people diagnosed specifically with schizophrenia were viewed most negatively. The perceived incurable nature of the condition seemed to elicit a more negative response, whereas other mental illnesses were perceived as easier to overcome. A wide-ranging 2000 study in the United States found that perceptions of individuals with mental illness as dangerous have increased over time. People in 1996 were on average 2.3 times more likely to describe someone with a psychotic diagnosis as violent than people were in 1950. In 2015, Public Health England commissioned the National Centre for Social Research to perform a survey on social attitudes to mental illness, which showed stark differences between perceptions of schizophrenia and other mental illnesses. Seven in ten people said they'd prefer to move next door to or socialize with someone who has depression rather than schizophrenia. People are less likely to want to marry or have children with someone with either of these conditions. The majority said they think a person with a mental illness is less likely to be promoted. And only half said they'd be willing to socialize with someone who had schizophrenia. A 2012 survey in France found that 65 percent of people felt those with schizophrenia are a danger to others.

I think it can be very hard for people to accept this diagnosis precisely because of these public perceptions, and because they believe it suggests there might be something innately wrong with them. Similarly, there is often a desire to keep those with psychotic episodes away from other family members—especially children. This can cause even greater feelings of isolation and despair for those living with the condition. A common misconception is that those with schizophrenia have multiple personalities, that they spend a significant amount of time not being "themselves." This then gives those around them a kind of permission to treat them differently, like they would a stranger. The person is cut off, or their time with loved ones is limited. This was the case with my father. Plus, the fear of genetic susceptibility is real, even if the realities of genetic inheritance are more difficult to pin down.

Genetics do seem to play a significant role in Michelle's experience. "My great-grandmother was apparently schizophrenic," she says. "They lived in the tenements in New York City, fleeing Hitler. My grandmother was born on the kitchen table, and immediately after that they put [her mother] in a mental institution on Long Island and said she had schizophrenia. So who knows what happened to her, but she was there for the rest of her life." Her father also has a first cousin with schizophrenia. "When we were kids, we thought she was super fun. But as we got older, we realized she wasn't quite like other people."

I ask Michelle if she finds it helpful to know there's a genetic trait.

"Yes, I guess," she says. There's a sense that rather than alienating her from her family, in an odd way it gives her something in common with them and makes her feel less alone. But Michelle is focused on living a positive life as an example to others with the condition. She wants to change the way people see it.

"Having schizophrenia, you're more likely to be a victim of violence than a perpetrator," she says. "People think schizophrenia is the worst diagnosis. But that's because of the movies. Everything is on a spectrum. You can have severe schizophrenia, or high-functioning schizophrenia. There are people who are way worse off than I am who have other mental illnesses."

She says the media is full of stories about people with schizophrenia attacking people. "But you never hear, 'This person with schizophrenia got up in the morning and had coffee and went to work. After work, he went to drinks with friends and then had dinner with his family.' That's because crisis and mental illness is public, while wellness and mental illness is private. If you never share the good news, you're never going to know the good news. You never hear about the people completely thriving and doing well."

My father's life may have ended badly, but many of the years he lived were happy ones, full of joy and creativity. He was universally described as funny, a deep thinker, generous, and kind. These are not the characteristics many associate with someone who has schizophrenia. But he was all of those things, even when the illness took over. Speaking to Michelle reminds me of that fundamental truth. I may be writing a book about my father and his schizophrenia, but that was not all that defined him. She reminds me about all the other stuff—the equally important, perhaps *more* important, stuff—that I know I inherited from him. And her desire to change attitudes toward her condition, to be a thriver, is an inspiration. "It's so ridiculous that there's so much stigma around this. Everyone is related to or knows someone going through this stuff. Stigma doesn't make sense!" And that's another fundamental truth: If we all know or are related to someone who goes through this, why are we so quick to judge?

Michelle will be the first to tell you her experience is not universal. These conditions can make living a normal life impossible, both for those who live with mental illness and for the family members who take care of them. As part of my research, I knew it would be important to speak to people who became unexpected caretakers for family members with mental illness.

I was introduced to Matthew through a caretaker organization. In 2003, his mother, Rosemary, had a psychotic episode seemingly out of the blue at their home in south London and was taken into the hospital. She was forty-five. "You're not prepared at all," Matthew tells me. "Even if she had been given a diagnosis, I don't think I would have known what it meant."

Matthew is in his late forties now and is very soft-spoken. He gives off a calming, mild-mannered vibe. The news of his mother's collapse took him by complete surprise, he tells me. Rosemary had never shown any symptoms of psychosis. She'd had a hard life: a divorce, debt issues, and caring for his two brothers. But through it all, there'd been no signs of any mental illness—until one day she suddenly decided not to go out. "She'd just stay in her room," says Matthew, "too afraid to go anywhere. The doctors came to the house, and she'd just talk in riddles. When she went into the mental health ward, she seemed confused and afraid." Matthew says she started complaining of bad smells and thought he was someone else. "She became suspicious of me and didn't trust me as much. She didn't trust the medication she was on and started thinking they were poison. She'd even throw away clothes, thinking they were poisonous.

"You expect some form of love from your parents. But with an illness like that, it just pushes things away," he says. "It's difficult when your mum says, 'Oh, you don't care for me anymore, you're putting me in a mental health institution.' It was really terrible to see her hauled off by the police when she wasn't accepting treatment." Matthew says health services relied heavily on medication but didn't offer sufficient psychotherapy, which he thinks could have changed the situation.

Matthew was the sole caretaker for his mother for fifteen years. What followed was a traumatic, bureaucratic experience, even being accused by care coordinators of mistreating her. "You know you're going to have to start looking after your parents," he tells me, "but not so soon, and not in this way. Over the years, from the medication and side effects, she gained a lot of weight and had heart problems. She was sixty-four when she passed away. What made it more difficult was the services weren't really there." Matthew had felt a sense of duty to help his mother. But caring for her took its toll on Matthew, who ended up struggling with anxiety and depression.

In speaking to Matthew, I find myself thinking about my own mother. She became a caretaker, of sorts, for my father. His illness was not as debilitating as Rosemary's, but the responsibility Matthew felt for his mother's well-being echoes my mother's experience of looking after my dad. Accompanying him to the hospital after suicide attempts. Trying to make sure he had some kind of relationship with me, even though she knew it couldn't be what other children had with their fathers. And the heavy responsibility of making choices for someone you love, even if they don't agree with them.

My father's notes show me he was well supported by social workers and psychiatric nurses. People dedicated, like Matthew, to a very sick person's well-being. But Matthew's experience with the care system, more recent than my father's, lends credence to Dr. Salkeld's observation that the care my dad received almost thirty years ago might have been better than what he'd receive today. "Mental health caretakers struggle to get help and get included in care plans," Matthew says. "My mum was saying she didn't want care—but that was her illness talking. You can get some good care coordinators, but a fair number of them were really terrible. When resources started getting cut, that's when things would really start to go downhill.

"Genetics was a huge part of our story," says Matthew. "My mother's mother also had a severe mental illness. It was a form of schizophrenia." He says Rosemary told him her own mother started throwing things at her one day. But there was no medical intervention in those days. Rosemary seems to have suffered through her mother's abusive behavior the same way Matthew suffered through Rosemary's. "I stayed until the very end, until my mum kicked me out," he says. I ask him whether that sense of repeating history is something he thinks about. Is it always in the back of his mind? "Oh, it's in the front of my mind," he says. "Not the back."

For Matthew, and for me, and for many others, repetition through the generations is a real concern. I wonder if the behavior his grandmother demonstrated was enough to "cause" schizophrenia in her daughter. In other words, was this abuse, this environment, enough to trigger her illness? Or was there a deeper genetic trait? Rosemary's sudden deterioration suggests—to this nonscientist, at least—that something other than the environment is perhaps at play here. Matthew's own struggles with anxiety and depression mirror my own. But were these also caused by the traumatic situation he found himself in, or does he have a genetic predisposition that makes it more likely for him to become affected? These were questions I still wanted to answer.

I started my research for this book by looking for people to speak to, expecting them to fall neatly into various categories that I had naïvely imagined: someone with schizophrenia; someone who shares symptoms with a family member. But since I am my own worst critic, I don't mind telling you that my work as a journalist—especially a TV journalist—can make me a little too prone to formula. You can often set out to film a news story, for example, "knowing" exactly what you need, only to realize all your expectations were completely wrong, and the person who was meant to give you a neat little sound bite actually gave you something entirely different. The trick, which I have learned the hard way, is to lean in to that difference. That's where the good stuff is.

Theo is the good stuff. He is sixty-one, a San Francisco native who now lives in Florida, and has lived with serious mental illness since he was a child. He has at various times in his life been a "high-functioning" schizophrenic—able to successfully function as a husband, a father, and an employee. But at other times, not so much. He shows how kaleidoscopic, how uniquely brilliant and terrifying the world can feel to someone with his condition. On his website where he writes about his experiences, which is how I found him, he describes himself as "an offbeat librarian" who "speaks softly and carries a big pen."

"I lived a normal life up until about eight or nine," he says to me, "when I ran up to my mother and told her I had seen an angel in my room. That would be my first vision. I remember I was hugging a Snoopy that my grandmother gave me. It was about eight feet tall. It was beautiful and so vivid. It's been so many years. People tell me it was a figment of my imagination. But to me, it's real." He has attempted suicide a number of times. The first time, he was just twelve.

Like Michelle, Theo speaks very fast. Sometimes he loses his thread and goes on tangents. But he is at all times cognizant of his condition. He was first diagnosed with schizoaffective disorder in 1977 at age fifteen, after his first episode of what he calls "hardcore psychosis." He married and had children but found it difficult to keep permanent work and describes an unconventional, itinerant life, moving from place to place. He has often found work as an administrator in libraries—first on the West Coast where he grew up, now in Miami. "The library is beautiful," he says, "because you can be odd and be all right, because it's a library." As Theo speaks, I'm immediately reminded of my father; his creative and intellectual flair is powerfully evident. He is a deeply thoughtful person, and I wonder how he and my father, only a little more than ten years apart in age, would have got along.

For Theo, when episodes strike, they seem to strike hard. In one major incident in 1984, he says he loaded up his car in the middle of the night and drove for the border, explaining to his mother the next day that he had to leave the country because the government was after him. "I got into a fight with a chef in a restaurant and ended up on the roof of the place in my underwear. I don't have knowledge of a psychotic episode. I have to ask people after they happen." My father, too, had obsessions he had to fulfill. In one late-night incident, my dad drove to Scotland during a storm and was found a few days later in a snowdrift, shivering half to death. In this, he and Theo seem to share a desire to uncover something, find an answer, or simply escape.

"I have synesthesia," says Theo. "I see colors. Days of the week are colors for me. Each day has its own color." He lists them at speed: "Sundays are white, Mondays are yellow, Tuesdays are blue, Wednesdays are purple, Thursdays are gold, Fridays are green, Saturdays are red. Ever since I was little." There is something almost dreamlike, and faintly attractive, to his experiences, as though he has unique access to an alternative reality that is much richer and more meaningful than this one. In a similar way, my father told his social workers that his hallucinations sometimes emerged from the colors in his paintings. Of course, these are serious and often dangerous conditions, and I don't want to make light of them. But my father would sometimes describe his hallucinations as pleasurable. When the hallucinations were good, he wanted to be in them.

Like many others with his condition, Theo also smells things that other people don't seem to smell. "I was so happy when people had to wear masks during the pandemic. I have this thing about being poisoned." He says he hasn't been to a restaurant in over twenty years. "I'm scared about poison in food or water. I recognize the smells as danger. I recognize it as potent diesel or gasoline or burnt plastic. When it registers, it registers like death is imminent. I need to break away."

Despite medication, Theo still hears voices "once or twice a month." The voices are like commands. "This is where you get into the darker aspects. If you're told or directed to do something, that's not so good. I'll leave the house in the middle of the night in my underwear, to go on a mission." These days, the missions don't result in anything too dangerous. But for a long time, he had repeated run-ins with the law. "It's nothing I'm proud of," he says. "There are times, in my mind, I thought I was a lawyer. I think I took out two hundred lawsuits or something." He's experienced drug addiction, police standoffs, trips to jail, and restraining orders.

These more challenging moments in his life demonstrate how destructive the condition can be for Theo. “It’s like driving a stick shift,” he says. “You shift into another gear that you are unaware of. But the whole world will realize it. To you, the whole world is wrong but you are right. It’s only when you come out of it, and you realize it, that you feel really bad.”

Theo tried for a long time not to tell anyone about his condition. He was worried about the reaction—and still is. He says on being fired after an episode at work, “People started disconnecting me on LinkedIn.” He doesn’t have friends, though he implies that this isn’t an issue. But I sense his hurt. “Once you tell people, you’re in for a really rough ride. When the police have come to my house to do wellness checks—this is a small town, everybody knows me—they send seven, eight, ten officers. I don’t present a danger! I don’t! I try to use humor, that seems to help.”

Like others I’ve spoken to, he talks about misdiagnosis and the struggle to find the right medication. “I’ve had more than fifty psychiatrists,” he says. “It’s like a pendulum. You can be diagnosed with one, and then be diagnosed with another.” At one point, he was diagnosed with ADHD and prescribed Adderall.

Misdiagnosis is something almost everyone I have spoken to for this book has mentioned. And once again, Theo points to a history of mental illness in his family, as well as a repeating pattern in the next generation. Of his two sons, he says, the younger has now also been diagnosed with schizophrenia. “He’s twenty-four but has the mental capacity of a nine-year-old. Who knows what he experiences? He has no friends, he’s like me. He can’t be independent. He runs away two or three times a month. My wife will always tell me, ‘He’s just like you!’ He likes to run to the police station.”

Theo says his mother never admitted it, but she spent a year in a psychiatric facility. And when Theo began experiencing symptoms, his mother tried to have him hypnotized, rather than seek professional health care. Family shame played a huge role. "In my family, the worst thing you can do is own up to having a mental issue. You may not seek the approval of outsiders, but you want the approval of your dad. You want the approval of your mom." Theo is, however, keen not to repeat past mistakes, and wants to offer his son the kind of help he never got as a child. Would finding out more about his genetic predisposition help?

"That's something I would like more than someone just pointing to *DSM*," he says. "That would help me. I know that's what I have. But it sure would be nice if I had some hard science to back it up. If they could go into my body and point at a specific gene, then I could say, 'Okay, you got me!'"

In my father's medical notes, I see repeated references to his search for meaning. To his efforts to understand his illness. He wanted answers. I hear in Theo's voice a similar desire. Someone who wants to know why he is the way he is. He thinks the most common misconception of those with schizophrenia is the idea that they are dangerous. "We're mainly docile," he says. "Mistreated and marginalized in your world, we prefer to live in our own. People think we're violent. They're scared. Do you know how terrible it is for people to be scared of you?" To be honest, some of what Theo has described *has* sounded dangerous. Or, at the very least, unpredictable. But what his story shows is these are moments in as rich a life as anyone's without the condition. Understanding schizophrenia as more than any one adjective—not just *dangerous* or *unpredictable* or *disconnected*—allows us to view the people who live with it with much more complexity, and hopefully therefore with a little more compassion and understanding.

It is true that Theo, Michelle, Rosemary, and my father were all diagnosed with schizophrenia even though their experiences varied wildly. That's part of the reason a lot of people take issue with the term in the first place. Dr. Salkeld asked the same question: Why is it necessary to have a label at all? But one thing Theo and Michelle do make clear is that having a diagnosis—and therefore an idea of how to manage it—has helped them make sense of their lives.

What I hope you've seen in this chapter is something very simple: Schizophrenia is much more than you might imagine it to be. It is not simply a condition plagued by paranoia, hallucinations, or any of the other stereotypical—and often exaggerated—tropes from the movies. Yes, it can be all of these things. But the people who live with it often do so despite hurdles that those with other illnesses would never endure. They've been misdiagnosed, they've lived with the burden of intense stigma, and, in some cases, their own minds have turned them against the people they love and who love them. It strikes me that the last point is the most destructive. For the person with schizophrenia, fear and paranoia fix the family as their antagonist. For the family, the person with schizophrenia is a worrying marker of a deeper possibility they want to ignore. Both dynamics serve to distance people from their loved ones, just when they need them most.

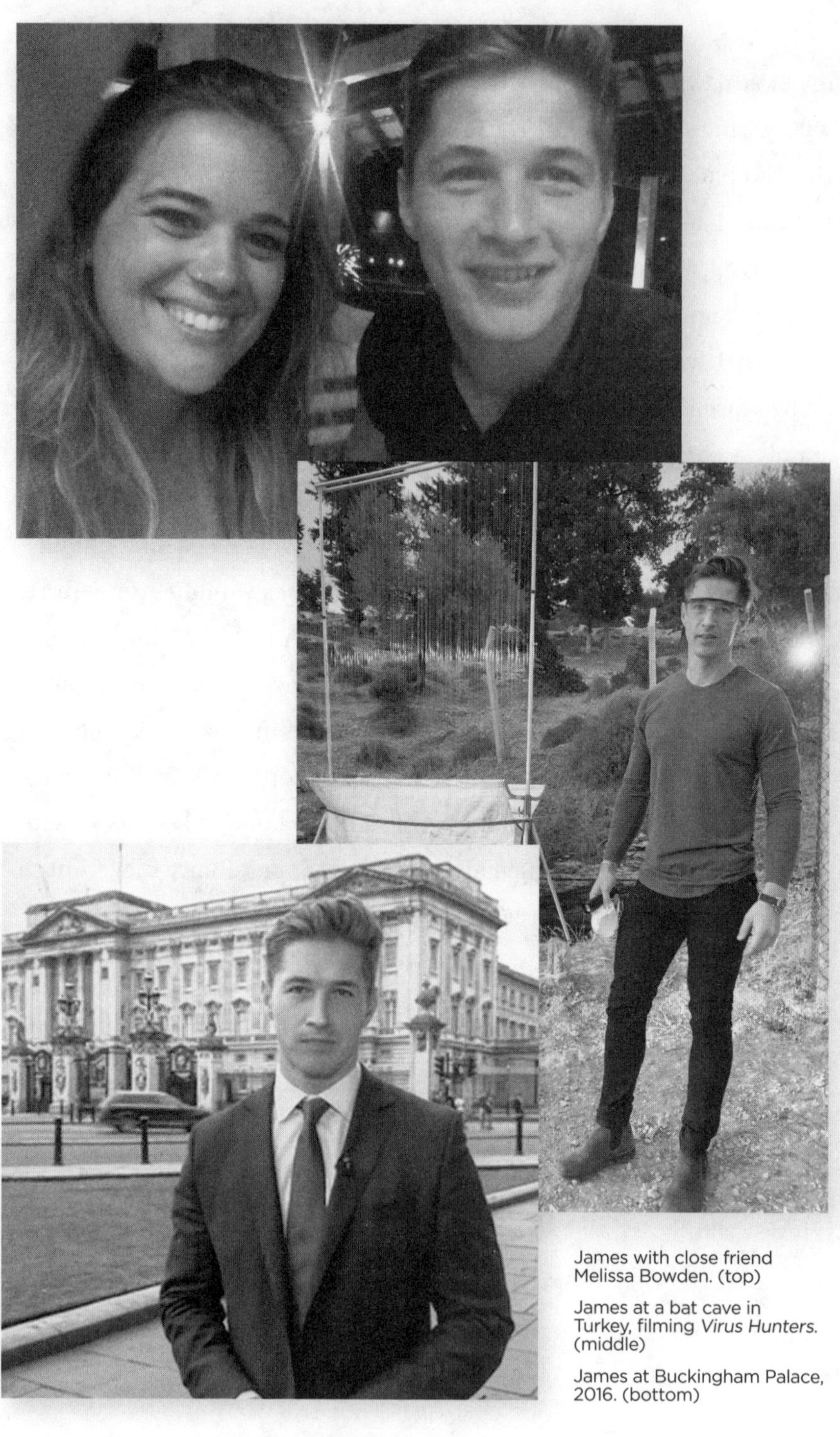

James with close friend Melissa Bowden. (top)

James at a bat cave in Turkey, filming *Virus Hunters*. (middle)

James at Buckingham Palace, 2016. (bottom)

CHAPTER 4

DEPRESSION: WHAT DOES IT FEEL LIKE?

I'll never forget how the depression and loneliness felt good and bad at the same time. Still does.

—HENRY ROLLINS, *THE PORTABLE HENRY ROLLINS*

I keep a work journal. It's a little smaller than printer paper, leather bound, with blue pages and gold edging. I did that thing we all do when buying stationery: imagine I'd make more effort to write in the journal if it was a bit fancy. Well, I mostly have kept up with it, and I'm flicking through it now, reliving some of my work trips, reminding myself how absurd this job can be at times.

A few years ago, I took part in a documentary for National Geographic called *Virus Hunters*, which took me to bat caves in various parts of the world where epidemiologists were collecting and recording new viruses. The hope was that they'd get ahead of the next pandemic, identifying the source before an illness could spread too far. Before I knew it, I was being lowered into a bat cave in southern Turkey.

Today, you may imagine a team of climbing professionals helping me, with medics on standby and strict protocols in place. However, just a few years ago, for shoot locations like this, that was typically not the case. In just a T-shirt and jeans, a mask, gloves, and a pair of plastic glasses, I scrambled down a ladder with a safety rope for protection into the darkness of a rocky hole by the side of a motorway. It was incredibly hot, and as sweat stung my eyes I realized what had seemed an unremarkable pit actually opened up into a huge chasm beneath the earth, and somewhere within an entire colony of bats lay in wait. In the gloom, my colleague and cohost Professor Chris Golden—a specialist in zoological diseases—warned me not to touch the walls.

"It's covered in guano," he said, with characteristic wisdom. Noticing my confusion, he translated: "Bat shit."

When I made out the faint outline of what looked like tiny winged rats bunched together in one corner, I momentarily lost my footing. The noise disturbed the sleeping creatures, and as they squawked in the darkness, I tried to push my plastic eye protection up my damp nose. But my hand slipped in the confusion, and with a guano-covered finger I poked myself directly in the eye instead. This was at the height of the coronavirus pandemic, when germ hysteria was as infectious as the virus itself. I immediately thought I'd self-administered a lethal dose of mystery bat poison straight into my blood system and, after scrambling up the shaky ladder, spent half an hour with my eye under a cold tap. When a few weeks later we went into a cave in Liberia where Ebola had been identified, our precautions included hazmat suits and gas masks. And I watched my footing.

As I've said, keeping my mind busy with the adventures of my working life helps to keep at bay my depression, which has over the years come and gone with various levels of severity. There's a big chance you picked up this book because you've felt depressed at one point in your life, too. There's a chance you're feeling that way right now. I started out by exploring schizophrenia because it is what my father experienced. But he had bouts of depression too, and it's something both my mother and I have dealt with. Later, we'll take a closer look at the overlap between the two.

Major depression is one of the most common mental disorders in the United States. The 2020 National Survey on Drug Use and Health showed some twenty million adults had experienced at least one depressive episode. The prevalence was higher among women than men—which is possibly because fewer men are willing to talk about it—and the rates were highest in younger adults ages eighteen through twenty-five. But again, that may be because younger people tend to be more comfortable discussing these conditions. The last major mental health survey in the UK took place in 2014 and found that one in six adults met the criteria for a common mental disorder. The largest killer of men under forty in Britain is suicide.

My first experience with depression came in my early twenties, when I was at university. I was struggling with my sexuality and felt deeply alone. In the back of my mind, I wondered if it was history repeating itself. I worried about my father's schizophrenia—a condition that normally manifests itself in the late teens and early twenties. I didn't know what schizophrenia would "feel" like if I was having an episode, just that there was a possibility this was it. There was no defining moment, no panic attack or incident that saw me falling off an emotional cliff. This was more of a slow journey into the gloom, which I could only really see once I'd emerged from the other side.

I remember a physical darkness that seemed to cloud my vision. Like the brightness had been turned down, the contrast reduced. The world felt dimmer, less sharp somehow. I could see what I needed to do, or what I felt I *should* do. But I had no energy to do it. Not to go to parties or see friends. Not to engage in much else outside of my studies. I felt the pressure mounting, the guilt at not doing these things. And yet at the same time, I felt a kind of dark pride at this otherness. A feeling of superiority. Of being better alone. A sense that others don't feel as deeply or think as cleverly. And then hatred would creep in—of others, and of myself. Hating myself for hating others. And the cycle continued.

Feeling depressed is a very difficult thing to articulate. You understand objectively that what you are feeling is illogical, and that the feelings of hopelessness and despair are symptoms of an illness over which you have little control. But because it affects the mind, you constantly doubt it. As though a road is being laid and only seconds later dug up, like Dorothy on the yellow brick road if the bricks were swept from beneath her feet by the tornado.

I know when I am well that this is my "less good" mind ensuring its better half cannot operate. It's the depression creating a home for itself in my mind, making itself comfortable. Expanding its territory. A kind of benign takeover of the brain. An evil army, marching on the rest of my mind not with anger or aggression, but with reason and benevolence. The attack is not hostile—it's a peaceful handover of sorts. One small part of my mind staging a nonviolent coup over the willing and exhausted masses. Until, finally, all my thoughts are controlled by this shady force.

To understand why some of us have what the actor Stephen Fry refers to as your own personal weather, I put out a call to social media for any professionals who wanted to help shed light on the question. Mark Rackley, a psychologist in London for the last ten years, responded. His podcast, *I Have Issues*, is as straight-talking as he is and aims to help inform teenagers and adults about some of the most common issues people bring to him in therapy.

I'm immediately interested to know if, like me, his patients worry about family history. My depression seems to me to mirror the low moods of my father—his distance, his solitude. Do other people feel this way? "Oh yes," he says when I ask him. "It's at the forefront of their minds. When I do an intake with a patient, I ask about family mental history because you must. But I'm asking that in a very broad way, because the patients get very scared. They think, 'Am I doomed? There's nothing I can do about this—I've just got dodgy genes!' But I explain this very clearly: This is not two and two is four. Just because you had somebody in your family with a mental health problem, it doesn't mean you're going to have it. But it is very scary stuff. If you're sitting in a psychologist's office and you're hearing voices or you're suicidal, it's really tough."

Even asking questions about family histories can be triggering. Family can often be a source of trauma rather than safety, and these questions are being asked at a time when the patient is at their most vulnerable. Mark is clear that these questions need to come as part of a long-term plan, not some quick Q and A session with a health professional you haven't met and will likely never see again.

My own experience with therapy has been mixed, to say the least. Not because the therapists themselves were not good, but because seeing one at all can be very hard. Mark spent seven years in Britain's National Health Service before he went into private care. He calls mental health services in the UK "a revolving door" because funding is around half of what other parts of the health service receive. With so much strain on public finances, he explains, NHS psychologists are considered a luxury rather than a necessity. And when they *are* offered as part of a treatment program, it's only for very limited times—even when the patient really should be seen for far longer. At the time of writing, waiting times for an NHS psychologist in many parts of the UK are over six months.

Humans have sought to understand our mental state for almost as long as we've had the power to write. In the Victorian era, as scientists gradually discovered more about our human biology, so too did they seek to understand the links between mind and body. Sigmund Freud is the man most closely associated with pioneering the new study of psychiatry, and his focus was psychoanalysis—understanding the unconscious mind. It is to Freud that we owe talking therapies—the one technique that seems to have had the most success in dealing with complex mental health needs. He believed all complex human behavior was directed by elements of the human mind, and through his influence, what was once variously described as a nervous breakdown, nervous exhaustion, lunacy, or melancholia eventually became more understood as a chemical reaction in the brain, related to but also separate from the reality of our lives.

Behaviorism evolved out of Freud's theories and became a dominant school of thought in the 1950s. It differed from Freud's psychoanalytic approach because it suggested that all behavior can be explained by external forces—or the "environment," to put it in modern terms. In response, cognitive psychology emerged, interested in how people think, remember, perceive, and learn, with a particular focus on children and their experiences growing up. Cognitive behavioral therapy is a product of this movement and is still practiced today—treating automatic negative thoughts and the behaviors they elicit, rather than unwinding childhood traumas as Freud's talking therapies would. Modern psychology as we know it is a blend of all of these approaches and more, and it's important to point out that our understanding of the field is changing all the time and differs greatly depending on who you ask.

If you have an interest in mental health, or you've ever been prescribed an antidepressant, you will likely have heard of serotonin. It acts essentially as a delivery service in the blood, carrying messages between nerve cells in your brain and throughout your body. It helps with all kinds of things, from bone health to sleep quality. But it is also a mood stabilizer, generating feelings of happiness and reducing anxiety.

First discovered as a naturally occurring substance in the body in the 1930s, serotonin only came to be understood as a treatment for depression by accident in the early 1950s. A ward full of tuberculosis patients, recently administered a new drug called iproniazid, found their moods transformed. Once glum and dejected individuals, often catatonic for months, were suddenly brought back to life. The side effect of iproniazid—increased serotonin levels in the brain—was found to be the answer. Serotonin was fueling electrical connectivity in the brain, and a lack of it, doctors discovered, caused depression. Prozac, the first available SSRI (selective serotonin reuptake inhibitors) to combat this chemical lack, quickly became one of the most popular drugs on the market. Today, millions—myself included—still take one of the many options in the new generation of antidepressants.

Doctors don't currently look for physical changes in our biology to identify depression; the signs of depression are diagnosed when a patient tells a doctor how they feel, and the doctor assumes serotonin levels in the brain must be low. The first of two cardinal symptoms clinicians now look for in people who may have depression is anhedonia: the inability to feel pleasure in normally pleasurable activities. The second is low mood. Normally, you need to display one of these, together with at least four of the following secondary symptoms: loss of sleep, change in appetite, lack of energy, low sex drive, irritability, feelings of guilt, or low self-esteem. Depression is an increasingly common diagnosis—about one in six or seven of us will be diagnosed with depressive moods in our lifetimes. However, the diagnosis is incredibly broad. Many people will enter a depressive period brought on by external forces—a death of a relative or close friend, the loss of a job, any traumatic event—and then recover. They may need medication for a short time and then never again. They may need to see a therapist, then feel that they have overcome their challenge. What scientists are more interested in, and what my own interest is focused on, is clinical depression that returns repeatedly, regardless of what is happening in your life.

I find it's not periods of change that greatly affect me, but periods of stability, which I often interpret as stagnation. I had found myself sinking into depression during my university years, but with therapy and medication I came out of it. Finishing university, heading to Syria, getting my first jobs in news—all of these things kept my mind alert, out of the gloom. But then, at the age of twenty-seven, the monotony of working life caused it all to catch up with me once again. I was at the BBC, where I had settled into a job as a producer. I'd already been feeling low for a few months; I'd interpreted the steadiness of my job as a failure, and I was unhappily single. In hindsight, I was dealing with all the same things almost everyone deals with in their late twenties. But I have the luxury of being well as I write this; when I get down, those rationales no longer hold weight. Depression became the obsessive source of my sadness, and the spring from which a sort of inevitable fate seemed to be materializing. Once again, I felt trapped in a cycle that began with my father and was being reproduced in me.

I was at my desk at work one day when I started to hyperventilate. Then I began to cry. I don't think I realized it, but I was having a panic attack. I called the nonemergency helpline in the UK and was given the address of a clinic in central London. It was a ten-minute walk, but I ran to the clinic. When I think about that run now, it feels very dramatic: It had started to rain and I could feel my heart beating fast. I was convinced I'd be safe once I arrived at the clinic. I had never had to access emergency mental health care before, and I think I imagined it as a place where I could just collapse and be caught by people who knew what they were doing. I thought people would be waiting by the door, maybe even prepared to give me a hug and sit me down somewhere comfortable.

"The mental health walk-in has closed," an angry woman behind a glass screen barked. "This is not where you're supposed to go." I was instantly crushed. She slotted a card under the screen and busied herself with another patient at what was now simply a doctor's clinic. Government cuts to mental health services meant this place could not help me. As I took out my phone to make the call, I heard her shout, "You can't make calls in here!" I dragged myself outside.

The number wasn't right. A kind South African voice on the other end didn't know why I had been given the number but said I should try asking the woman at the clinic again.

I hung up. I called my friend Melissa and left a message. I was a little rambling, I think. I don't remember much of what I said, but I know I kept thinking I didn't know what was happening to me, and I imagine I kept repeating that. And then I sat on the curb with my head in my hands, out of options. I felt entirely helpless. My breathing had slowed, but tears still rolled down my face. I'd used up all the energy I felt I had. It was as though the panic attack had given me an adrenaline rush that had worn off all at once.

And then, for a few minutes, I seriously considered walking out into traffic. I wondered what it would feel like and how quick it would be. I thought about what road I would need to get to where the traffic might be going fast enough. I looked around at the quiet street and realized it would be a few minutes' walk until I could get to Tottenham Court Road, where maybe there'd be a bus. I sat there, wondering if I had the energy to get up and go there. It was a horrible thought, and didn't last long. Later, when the doctor asked me why I hadn't gotten up, I told him that I couldn't be bothered. I had lost the energy even to want to end my life.

I stayed there for a while—I'm not sure how long—and then Melissa called and dropped everything to come find me. She was, and still is, a guardian angel. She took me to my doctor's office and insisted to a not particularly cooperative receptionist that he see me as soon as possible. The doctor started by congratulating me on coming to see him. "Well done for seeking help," he said, looking at me over his glasses. "A lot of people don't make it this far." *No shit, mate,* I thought. *Not if every service meant to help a person becomes a barrier.*

And then, I kind of just got on with life. It's rather strange how much like going over the edge a moment like that can be: One second you're okay, and the next you're not. And if you're caught, you're back up and running, away from the precipice again. It's a bit like how Ernest Hemingway describes bankruptcy in *The Sun Also Rises*: "'How did you go bankrupt?' Bill asked. 'Two ways,' Mike said. 'Gradually, then suddenly.'"

I think I was scared by how I had felt, and I did my best to make sure I wouldn't feel like that again. More pills and more therapists and, crucially, sharing the story with my closest friends. Oddly enough, some people take it personally when you admit to having been in crisis, similar to the response some have to being told a friend is gay: "Why didn't you tell me?!" It's a loving refrain, but also unwittingly self-centered. Fortunately, my friends' responses were exactly as understanding and nonjudgmental as I imagined they would be.

It's incredible what a release that can be. A pressure valve being relaxed, the burden lifted. It's like a magic trick.

I don't know why, but shame never really came into this experience. My father's family was burdened by the shame of his death, of his condition, of his father's suicide, and of the mental illness that they could see pulsing through the family. It was perhaps my earlier experience with depression that gave me the perspective I needed to realize, subconsciously, that I should not keep this a secret. It is also clearly a generational difference. Conversations about mental health might never really have taken place around my father, or his father. I am fortunate to have been born at a different time, in which attitudes are shifting. I knew that if I wasn't going to repeat the patterns of my family, I had to destroy any feelings of shame or embarrassment.

It was this experience that spurred me into examining the genetics of mental illness and to learn what had happened to my father. I realized that being a journalist and working at the BBC would open doors I might otherwise have found closed, and even though I don't have a single scientific bone in my body, I became focused on my biology. What is it about me that causes this to happen? Why had I gone through this twice now, before the age of thirty? Where had these feelings of inevitability come from? And, of course, what really happened to my father?

A year after sitting on the curb with my head in my hands, I was filming a short documentary for the BBC on the inheritance of mental illness. I was lucky enough by then to be working on a current affairs show called the *Victoria Derbyshire* programme, and the editor there, Louisa Compton, was one of the best bosses I'd ever had. We'd shared our own private battles with each other, and when I suggested I was interested in whether my father's illness might have traveled to me somehow, she thought it would make a great piece for the show.

I was paired up with a producer—the incredible Sarah Hatchard—and together we went about finding the genetic specialists who I hoped could give me some answers. As it turned out, one of the most prestigious centers for the study of genetic mental illness is based at King's College London, and so I met with Professors Cathryn Lewis and Roland Zahn. My interviews with them formed the basis of this book.

The whole process of making the piece was extraordinarily cathartic and revealing. It forced me to think about my dad as a person independent of me—as "John Longman" rather than "father of James." And that, in turn, helped me to separate his illness from what I wondered might be mine. I was able to come to grips with the distinct nature of schizophrenia, how living with it might have made him depressed, and how our experiences could be just as influenced by our respective environments as by any genetic susceptibility. I was also able, for the very first time, to sit down with my mother and talk about my dad. I've asked her to put in her own words what life with him was like. (You'll read that later.) But taking action, finding answers, asking questions—that is what I have found helps me. That, and working on this book.

Moving past a depressive wave—as a lot of you reading this will know—doesn't necessarily make you any better prepared for the next. And over the course of writing this book, the feelings I describe here returned. Toward the end of 2022 and into the first months of 2023, I could feel myself retreating again.

This time it was different. My sadness was compounded by anxiety. I could feel anger raging through me at the slightest inconvenience. If someone was walking too slowly in the street or I missed a green light while driving, I could sense what felt like waves of electricity shooting through me from my feet to my head. I could feel my heart racing and my breath becoming shorter. And I could not stop thinking. Thoughts about my work, my life with Alex, my friendships—all of it would rush around my head all day, every day, so that when I wasn't angry, I was just exhausted.

I felt I'd essentially failed at my life, and thoughts of ending it returned. I'd walk around London glancing up at tall buildings, wondering if they'd be tall enough. What the experience would feel like. If I'd regret it on the way down. When a close friend told me about the suicide of someone close to her, she looked at me, stricken, and asked, "How can he possibly have gone through with it?" But my reaction shocked even me. I felt I knew exactly what he was thinking and feeling. I felt I knew that he didn't believe what others saw in him was real, and that the disconnect even with those he loved had become so permanent and painful that suicide actually felt like the only option. When the doctor asked me why I had not acted on these thoughts, "Alex" was my only reply. It made me cry to know that I loved him so much, but it deepened my own sense of worthlessness that I couldn't find a reason in myself to stay alive.

One thing a previous experience of depression does give you is an understanding that you've got to go through the motions of recovery, even if at first you think they're of no use. It did take me some time to reach this conclusion, and even when you're doing all the right things, you may still be thinking all the wrong things. But it doesn't matter—you've got to keep going, even when you feel you're using what little energy you have for no reason. And if you're lucky, you'll have someone like my Alex to encourage you along the way. So it was back to doctors' appointments, psychologists, and medication, just as before.

I'll be honest with you: I had to stop work on this book for a while to get my head straight, to simply regain some energy. But since returning to it, learning about some of the latest science around recovery has really given me new hope. In only the few years between my last dip and this one, the breakthroughs in research have been extraordinary. They go beyond changes to medication. Our newfound understanding of our biology, and the interdependent nature of our physiology, makes me feel in much greater control of my mind and my feelings. And that is so liberating.

James at Hill House school, 1993. (top)

John Longman with newborn James, December 1986. (bottom)

CHAPTER 5

THE GENETICS OF MENTAL ILLNESS

Isn't it odd. We can only see our outsides, but nearly everything happens on the inside.

—CHARLIE MACKESY,
THE BOY, THE MOLE, THE FOX AND THE HORSE

The only major physical health scare I've had was when I broke my leg when I was a kid. I was eight years old, and I was thrown into the aisle of the school bus when it stopped suddenly on the way home, and a bunch of my classmates fell on top of me. I landed so awkwardly that I broke my femur, the largest bone in the body. I remember looking up to see my mother bounding onto the bus and ordering all the other kids to the back. She swept me up, put me on her knee, and told the ashen-faced bus driver to go directly to the hospital. So off we all went to the emergency room (along a route with speed bumps), where I ended up in skeletal traction for six weeks. My mother slept on the floor of the hospital by my bed for the duration.

When I was finally able to get up, I was given a wheelchair for two weeks so I could move about the ward. It was at this time that I got to know a young boy about my age who lived there. His name was Absar, and he had severe physical disabilities. It's possible his parents had only realized his condition once he was born, and he had been tragically left behind at the hospital. It may not be common practice now, but he just stayed there. He couldn't speak or move most of his body. He only had the use of one hand to direct his electric wheelchair, but with his head tilted to one side, he could move his mouth and eyes to communicate. The children's ward was his home.

Absar was an entertainer. He'd play tricks on hospital staff, and he and I would race our wheelchairs around the place, bumping into things and causing all kinds of mischief. He really loved fruit yogurt, and when the nurses came with his food, he would pretend not to want any of it, turning his head away. Finally, when their attention was elsewhere, he'd lunge for the spoon, and the yogurt would end up all over his face. He thought this was very funny, and I did, too. Everyone in the children's wing loved him—he was part of an adoptive family.

I thought of him often and went to visit him a few weeks after I'd been discharged. He was so happy to see me, and I remember even now feeling a pang of sadness that he had to stay at the hospital. Sometime later I went back to visit him again but was told he had died.

I don't know what condition Absar had, or whether it was genetic, or whether something had gone badly wrong during his mother's pregnancy. But I often think of Absar, and the biological lottery in which so many don't fare well. I wonder about Absar's family, and whether they passed down some genetic marker, a kind of kink in the code. I also wonder about my own family and if they did the same to me—but with my mental health.

When I talk about depression, people often tell me about someone they are related to who has some form of mental illness, too: "Oh, my brother got depressed for a while." "My aunt has bipolar disorder." "I think a cousin of mine is on antidepressants. Not sure what for." In my experience, there's a fleeting moment when the person then supposes that the illness or condition afflicting their relative might also impact *them*. It's a kind of stare into the middle distance, as they consider for a split second that they too may "have" whatever "it" is.

I am lucky that talking about mental illness at ABC is not only tolerated, but celebrated—both as a personal issue and editorially. We aim to produce stories about these issues and get as many people as possible to see or hear them. Dr. Jen Ashton, a physician and ABC's former chief medical editor, has been very open about her own experiences of suicide. Her ex-husband took his own life in 2017, and since then she has become an advocate for suicide prevention. A few years ago, I was interviewed on Dr. Jen's podcast, *Life After Suicide,* which takes its name from her bestselling book, and afterward was contacted by a lot of people with stories similar to my own. One of them was Kim, a thirty-seven-year-old designer and art director who lives with her family in the Netherlands. She got in touch to tell me her mother had ended her life, and that twenty years earlier, her grandfather had done the same.

"It's been such a huge part of my life," she tells me. "I was my mother's counselor from the age of fifteen. I found her trying to end her life. She spoke to me about it all the time. When my grandfather ended his life, he called us before to say goodbye, and then hanged himself in the garage." Her mother killed herself the same way.

"I have always felt these issues of mental health have been hanging over our family. I've been trying hard to make sure I don't become my grandfather or my mother. I think positively, I've got all the tools. But still, I see some of the bad stuff repeating in me. I've had this huge fear that I somehow will turn out like them.

"Everything you said on the podcast and everything I've listened to made me so happy because I was, like, 'Oh my god, there is somebody else!'" We speak about the feelings of depression she sometimes gets, and the sense that these have been passed down. In Kim I see a kindred spirit—someone who is aware of her past and wants to know more. "I totally know that it comes from her," she tells me. "I can feel what I saw in her."

While speaking to Kim, I'm struck by what a big word *depression* is, and how it's not an abstract, objective sense of being sad that I sometimes feel. It's much more specifically my father's sadness, or what I imagine it to be. My father's schizophrenia was also characterized by low moods and a penetrating desire to be alone. I feel his need to be isolated reflected in me. It's almost like I don't have depression—I have *his* depression.

As you can imagine, nine years is not a lot of time to gather memories of a person, particularly when most of those years are impossible to remember. I also know I only saw a small fraction of my father, both in a literal sense and emotionally. I was a child and was protected as much as possible from his illness. So it was to others that I went for answers, specifically the relatives on his mother's side.

My grandmother Nancy had a sister, Rosemary, and while Nancy decided to marry an Englishman and move south, Rosemary married a Scot and became the doyenne of an entire Scottish clan. Aunt Rosie—as I knew her—had all the same mannerisms as my grandmother: the same smile, the same hand movements, the same faint Scottish "och yes" or "och no." And she had the same big white hair. But where my grandmother was the more reserved, spindly sister, Rosie was plumper, more smiley, and chirpier. While between my father and his brother there was only one child (me), Rosemary and her husband, Sandy, had three children, all of whom had three children of their own, who in turn have had many more, making Rosemary a great-grandmother many times over.

I've often felt very isolated as far as family goes. I envied these Scottish cousins, who I imagined led the kinds of busy TV-family lives of my dreams: full breakfast tables, frenzied school runs, loud birthdays and anniversaries and Christmas festivities. And Rosie's daughter Karen, my dad's first cousin, has long had an instinct for this, and has tried to include me as much as possible over the years. On visits to Scotland, she was always the one to pull out the photo albums, to show me my dad on family holidays, to tell me about him as a boy and as a young man. Many of the memories are fuzzy, but they've been my only real clues into my dad's early life. And in our baby photos, we look almost exactly the same.

Karen and the handful of others who knew my dad well all have remarkably similar memories of him: A man who could light up the room with his wit and humor. Someone who enjoyed making a fool of himself in front of the people he trusted. An intensely withdrawn person who wanted to hide away from the world. I like to see the former qualities in myself, but I also fear the latter has its way of taking over. In my father's medical notes, professionals explain repeatedly how badly he wanted to retreat from the world. When he was well, he would tell them that he wanted to try to reengage, that he knew socializing would likely relieve his symptoms. But when he was unwell, he was convinced cutting himself off was the only way forward.

There is a comfort to seeing your parents reflected in you. And I imagine an even deeper pride in seeing yourself reflected in your children. It helps us make sense of our place in the world and gives us purpose. We feel part of something bigger than ourselves—a personal journey through time that is unique to us. Depression has been an isolating experience for me, compounded by the reality of having very little immediate family. I imagine that's why I hold on to memories of people I love so keenly and have always found my grandparents' lives deeply fascinating. I think it's why I ended up working in the Middle East, following in their footsteps. When I was the BBC's Beirut correspondent, I often marveled at how history had come full circle. Perhaps in her day, I thought, after Gabrielle had fled Lebanon, she'd listen on the radio to the voice of a well-spoken British man telling her about the war ripping her country apart. Some forty years later, her grandson had become that person, in no small tribute to her.

Our family history, and what it represents to us, is one of the ways we form our own personal identities. And the specter of mental illness has long been part of those calculations. In her book *"Shattered Nerves": Doctors, Patients, and Depression in Victorian England,* Janet Oppenheim explains how attitudes surrounding mental health shifted throughout the nineteenth century and evolved into our current understanding. It was an obsession with the family that gripped Victorian scientists. British class systems revolve around the family and its status, and no amount of money can move you from one class to the next. And so a focus on family health was perhaps natural for a generation of scientists who viewed life through this lens. It's easy to see how shame became so intertwined with mental illness—and how the connection persists today—if a family's entire future could be lost through the public revelation of some kind of genetic deficiency. The issue of hereditary health comes into sharpest view in the stories of Europe's royal families, including most infamously two of the late Queen Elizabeth II's first cousins. Nerissa and Katherine Bowes-Lyon were the children of Elizabeth's uncle, and were both born with learning difficulties. Very little was publicly known about them other than their reported deaths in 1940 and 1961, respectively. But a scandal broke in 1987, revealing that the sisters were still alive but had been put into permanent psychiatric care. When Nerissa died, it was reported only hospital staff attended her funeral.

"The unit of degeneracy is the family," wrote P. C. Smith, a physician from Tunbridge Wells, in the early 1900s. "A degenerate family is one in which there is imperfect heredity." I certainly don't think of mental illness as "degeneracy"—and the scientific community has obviously moved on from such negative terminology. But observable patterns of behavior through generations of families continue to fascinate.

In the late twentieth century, German psychotherapist Bert Hellinger pioneered a method of therapy called Family Constellations, in which participants attempt to understand how our family histories are repeated through time. He theorized major events like murder, death, suicide, war, or any other massive trauma can reverberate through the generations, and it is up to us to untangle these traumas in order to be free of them. His work sparked a worldwide movement of alternative therapy and healing that is variously dismissed as quackery in some quarters and revered as spiritual enlightenment in others. It is still practiced as a therapeutic treatment today, in which actors take on the roles of family members so the therapist can observe the responses of their client. Hellinger's theories were spiritual in nature, focused more on the psychoanalytical school of psychiatry's view on learned behaviors than biological explanations. But tracing genetic susceptibility to depression and other mental health conditions is a natural next step for his work.

Much of the most basic science of inherited mental illness is based around observable patterns. The so-called 2-4-8 rule is a long-established one. It means that if one of your parents has depression, you are twice as likely to have it. The offspring of those with bipolar disorder will have a fourfold risk of receiving the same diagnosis. And for those with a parent with schizophrenia, it's eight times. (In fact, the most reliable predictor of developing schizophrenia is having a parent with the condition, which is not the case for depression or bipolar disorder.)

Genetic research largely revolves around twin studies. When studying two biologically identical people who have likely been raised in the same environment, scientists can identify the processes that cause a change or fault in one and not the other, which can help disentangle the influences of genetic and environmental factors on a particular trait or disease. The twin design involves monozygotic twins (identical twins) and dizygotic twins (nonidentical twins), with the underlying assumption being that monozygotic twins share 100 percent of their genes and dizygotic twins share only 50 percent of their genes, but both will have had the same environmental exposure. This means scientists can look for sets of traits or characteristics—in this case, the symptoms of severe mental illness—which they call the phenotype. If genetic factors are indeed important to the phenotype, then monozygotic twins should resemble each other more than dizygotic twins do.

The word I come across over and over in this research is what scientists call *heritability*. While you may directly *inherit* blue eyes from a parent, heritability is all about statistical probability and takes into account much broader trends across a larger population. So, while *heredity* is the ability of traits to be inherited by children from their parents, *heritability* is a measure of genetic influence—the degree to which variations in a trait or characteristic can be attributed to genetics. For example, a 2017 Danish twin study of schizophrenia found a heritability estimate of around 80 percent. That does not mean 80 percent of people with a parent who has schizophrenia will also have it. It *does* mean schizophrenia is likely 80 percent a matter of genetic inheritance. Meanwhile, the same study found depression to have a heritability estimate of around 38 percent. Because more than half of the variance in depression cannot be explained by genetic factors, the Danish study found that environment plays a greater role than genetics in depression.

(Crucially, twin studies assume either a genetic factor or an environmental one and kind of add them together, and they can therefore overestimate the importance of genes. What they don't do is explain how genes and the environment might *interact*. How the environment activates those genetics is a fascinating newer area of research we'll explore later.)

The numbers here may sound high, but the chances are very low to begin with—1 percent of the population has a chance of developing schizophrenia. This means I have an 8 percent chance. Still, given that my uncle Tony was also in and out of psychiatric wards, and my grandfather Jimmy also ended his life, *and* my mother has also had difficulties with her mental health, I can't help but feel attacked from all sides.

All this science might be rattling your brain. Writing it down has certainly rattled mine! Thankfully, there are scientists who are able to explain genetic susceptibility in digestible ways. Jehannine Austin, a professor of medical genetics at the University of British Columbia, developed a model that helped me grasp it: the jam jar. First, she puts a certain number of stones into her jam jar. These represent our genes that increase our likelihood of having mental illness. The number of stones is fixed at birth. Some people will have a lot of stones in their jam jar, to the point of being almost full, while others will have a very small number.

She then adds the environment, which is any traumatic life event: a death, a major breakup, the loss of a job. In her analogy, she sees this as pouring water on top of the genes. The combination of stones and water is what makes up your resilience, your personal buffer against depression. When the jar overflows is when you've gone over your limit. That's when you're diagnosed with depression. The fewer stones you have in your jar, the more water you're able to take on. But if your jam jar is already full of stones, there isn't much room for anything else.

This is a helpful way to understand why we all differ in our abilities to take on what life throws at us. I first came across the analogy in a BBC documentary, *Depression and Me,* by former Downing Street head of communications Alastair Campbell. He has spoken very openly about having depression. In the program, he spoke about creating what he calls rings for the top of his jam jar, ensuring it could take on more and more water if needed. Each ring was something that made him happy, whether that was exercising, spending time with friends, or walking his dog. In other words, he was able to implement mechanisms to stop the jar from overflowing. This is certainly a worthwhile strategy, but I'm especially interested in those stones at the bottom of the jar. How exactly did they get there in the first place? And given that they *are* already there, how can I avoid taking on water?

Another useful analogy, coined by Nathan Filer, is to type 2 diabetes. Type 1 diabetes is a fundamental issue with insulin production, meaning no matter what you do, you'll need a lifelong supply of it to keep you alive. Type 2, on the other hand, is what he calls "a more variable biological state," not attributable to any one issue. The body may not be as responsive to insulin as it should be, but there are other hormone imbalances at play, too. So it's this *collection* of problems that combine to put you at risk. If you eat badly or don't exercise, for example, your risk level increases, and you may develop serious illness. But unlike with Type 1, altering your environment can mean you can beat type 2 diabetes—maybe for good.

In the same way, changing our environments can lessen our

susceptibility to mental illness. It all comes down to how those environments interact with our DNA. So, before we go any further, let's return to the basics. What are genes, and how do they work?

DNA (deoxyribonucleic acid) is the basic coding for all life on earth. It carries the genetic information for the development and functioning of our bodies. DNA sequences must be converted to messages that produce certain proteins, and those proteins form the cells that do most of the work in our bodies. Each DNA sequence containing instructions to make a protein is known as a gene. The image you're probably thinking of now—the twisted ladder with pairs of balls on it, which represents each piece of DNA—is the genome—the complete set of DNA instructions.

These precise base pairs were first sequenced only at the turn of the century. There was an immediate explosion of optimism about how many secrets could be unlocked; for the first time in history, researchers could categorize each part of the human genome. That is, they could differentiate between coding and regulation: genes that cause characteristics, and genes that regulate the degree to which they function. The ability to compare healthy DNA to that of patients suffering from all kinds of physical illnesses meant new possibilities for disease treatment and prevention. Cancer research, for instance, has made huge strides in recent years because scientists can now identify mutations, understand how specific genetic processes are being activated, and develop medications that target them.

However, it became apparent very quickly that discovering the genome wouldn't be an automatic panacea. There is much more at work when it comes to how our genes actually function. It turns out that only 2 percent of our DNA is coding for proteins. Scientists had no idea what the other 98 percent was doing. They even called it junk DNA for a while.

I'm conscious of how much science I'm throwing at you, and I hope you're following along. Science never made much sense for me at school, and to be honest, I can't really believe I'm halfway through writing a chapter about genes. When I told a friend I was writing a book with a lot of science in it, she started laughing. I might as well have told her I'd be translating the complete works of Homer. But while chemistry had too many numbers, and physics might as well have been ancient Mayan, biology did appeal to me in school. So often it's about the teachers we have. One of my earliest science teachers, Mr. Fagan, taught me when I was eight through to about twelve. He looked like Father Christmas, but a five-foot version, with rust-colored beard and hair and a slightly less cheerful demeanor. Father Christmas's evil twin, perhaps. He had a habit of throwing our exercise books back to us across the room after he'd done some marking in them. The books were huge. It was like having the phone book thrown at you twice a week.

But behind his occasionally gruff exterior, Mr. Fagan was deeply kind. Not long after my father died, I was in his class Thinking Skills—my Catholic school's version of "philosophy for kids," with the occasional bit of sex education. I would have been nine at the time, and I was sitting quietly at the back of his lab, looking down at the desk in front of me. After the general din of a new period was over, and the other boys had finished scraping their chairs noisily under their tables and settled into their exercise books, he walked over to me. Without drawing any attention, he slid his hands across the desk to alert me to his presence. I looked up and saw his bright blue eyes shining from beneath bushy eyebrows. He mouthed, "You're okay," nodded at me with a smile, and silently walked on. It wasn't really a question, although it could have been. He was just letting me know he was there. It was the kind of subtle recognition and reassurance I needed. I don't remember much from science class, but I do remember that. All these years later, I wonder what he would have made of this book. (He'd probably have crossed half of it out with his red pen and thrown it back at me.)

All that is to say, I'm doing the best I can with the science. Luckily, accomplished scientists are as eager to share their research as I am to learn from it. Professor Cathryn Lewis at King's College London is a geneticist studying the genes involved in mental illness. Cathryn was the first scientist I met when I began looking into this topic, back when I was filming the story for the BBC. Twin studies have given her team the basis from which to understand the "heritability" of depression and other mental illnesses.

"Depression is about 40 percent heritable," she says, referencing twin studies like the Danish one I mentioned earlier. "Bipolar disorder and schizophrenia are much more genetic—in those cases it's about 70 percent or 80 percent."

Although twin studies have played a pivotal role in highlighting the importance of genetics in psychiatric disorders, they do not tell us anything about the genes or genetic variants that are potentially involved in those psychiatric disorders. In the last decade, developments in DNA technology have allowed researchers to identify the potential genetic variants that increase the risk of developing illness. Genome-wide association studies (GWAS) are now widely conducted and have been instrumental in identifying the genetic variants that contribute to traits and diseases.

Professor Lewis says doctors have known for the last twenty or thirty years that there is a genetic component to depression, but only in the last four or five years have they been able to identify which genetic variants—which "snips"—are common in people with mental illnesses. "It's clear that there is no single variant that has a very major effect," she says. "In school we learn about genetics like Huntington's disease or cystic fibrosis, where there is a single gene and that's the one that's important. There is nothing like that in depression. You cannot say you have the gene for depression."

She describes depression as instead being a polygenic disorder, which means multiple genes are involved. Researchers suspect that there are possibly tens of thousands of genetic variants that all combine to determine someone's risk of depression. (Remember, we're talking about risk factors here, rather than definite predictors.) For depression, the number of variants identified is currently at 178. Genome-wide association studies involve thousands of participants, and as their number increases, so too do the number of variants that have been identified. For example, the study that identified 102 variants was published in 2019 and had 807,553 participants (246,363 cases and 561,190 controls). The study that identified 178 variants was published in 2021 and had 1.2 million participants (around 365,000 cases).

The key, for me, is that Lewis says many of the variants identified are associated with all three of the major mental illnesses we are discussing: depression, bipolar disorder, and schizophrenia. This means that some of the same variants that combined to cause schizophrenia in my father may also have combined to cause depression in me. (It's worth stating: Lewis is not saying my depression was some "weaker version" of my dad's schizophrenia. It's important not to view these conditions on a sliding scale. His depressive moods might have been an aspect of his schizophrenia, or perhaps a response to the knowledge that he had the disease. Whatever was transpiring in his mind and in his body might very well have been a reaction to the combination of genetic variants he carried, while some of those same variants might have caused something different in me.)

Five years ago, nothing like this had been discovered.

Genetics cannot predict mental illness in a person, but Lewis hopes in the future her work may improve diagnosis. The number of different diagnoses people receive throughout their lives is often quite surprising. My father was told he had schizoid personality disorder, sociopathic personality disorder, and schizophrenia at various times in his life. Michelle, the schizophrenia activist in New York City, was told she had bipolar disorder and was prescribed medication that actually made her symptoms worse. It can be really difficult for the doctor, but most importantly the patient, to have any clarity about what is actually going on.

One significant example of this is the difference between depressive episodes and those that come as a result of bipolar disorder, or what used to be called manic depression. Depression is mostly associated with low moods, while bipolar disorder is associated with shifts between low and high moods that the person finds uncontrollable. But because the low moods tend to start first, depression can be diagnosed by mistake and "treated" with antidepressants—the wrong treatment for someone with bipolar disorder. It is of course the case that many people find these terms too fixed, and a lot of human experience varies. But while the behaviors and therefore the diagnoses may be easily confused, genes are easier to read.

Lewis keeps repeating that this is early-stage science, but researchers are now more capable of distinguishing between genetic predisposition to depression and genetic predisposition to bipolar disorder.

Researchers are hoping better genetic understanding will mean better treatment. For example, in schizophrenia and depression, around 33 percent of patients are treatment-resistant—they don't show any improvements after being prescribed their first line of treatment. Researchers are now trying to see whether they can predict if someone will be treatment-resistant, based on their genetic profile. Outside of psychiatric disorders, there has already been success in this respect. Hepatitis C, for instance, is commonly treated with two medications, which don't cure all patients. What researchers have found is that there is a genetic variant in a gene that can predict whether someone will respond well to the medication. The implications of this kind of research for mental illness are huge; doctors of the future may one day be able to determine which antidepressants will work best for any given person.

When I started thinking about this book, and in my earliest conversations with Professor Lewis, the idea of publicly available genetic testing for depression sounded like science fiction. But in the intervening years, some companies have begun offering just that. You may know 23andMe as a DNA-mapping service that tells you about your genetic makeup and helps link you with long-lost relatives. But it now offers genetic screening for all kinds of conditions, too, from blood markers for certain diseases through to genetic predispositions to depression and anxiety. These services are not uncontroversial. When I told friends I was going to see what 23andMe said about my depression, the news was met with real skepticism. "You have no idea what they are going to do with your data!" was the general reaction.

While I am slightly concerned that there is, as we speak, a version of me being grown in a Chinese lab, I thought it would be worthwhile. So I packed up a spit sample and sent it off for testing. A few weeks later (plus the necessary subscription to their premium service for depression results—*eye roll*) and I have now been told I have a "typical likelihood" of developing depression. "An estimated 25 out of 100 people with genetics like yours have been diagnosed with depression by their twenties," says my app, with a neat little graphic of twenty-five little men grayed out in a grid of one hundred. It strikes me as quite simplistic. They are presumably making this assessment based not just on my information but on wider statistical data, and there don't seem to be many specifics in this result. It doesn't feel especially precise or tailored to me. But that this service is even available does feel like the start of something important and like part of the future of diagnostic services for all kinds of health complaints.

As I have repeated throughout this book, there is nothing uncontroversial about the study of genetics in relation to mental illness. There are many scientists who completely disagree with Cathryn Lewis and others who place an emphasis on the heritability of these conditions. One of the more high-profile objectors is British clinical psychologist Dr. John Read, who worked for more than two decades in mental health services in the UK and the USA before committing full-time to academia. He has called these results from genetic research "laughable," and instead places much greater emphasis on childhood trauma as a cause of major mental illness. He also believes psychoanalysis is a preferable treatment to drugs. But while Lewis and Read approach the issue at different angles, they don't necessarily stop at wholly different points. Lewis and researchers like her are also interested in the way genetics and the environment interact, acknowledging that they are not, in fact, two separate forces in a simple equation of addition or subtraction.

Genetics is already a big part of the diagnostics process in the UK. The 100,000 Genomes Project, an initiative started in 2014, gathered DNA from around 85,000 National Health Service patients affected by a rare disease or cancer. They then used what they call whole genome sequencing to identify new genetic causes for conditions ranging from common cancers to the rarest autoimmune disorders. Now, when certain patients present to a health professional with complaints that match symptoms of that study, they are offered genetic testing. The impact can be life changing. A 2021 analysis of the initiative studied over four thousand people from over two thousand families who were early participants in the project. It found that using whole genome sequencing led to a new diagnosis for 25 percent of participants, and of these new diagnoses, 14 percent found variations in regions of the genome that would have been missed by other methods. Given these extraordinary results, it is hard to see why investigation into the genetics of mental illness would not be worthwhile.

I wanted to speak to someone who is at the cutting edge of this research. Someone who is using these new technologies to actually change people's lives. Mark Philip is a neurogenetics clinical nurse at St. George's Hospital in London, where these tests are carried out. He is assigned to patients who may be demonstrating symptoms of a rare disease, and who therefore may benefit from genetic testing. "We are mainstreaming genomic medicine as part of diagnostic care," he tells me. "More often than not, people are happy to understand their genetic susceptibility. But my job is often to manage expectations. They think finding *the* gene is going to happen. But that's not the case, mostly."

The National Genomic Test Directory is an open resource in which symptoms, conditions, and even specific genes can be searched. Groups of genes, called panels, are listed for different categories, but there is currently no individual panel for mental illness conditions. "The science that links specific genes to specific mental illness isn't there yet, but there is a lot of overlap with existing conditions," says Mark. "So, for example, one category of genes is listed under adult-onset neurodegenerative disorder. That takes in conditions like Alzheimer's and Parkinson's disease." These aren't conditions that depend on only one gene. Like schizophrenia, for example, they are polygenetic, meaning they require a number of genetic variants to be present. "The directory is growing on a daily basis," says Mark. As with 23andMe, more data collected by initiatives like the 100,000 Genomes Project could lead to better results, helping to improve the ability to map genetic variants for mental illnesses.

Skeptics like Dr. John Read may say my father and his brother received schizophrenia diagnoses not because of genetics but because of the environments they shared. His argument could be further strengthened because I did not develop schizophrenia, and I have experienced none of the symptoms normally associated with the condition.

But I keep coming back to Professor Lewis, who says a number of the genetic variants she has uncovered *are* common in all three major mental illnesses, which means schizophrenia and depression share many of the same genetic variants. I may have received some of these variants from my father. My jam jar, as it were, might already have been filled with those rocks, so when water was poured in—life stresses, work challenges, relationship difficulties—my jar spilled over. One day it may be possible to run my mum's and dad's DNA through a system like 23andMe, and establish which variants came from which parent. This kind of detailed forensic analysis isn't available right now. But it may be very soon.

Since genetic susceptibility accounts for 40 percent of the risk for depression, I'm interested in how the other 60 percent—the environment—could have played a role in my life. What impact my upbringing and the knowledge of my father's death might have had. We generally understand the causes of depression as split—part genetic, part environmental—but there is increasing evidence to suggest our environments don't just have an emotional impact on us. They can affect us on a genetic level, too, meaning the effects of environmental traumas can also be inherited.

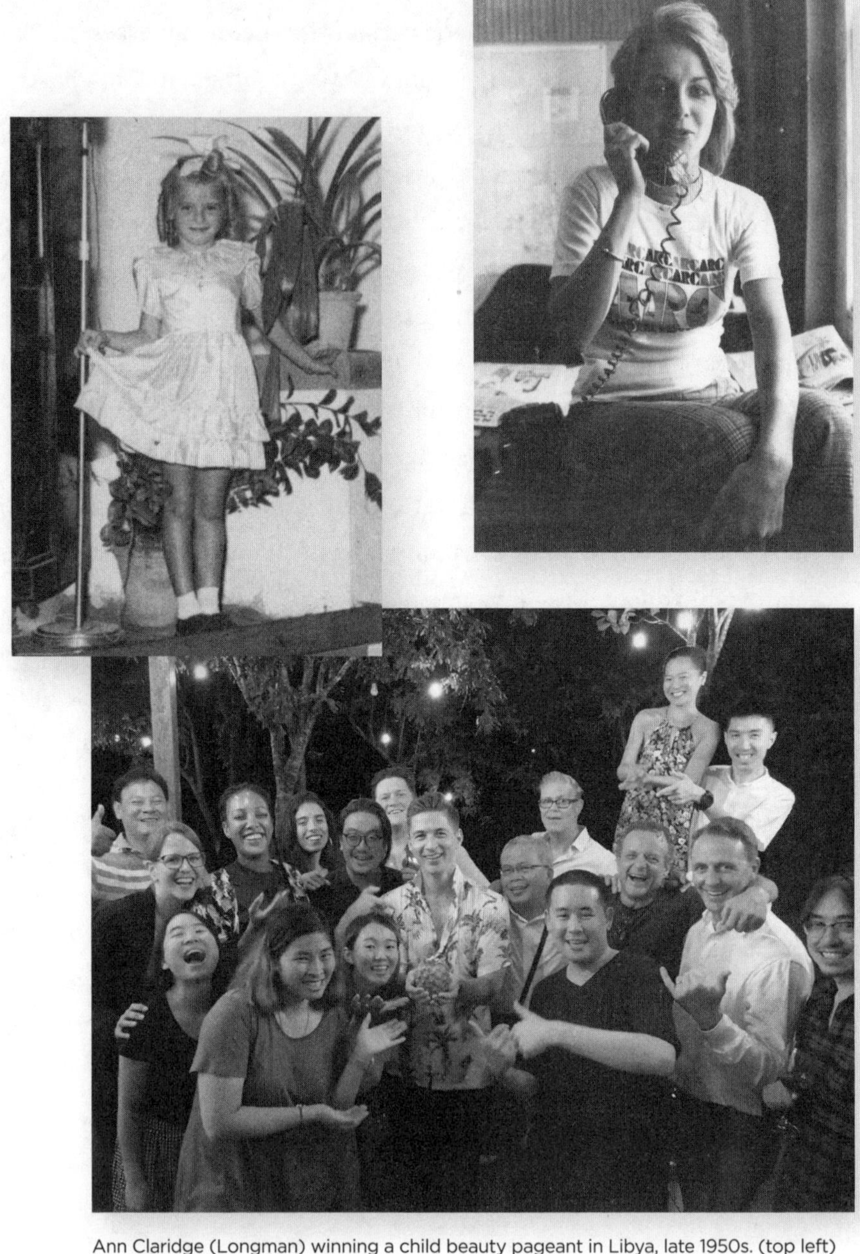

Ann Claridge (Longman) winning a child beauty pageant in Libya, late 1950s. (top left)

Ann in London, 1970s. (top right)

ABC team in Thailand covering the cave rescue. (bottom)

CHAPTER 6

FAMILY LIFE AND GROWING UP FAST

Biology is truly a land of unlimited possibilities. We may expect it to give us the most surprising information, and we cannot guess what answers it will return in a few dozen years. . . . They may be of a kind which will blow away the whole of our artificial structure of hypothesis.

—SIGMUND FREUD, *BEYOND THE PLEASURE PRINCIPLE*

Family? What are you calling family, darling? We're hardly the bloody Waltons!

—EDINA MONSOON, *ABSOLUTELY FABULOUS*

You may have heard of the phrase "big in Japan." Well, I'm kind of big in Thailand. They call me "Mr. Pineapple," and it's all because of our coverage of the Wild Boars soccer team, who got stuck in a cave in the north of the country in the summer of 2018. ABC was the first foreign news team at the cave site, and we spent weeks in the rain-soaked jungle landscape tracking a rescue effort that had gripped the world's attention. Because we had been so quick to respond, Thai news media took an interest in our coverage, and soon our reports for *Good Morning America* and *World News Tonight* were being broadcast on local news stations and shared on their social channels. The cave was in a remote area, lush with all kinds of fruit farms, and our live position was right in the middle of a pineapple field. Producer Angus Hines took a photo of me holding one of these pineapples, which I posted to Twitter. Not long after, a Thai teenager drew a cartoon version of that photograph. And in keeping with the inexplicable nature of so much internet content, the cartoon went viral.

From that moment on, everywhere I went, people would call me Mr. Pineapple. They'd call it out on the street, in restaurants, in shops, and in cafés. And not just in that remote town. The national news started using the phrase. I was greeted off the plane by Thai Airways staff with a whole tray of pineapples. Restaurants in Bangkok would put random chunks of pineapple in my food, and one café served me a coffee with an entire slice in it. ("Pineapple coffee!" came the excited refrain from the barista.) When I was asked by a fruit juice manufacturer to put my name and face to a line of pineapple juice drinks, I realized things had really escalated. Apparently, I was being credited for a rise in the wholesale price of pineapples; I was told a member of the Thai parliament who represented a rural area had made a speech saying as much. On a vacation with Alex more than four years later, I found the pineapple magic was still alive. At the end of our stay, as we finished loading our bags into a cab to take us to the airport, a hotel porter broke his silence. "You are always Mr. Pineapple here," he said quietly.

I like to think it had something to do with our respect and admiration for the people of Thailand, whose response to the disappearance of those twelve boys and their coach was a real inspiration. When the world assumed the worst, they all kept their faith. When the team was located but the rescue looked next to impossible, they were adamant it could be done. And they were right. Fundamentally, it was a story of hope and courage, which is probably why it kept so many people riveted.

It was also a story of children surviving the unthinkable. But the joy and relief so many experienced back then didn't last for everyone. Very sadly one of the boys in that cave has since ended his own life. Duangphet Promthep—Dom—was the captain of the soccer team, and had been studying abroad in the UK when he was found unconscious in February 2023. He was just 17 years old. An inquest ruled suicide, and there is no way of knowing what caused him to do this, but it is the case that the traumas we endure in childhood can stay with us for the rest of our lives. Early adverse experiences are often associated with adult mental illnesses.

When you think about childhood trauma, what you think about, whether you realize it or not, is the work of Sigmund Freud. He introduced the world to the idea that what happens in our childhoods reverberates through the rest of our lives. His work focused on pseudo-hereditary illness—the idea that mental illness is passed on through families, but not through DNA. He observed the impact of trauma in the early years of a person's life and sought to demonstrate how cycles of what he called neurosis or hysteria are passed from one generation to the next. One of his most famous cases was that of "Little Hans," a boy who had a phobia of horses after seeing one fall down and die near where he lived. His father sought Freud's help in curing the phobia. Freud's conclusions typify the kind of analysis he would become famous for. Among them: that horses, with their blinkers and dark mouths, put Hans in mind of his father, who wore glasses and had a mustache, and that the arrival of a younger sister in the household had made him subconsciously competitive with his father for his mother's affections. Freud's famous Oedipus complex—named after the main character of a Greek tragedy who kills his father and marries his mother—was applied to Little Hans.

Since Freud, psychologists have sought to build on these behavioral observations and find biological explanations for them. They want to not only understand the causes of mental illness but delve into the brain and uncover what is happening on a granular level. Bessel van der Kolk is a leading voice in the study of childhood trauma and what it does to the brain. In *The Body Keeps the Score*, he states that trauma is universal. Acute traumas—things like the physical or mental abuse of a child, rape, near-death experiences, and the like—are shockingly common. According to the Centers for Disease Control and Prevention (CDC), the overall rate of depression in the United States would drop by half were child abuse to be eradicated. But there are subtler abuses suffered in childhood, and van der Kolk says these can be just as damaging as the more extreme cases.

Brain mapping for mental illness focuses on two areas: the insula and the amygdala. The insula is the part of the brain that interprets sensory information from what we take in through our ears, eyes, mouth, nose, and skin. It's often called the *feeling* part of the brain. In people who have lived through trauma, the insula is not only firing when it's stimulated by an event as it is meant to; it is firing all the time. The result is a constant feeling of impending doom or that something will go wrong. The amygdala is primarily associated with memory and the fight-or-flight response. The impact on the amygdala is less well understood, but some studies have also pointed to overactivity in that area, too, meaning bad memories are potentially rendered in higher definition. Van der Kolk says early life trauma essentially rewires the brain from a young age to respond in this way, and that the effects last a lifetime.

My story is about more than just my genetic predispositions. It is also about the trauma of my childhood. And to understand that part of the story, you need to understand my mother.

Ann Claridge was born in Cairo to the glamorous Lebanese woman Gabrielle, who I told you about earlier, and her dashing husband, Harold. Ann's teenage years in Lebanon sound full of fun and laughter. She was educated in the UK, away from her Beirut-based parents. Family photos of her trips back home, to Lebanon's sun-drenched beaches and snowy mountains, look dazzling. One photo is taken at the Casino de Beyrouth: My mother is in a short shift dress with a sixties bob haircut, holding a coupe of champagne, balancing on the edge of a table and laughing with someone off-camera. There's something more than a little James Bond about the whole thing.

But the reality of helping her parents escape the war-torn Middle East by the time she was in her thirties must have taken its toll. Civil war had struck Lebanon, and her parents were left with nothing. My grandfather's Kiwi passport got them a ticket to the UK, and the family settled in England. My mother went on to meet my father in the rather bleak gray London of the 1970s, where her internationalism must have been a stark but attractive change to his life. She was a successful business executive and interpreter. He was working as an artist and experimenting with the burgeoning Transcendental Meditation that was spreading around Europe at the time.

My mother was forty-one when she became pregnant with me. But that was only after ten years of a rather rocky relationship with my father. He had already called off their engagement once and had all kinds of breakdowns, which she says she saved him from. She was very keen to start a family, but my father's mental illness caused him to retreat from the world rather than take part in it.

My first memory of boarding school is my first visit there, in the summer of 1995. "Oh, we're very international." My mother is replying to a question about where we are from posed by Matron, who clearly hasn't understood and is giving the kind of vacant look I recognize in people who have just realized we're not quite what we seem. My father is holding my hand, and I look up at him. We share our knowing smile.

"Let's go and find Mr. Owers, shall we?" Matron says. She has neat, curly brown hair, piercing blue eyes, a blue cardigan, and a happy Irish accent—the central casting version of a boarding school matron in Britain. I'd never been on a cruise ship, but the room made me think of one: wooden and metal stairs floating up from the tiled floor and, on a mezzanine above our heads, a ship's wheel inexplicably attached to the balustrade. Through big wooden and glass doors, we set off along a corridor of worn-down parquet and dull white walls.

Worth wasn't a school my mother could afford, but she was adamant that I needed to go to a boarding school because she wanted to protect me from my father's illness. It was agreed my grandmother Nancy would help pay. There was something quite Evelyn Waugh about my younger years: a boy from the faded grandeur of a ruined family, shunted into high-society life by a mother desperate to protect him, wanting him to relive the splendor of her childhood but unable to provide it. My grandmother fit the role of Victorian matriarch and sponsor of the young ward, and my father that of absent cad.

"It's very important, darling, that you go somewhere Catholic. You must be surrounded by *people like us*." My mother is talking over the back of Matron's head as we follow her down the corridor. The word *Catholic* comes out slightly louder, to make sure Matron hears. And she almost hisses *people like us*. All I can think is how unlike the people at this school we are.

If my childhood has a smell, it's Chanel No. 5. My mother loves it, and she always has little tester bottles of it strewn among the tissue paper and change at the bottom of her handbag, forever squirting it on her wrists and rubbing them together. Today, I follow the smell and her familiar silver bangles jingling on her wrist as she walks. Whenever she dresses up, like on this day, I feel proud of her. Deep red lipstick, always applied in a hurry on a train or in a taxi, hair clipped up at the back of her head, and a smart little blazer. She can move effortlessly between languages, between cultures. Her Britishness was always for others. But she spoke to me in French most of the time, and as we walk, she's giving me clipped orders. "Comporte-toi bien." *Behave yourself.* "Parle comme il faut." *Speak properly.* These little asides always prompt people to ask where we're from and my mother to give her grand answers in the style of Hyacinth Bucket.

It is August, and through each window we pass I can see massive horse chestnuts, little white blossoms blowing around in the air, dancing leaves a translucent green in the bright sunlight. We head outside and walk down the hill, arriving at the main building, a rather solemn, Gothic house with turrets, tall chimneys, and strange statues peeking out at various spots on the facade. It is certainly beautiful, looking out toward tennis courts and the many acres of woodland the school owns. But the rest of the campus is more like a suburban hospital: rather ugly mismatched buildings dotted around the place; the school motto ("Do It with Thy Might") emblazoned over fireplaces; large drafty corridors; endless lines of hooks waiting idly for the endless lines of children to come back in the autumn to use them. It has a ghostliness to it not unlike the hotel in *The Shining*. (But a little less murder-y, I suppose.)

We find Mr. Owers in his office. I remember his kind eyes finding me huddled slightly behind my father. "It's okay, son," he says. "Why don't you sit here and answer a few questions while I chat with Mum and Dad?" His desk is a mess of books and papers, and he scrambles around for a pencil and something to write on, writes a few things down on the paper, and sets them on a table in front of me. "There you go." I sink into a comfortable beige corduroy sofa and look at the paper. There's a question about Shakespeare, a history question, and an equation. Ten minutes later, Mr. Owers returns with my parents. He looks over my shoulder at the answers. "Well, two out of three isn't too bad." And that, it seems, is my entrance exam. I am in. My math never improves.

School became a haven for me. Over the years that followed, I developed close bonds with my teachers, who became surrogate parents, as my mother had hoped. I was aware on that first day that the three of them had had a serious conversation while they were out of the room together. I could tell my mother had been crying, which was fairly usual, but it felt like something important had been decided. I understand now that sending me to this school was the first part of my mother's plan to "save me" from my father. Even then, I knew things weren't quite right at home. My father was more of a grown-up friend than a parent. He was there to hang out with or go for walks or days out with, but he wasn't responsible for the everyday needs of our lives. I don't remember ever going to a supermarket with him or running an errand, and even though he came with us to the school on that first day, he was there more as a friendly observer than a reliable parent.

My mother is a complicated but fascinating person. Deeply intelligent, she speaks three languages fluently, and it's from her that I get my interest in the Middle East and travel. She's charming and funny, and most people when they meet her are enthralled. It's Eddie Monsoon—Jennifer Saunders's colorful, hilarious, and in every way totally over-the-top character in *Absolutely Fabulous*—who most people think of when they meet her. In one scene, Eddie shouts up the stairs to her long-suffering daughter Saffy, whose birthday she has only just realized she missed: "Darling, it's my birthday, not yours. I gave birth to you! When you have a child, it'll be your birthday!" My mother says the same thing to me every year. That said, she would never miss my birthday. She would send me poster-size birthday cards with songs that played when you opened them. I remember their tunes reverberating around the school breakfast hall, my friends looking on confused. (I had *Absolutely Fabulous* on repeat for most of my childhood, by the way. It's still a mystery why I needed to come out to her.)

My mother also absolutely loves adventure. During the Arab Spring in 2011, she lived in Egypt and went down to Tahrir Square to protest alongside the thousands of people demanding freedom and getting teargassed. There's a picture of her flicking the peace sign with some newly made friends as chaos swirls around her. She's unpredictable in this way. I once took her to a rather nice country hotel for a weekend and left her in the salon to get her hair done for a treat. When I returned, the stylist looked rather sheepish, worried about my reaction. With a half smile, he pointed over to his station, and my mother swung round in her chair to show off her new cornrows. The woman is in her seventies. Naturally, everyone in the salon loved her. She spent virtually all her money on my education—even selling her home to fund it. She is generous to a fault, and has been singularly committed, in her own way, to making sure I am happy.

I know she has reason to feel hard done by. I can't imagine what it would be like for my own husband's mental health to disintegrate, then to find myself all alone in trying to save his life. But the trauma of that experience does seem to have carried into every part of her life, with me being the focus of her anger and sadness. I remember sitting in front of the television when I was a kid, and those fundraising adverts for starving families in Africa would come on. We'd sit and watch the three-minute film, mothers holding their malnourished babies, gazing up at the camera. After the mournful music faded and the number appeared for viewers to make donations, my mother would exhale sharply, look over at me, and say, "Well, at least they've got each other. I've been abandoned." When I was at university and didn't return her calls for a couple of days, she told the police I was dead and had them break down the door to my apartment. Her need for company was so intense that during my teenage years I would often come home to find homeless people in our flat. One of our visitors stole our cat.

There are countless stories. Our lives are both intensely intertwined and completely divided, characterized by years of cat and mouse as she fought her way back into my life: Her, believing her love is enough to sustain a relationship and that nothing else matters. "I'm your mother, I can do no wrong" is her mentality, and a verbatim mantra. Me, feeling stability, order, and calm are what's needed. She was, and remains, full of love and pride for me. Her home now is papered in photographs of me and copies of articles I've written. But the damage done to our relationship is massive.

"You mustn't end up like your father, darling" was repeated at every available opportunity. Even in front of him. I'd fail to take the rubbish out when asked or to get her a cup of tea, and she'd say, "Darling, you really mustn't end up like your father. I don't think I could cope." It wasn't always said in anger or with malice, but often in a matter-of-fact way. She was obsessed with making sure I turned out like her and escaped whatever inevitable darkness was creeping in from the other side of the family. "I'm the only one who is truly able to love you, darling," she would tell me. Everything she asked me to do—however mundane—was to her, somehow, a marker of how much like him or like her I was.

I remember trudging home with her to our top-floor flat in Notting Hill on rainy afternoons with heavy shopping bags cutting into my hands, having to take multiple trips to the top. This was west London in the 1990s, before Hugh and Julia's movie and the tourists and the trendy juice bars. No one had heard of downward dog or acai bowls. It was still a fairly gritty part of town, in the days when London in general was a lot less shiny than it is now. We lived opposite a Texaco garage on Westbourne Grove, and my mother would often go downstairs to argue with the drug dealer who would stand outside it repeatedly kicking his dog.

The flat was my father's place when he met my mum, and when they married, she moved in. He smashed through the loft to create space for our bedrooms and a small roof terrace. It was a jumble of Oriental rugs, plants, and hand-me-down furniture. Both my parents smoked, and there seemed to be endless half-empty cups of tea on tables or balanced precariously on piles of books. My father's painting experiments were dotted around the place alongside my mother's eclectic Middle Eastern throws and cushions, and I remember the sound of the *Archers* theme tune on Radio 4 drifting from the bathroom at the end of the corridor when my mum was in the bath. All kinds of different lodgers stayed in a bedroom downstairs, most of them foreign students with very little English. But fights are obvious in any language, and I remember plenty of polite retreats to the bedroom when they'd break out.

Don't get me wrong, I wasn't growing up in the roughest part of town. But I do remember my life there as occasionally chaotic and unpredictable, with a variety of colorful characters moving in and out of my parent's quasi-hippie existence. There was one neighbor, Toots. She was about as tall as I was at the time—so no more than about five feet—and had short silver-gray hair. She smoked so much that what I think would ordinarily have been white skin was a much darker shade of gray, and she had black rings around her eyes. Always wearing black, she looked a little like a badger. A badger with a deep smoker's cough. Then there was Tony—or Fat Tony, as my mother would call him. He lived across the hall from my dad after my parents separated. My only memory of him is when he was carrying me down the very long wooden stairs from our bedrooms and fell, taking me with him.

For years, it felt like my mother was my whole world. It was just the two of us, with my father's satellite-like presence and this odd collection of local characters in orbit around us. I knew she was completely dedicated to making sure I was happy, but it came with a neurotic obsession that made me extremely self-conscious. There was certainly a charm to her eccentricity. Once, at my prep school, parents were instructed to provide Buckingham Palace Guard outfits for a school musical production of *The Grand Old Duke of York*. My mother couldn't afford to buy an outfit, and so I was put in one of her cropped red blazers, oversize black trousers, and an enormous boat-shaped military hat in the style of Napoleon that she'd found at a thrift store. "I'm pretty sure this wasn't what they asked for," I tried to tell her, already embarrassed. "Oh, don't be so silly, darling. You'll look the best." Complete with my grandfather's war medals pinned to my lapel, I arrived onstage to find a rather startled assistant teacher, who decided at the last minute to put me in the middle of all my peers in their perfectly pressed red-and-black soldier uniforms. The curtain was raised, and there I was, standing in the middle, the mortified accidental Duke of York. And my mother in the audience, beaming. Some of the other parents and children were unable to hide their amusement, but there was also, I'm sure, more than a little envy. A few years later, when I played the gold-bringing king in the school nativity play, she put me in one of her gold-sequined mini dresses, which came down to the floor on me. To this day, I probably remain the only king who ever brought gold to the baby Jesus in a disco dress.

My mother was—and still is—like a lioness when it comes to what she sees as her role to protect me. After my father died, though, her eccentricity turned into a deeper instability, and her sadness fueled heavier and heavier drinking. Students were allowed home from school on the weekends, and on Saturday afternoons I would go to the station to catch the train back to London. But I'd always make sure to call home from the pay phone on the platform before boarding. If the words at the other end of the line were slurred, I'd hang up, head back outside to the taxi stand, and find a car to take me back to school. This was a habit I got into from the age of nine or ten, and continued until I was old enough to make my own plans. I would go back into Matron's room, letting her know I would in fact be in that evening, and with a warm smile she'd open a tin of biscuits and make us cups of tea. I found myself gravitating toward classmates with large, rambling families. The kinds of families you see in Christmas movies in which hundreds of cousins turn up and chaos ensues. I wanted the inviting glow of a large home, full of food and joy and happiness. But instead, when I did go home, it was often to an enormous fight.

I would get so angry at finding bottles of wine or vodka hidden under the kitchen sink or behind pillows on the couch. I had an instinct for drink. Like a bloodhound on a hunt, I could smell even the faintest hint of it. My mother could do what she liked to try to hide her habit from me, but I would know immediately. I could see it in the too-wide grin on her face, or in her eyes, blinking half a second more slowly than usual. In my early teens, she began to appear at my school drunk. On one occasion, she fell out of a car and lay on the green in front of my boarding house. I was thirteen years old and remember having to help carry her inside with my housemaster. He took her legs, I took her arms.

Keeping to the Evelyn Waugh theme, my mother moved to Nice when I was fourteen, hoping to start a new life in the south of France in a culture and climate she preferred. "The English don't understand us, darling!" she exclaimed. But the drinking followed, and since I would only fly home for the holidays, our separation deepened. In my later teenage years, with all the extra angst they bring, and the creeping realization that I may be gay, I started to stay away. As I got older, once the fights started, I'd just leave and go to friends' houses. My mother, in turn, could feel me drifting away from her. Many of our arguments descended into physical fights over my keys, which she would hide so I'd have to stay with her. By the time I was nineteen, she had moved back to the UK but had become homeless, and each time I visited her, it would be in a different small flat or room provided by local authorities. Each space was packed full of the furniture, photographs, trinkets, and memories of a fascinating life. But none of it could make up for my increasing absence. As I write this now, I feel deep sadness for her, and for our wasted years. She'd lost her husband, and she felt she was losing her son, too. But as a child, I couldn't handle or really understand what she was going through. All I knew was my father had left us, and now my mother was not the dependable person I needed her to be.

The other uncertainty I was dealing with was my sexuality. Or rather, realizing that I might be gay, and feeling that I needed to hide it. I suspect my coming-out story is much the same as many others. I was sixteen when I told my friend Stephanie. We had "dated" for a little while, in that preadolescent, holding hands kind of way. I was an incredibly spotty and still rather pudgy boy-child who had an unfortunate obsession with a camouflage fleece. And it was probably in that horrid top, sitting in Steph's family kitchen, that I told her through big sobs, trying to make sure her parents couldn't hear from the next room, that I thought I might be gay. I don't think I used the word *gay*—that still felt too dangerous. The whole experience felt like I was admitting a crime somehow. I just hoped she wouldn't judge me as I had come to judge myself. I found it very hard to tell anyone else afterward and spent years trying to push it down, to ignore it. (Steph, by the way, didn't judge me, but stayed a very close friend. Years later, I gave the reading at her wedding.)

I went through a few stages of acceptance. Initially, I thought I could just pretend I was straight, get married, have kids, and just think it all away. I slowly realized this wasn't going to be possible, and so I thought I could simply be celibate, or asexual. I thought I would suffer in silence. By the time I arrived for my first week of university, I was still very much in the closet. The only person I was forced to tell was my "girlfriend" at the time, because she was literally in my bed one evening in the first week of classes. I had met her, a girl named Emily, in the year I'd spent in China between school and university. It had been a mesmerizing year, teaching English in Sichuan province. Like all the girls I'd "dated" in school, she was completely stunning. I always thought if people hadn't already guessed I was gay, they could have figured it out by just looking at the girls I tried to date: always the most glamorous. And Emily was bright and gifted to boot. But that evening, she was in my single bed, and I was staring up at the ceiling in the darkness, completely terrified. I remember sweating an unnatural amount and trying to keep small talk going for as long as possible, feeling all the time that I was delaying the inevitable. I know what you're thinking—*lucky Emily*!

Eventually, I jumped up and went to the sink in the corner to wash my face. I carried on talking absolute rubbish. I don't remember what I was saying. But at the end of one of my ramblings, with my head in the sink, I crowbarred in ". . . and that's when I knew I was gay." The silence in the room was so heavy I could feel the pressure in my ears.

"What?" came Emily's uncertain reply. She either hadn't heard, or thought she had and needed it repeated. But now that I had said the word, I found it easier the second time. Like it was already floating in the air—I just needed to push it toward her. "I think I might be gay," I said again. I couldn't see her reaction because it was so dark, but she was clearly shocked. Looking back now, I imagine she might have felt embarrassed and more than a little stupid. I don't know. I do know I still feel bad about it now. To her enormous credit, she wasn't angry or upset, and I think we just chatted until we fell asleep. I saw her once more a few years later, but we eventually lost touch. Wherever you are now, Emily, thank you for being as kind as I remember.

I did manage to tell one other person, Seyi, in my first year at university. She had that quality in a friend that I needed at the time: unrelenting goodness. I knew Seyi knew I was gay. But I knew she knew she couldn't actually ask me, because she didn't want to put me on the spot. Instead, she'd keep telling me about girls who fancied me and ask what

I was planning on doing about it. Like an annoying but loving sister, she prodded and poked until eventually I told her. I felt huge relief in telling her, and the knowledge that at least one university friend knew was enough to sustain me for years. She took me for me, and remains a dear friend to this day. As I write this now, I'm getting messages about how she needs me to take her to the Eurovision Song Contest and won't accept any excuses to the contrary.

Eventually, I wrote my mother an email when I was twenty-four to tell her the truth. I have looked for this email in order to recount the words I used, but I've had no luck. I wanted to write it all down, rather than call her or tell her in person, for a number of reasons. First, I didn't want a fight or tears or melodrama. Second, I was still ashamed, and felt the distance of an email would keep me from seeing her face, which I assumed would be etched with disappointment. Third, I wanted to choose my words properly, and for her to completely understand what I was saying. "Darling, you're probably bisexual" was part of her response. "It's a phase! You'll get over it." I believe at one point she suggested I marry a lesbian. If I had hoped for immediate understanding, I did not receive it. But I don't remember feeling upset by her response. I think, in truth, I had expected it. Thankfully, she has since embraced my sexuality, and I was proud to walk into my wedding to Alex with her on my arm.

At every milestone of my life—leaving school, going on a gap year, starting university—I told myself I'd tell more people, but I could not bring myself to do so. And as a result, every interaction I had felt like a lie. Whether talking about relationships and having to specifically deny being gay, or just simple things like buying milk or chatting about the weather, I just didn't feel like myself, as though I wasn't presenting the real me to the world. It made me feel like less of a person. Of course, feeling that you are "less" than other people, that you are essentially worthless, is a fast route to a mental health crisis.

Members of the LGBTQ+ community are more likely to experience a mental illness. A 2018 Stonewall study in the UK found more than half of the LGBTQ+ people asked had experienced depression in the previous year; one in eight age eighteen through twenty-four had thought about taking their own life; and one in seven avoided getting help because they were worried about discrimination from staff. And, as I have mentioned, it wasn't that long ago that the *Diagnostic and Statistical Manual of Mental Disorders* listed homosexuality as a disorder. Homosexuality began to be decriminalized in the United Kingdom in 1967, and with the passing of the 2013 Marriage Act, which finally allowed same-sex couples to get married, it seemed—politically, at least—that the UK was becoming a more accepting place. In the United States, however, gay rights are one of a series of contested social issues, along with women's reproductive health and the right to die. And then, of course, there's the rest of the world, in much of which it is either difficult or illegal to be gay, lesbian, transgender, or any identity that falls outside of the heteronormative ideal.

Whatever the legal context, and however accepting your own friends and family are, to be gay is to carve out a place for yourself in a world built for straight people, where everything from movies to commercials, public spaces, and all you see, hear, and read as you grow up aren't meant for you. Whatever the relationship with your family, hiding your sexuality from them still makes you feel like you're in the closet, even if you live an open and happy life with your friends and "chosen family" for much of the time.

I suspect my job as a journalist and foreign correspondent is in large part a product of the habits I formed while needing to escape a difficult family life, and the truth of being gay. I became independent at a younger age than most, and formed an ability to rely on my own wits. Journalist or not, I think this is the experience for a lot of other gay people, too. A few years ago, I read Bruno Bettelheim's book *The Uses of Enchantment,* which analyzes the meanings of well-known childhood stories and explains what certain fairy tales mean to children. I gave the book to my mother, and I remember her flicking to the glossary to find Rapunzel, who lived locked at the top of a tower and let down her long hair for her beloved to save her. It was my favorite story when I was a kid. "Overwhelming desire to escape," my mother said after scanning the text briefly. "Charming." Then she handed the book back to me. But it was true. I did want to escape, and a lot of that was to do with being gay.

That brings me to Alex, my husband. If I felt I had very little family growing up, the prospect of building a new one with him is one of the great joys of my life. We met right at the end of 2016, on Tinder. I was thirty, which can feel like retirement age to a gay man, and there wasn't a dating app I didn't have. I *really* wanted to meet someone. Alex and I had been chatting for a couple of weeks online by the time we did meet in person. I asked to meet in a coffee shop next door to my gym and turned up in my training gear. I wasn't going to have my workout interrupted by a date! Thankfully, he wasn't too put off. We met just as I was starting my job at ABC, which made it immediately clear to us both what being in a relationship would mean: constant compromise, more on his part than on mine. Having your plans ruined by a call from work and a last-minute dash to the airport can be irritating. But it's worse for the partner: Their lives are turned upside down, but there's no payoff, no exciting work trip or fulfilling career experience. But he doesn't just sit by the phone waiting for me. He has his own career, his own full and exciting life. All this means—I hope—that we are equal partners, and we respect each other.

Very simply, Alex is the best thing in my life. I've learned that healthy relationships are not about finding someone like you. I think many people can fall into this trap—looking for a carbon copy of yourself, perhaps as a form of self-protection. I tried to do that for a while. But Alex is all the things I am not: detail orientated, a perfectionist, totally committed to his family and his obligations. He has a strong moral compass, an absolute sense of right and wrong. I don't know anyone better. He understands what it means to work as a team and reminds me to be less of an only child about everything. (I don't always remember.) He also has a lot more patience than me, especially with my mother. A couple of years ago, I called her to let her know I'd asked Alex to marry me. "I learned years ago all my dreams would die" was her cutting response. I handed the phone to Alex. He broke through to her with his kind heart and warm words.

Alex has also been the force for good in my life when I've felt that everything was turning bad. His sanity, his balance, his calm have been a much-needed tonic to the hysteria of my childhood. My upbringing is a large part of the reason I wanted to write this book. I've long wondered if, along with the "curse" I might have received from my dad's side, undiagnosed mental health issues from my mother's side have been reproduced in me—both inheritances intensified by the lasting impact a childhood like mine can have. Bessel van der Kolk is part of a field of study called Early Life Stress (ELS), a broad term encompassing a range of traumas—from abuse, to parental divorce, to neglect—experienced during childhood and adolescence. In the late 1990s, the term Adverse Childhood Experiences (ACEs) was coined to define a set of potentially traumatic events a child under the age of eighteen might experience. These include parental substance use, incarceration of a household member, parental death by suicide, domestic violence, and having a parent with mental illness.

People who experience ACEs become more prone to health problems, both physical and mental. One study found that when compared to those who had experienced no ACEs, those who had four or more accounts were at higher risks for substance use disorders (both alcohol and drugs), depression, suicide attempts, and poor self-rated health. In the National Comorbidity Survey published in 2010, it was reported that childhood adverse experiences are associated with up to almost a third of psychiatric disorders, and even more so (44.6 percent) with disorders that have an onset in childhood. More specifically, evidence shows early life stress as a clear predictor for adulthood depression. Studies have shown higher risks of more severe courses of depression, longer and more frequent lifetime depressive episodes, earlier disorder onset, psychotic symptoms, and suicide attempts in adults with a history of ELS compared to adults without an ELS history.

These are observable trends, but scientists have sought to understand what *happens* to the biology of our brains when we experience trauma. One such scientist, Nobel Prize–winner Eric Kandel, has demonstrated that the effects of trauma in early life are intimately associated with memory. "Without the binding force of memory," he says, "experience would be splintered into as many fragments as there are moments in life. Without the mental time travel provided by memory, we would have no awareness of our personal history, no way of remembering the joys that serve as the luminous milestones of our life. We are who we are because of what we learn and what we remember."

His work builds on the case of one of the most famous patients in neuroscience history: Patient H. M. He was known only by his initials for decades, but his full name was Henry Molaison. Knocked down by a bicycle when he was seven, he began, as a result, to have seizures when he was ten. By the age of twenty-seven, his condition was so severe that doctors removed part of the hippocampus region of his brain—a treatment for epilepsy in the 1950s. The result was that he lost his memory. Or, to be precise, his ability to form short-term memories.

Molaison became the subject of a decades-long study by neuroscientist Brenda Milner, who found that Molaison could not remember having met her the previous day but was able to build certain skills over time. She would return to find, for example, his ability to draw a star had improved, though he still couldn't remember the names of people he had just met. This work established that memory is a distinct cerebral function, separate from other cognitive and motor abilities, and that the temporal lobe—which Molaison had had removed—is particularly important for memory. Crucially, Molaison's case showed that different parts of the brain are important for different types of memory: short-term and long-term, but also what has come to be known as declarative and nondeclarative memory. The former refers to immediate recollection of people and events, while the latter is an umbrella term for learning skills and habits.

The parts of the brain Milner, Kandel, and others identified have since been the subject of intense research into mood changes and depression. Kandel's work focused on the central role that synapses play in memory and learning. Synapses are transmitters in the brain—they are the gap between neurons, where information is stored for transmission from the brain to other parts of the body, through the central nervous system. By studying a sea snail, Kandel revealed that as the creature learned, chemical signals changed the structure of the synapses between cells. Repeated stimulation made these connections stronger: The neurons were *learning* to modify their response, until movement became a reflex. Applying this fundamental principle has given generations of researchers greater insight into depression and other mental illnesses. Modern brain-mapping technology has identified changes in connectivity between brain cells in those with mental health problems. So regulating those connections can help relieve symptoms. There is also a growing body of evidence to suggest depression can impact memory function, as processes in the relevant part of the brain become overstimulated. We store our memories and our emotions in close proximity, and understanding the relationship between the two is at the core of mental health science.

Former BBC correspondent Alex Bushill also grew up in what he calls a loving but occasionally chaotic household, with a mother who was diagnosed with schizophrenia before he was born. It's safe to say he and I have both been affected by our upbringings, but he feels his experience has made him stronger. And, unlike everyone else I've spoken to for this book, his mother, Monica, is not medicated and lives an independent life under the watchful care of Alex and his siblings.

"My story is very positive, for those who understand serious mental illness," says Alex. "For a lot of people who don't, it might be shocking or upsetting. But actually, Mum has been a remarkable example of someone who themselves has coped amazingly and has been privileged to have a real support network. Although there have been real crises." It is clear to me how much Alex loves his mother, and, at various times as we speak on Zoom, he turns off the camera as he becomes emotional. I get the sense he is moved by his own feelings of pride for his mother. "I have huge love and respect for my mother," he says, "who I think is one of the most powerful and dynamic forces in my life. But because of her illness, she has also forced me to build real resilience."

Alex was born into an affluent British family and grew up in the south of England in a large house that had itself, oddly enough, been part of a Georgian psychiatric facility. Alex calls his mother the "powerhouse" of the family; his older brother and sister were born ten years before him and grew up as a kind of separate family. "But she wanted to have more children, because children and her illness have given her a point to her life. She has only really been motivated by those two things: loving her children, and her conspiracy theories about the world."

Alex says he was aware as a young child that his mother was different. "We are not a secretive family, and by the time I came around, Dad had already been through this with my two older siblings. The family folklore is that Dad and her fell in love on a skiing trip back in the 1960s. Quite quickly after they met, she got a diagnosis of schizophrenia. And before that, she had tried on one occasion to take her own life. He knew she was special. By the time I was born, she'd been sectioned [committed] at least once or twice."

Monica's illness is characterized by extreme paranoia and conspiracies—often about the British establishment. "Back when I was a kid, the fervor of the paranoia was really powerful. The positive earliest childhood memories of Mum I have are of someone who was really powerful. She was charismatic, she was funny, she'd boss Dad around. Interestingly, when she had to engage with someone outside of the family, she'd change. She'd become quite formal, quite nervous, even, or brittle. But in the family unit, she was wonderful. And very eccentric. Also, because she was Danish, she cut a different figure to any of the other mums I saw."

But he also has strong childhood memories of a different kind. "I'd remember her screaming at the walls every evening. She had this powerful view of the world that she was under constant surveillance. It was MI5 that was doing the surveillance, and it was because she posed a threat to national security. It was all totally ridiculous, but you don't know this when you're four, five, six.

"She would write to MPs saying she was going to get murdered and they needed to do something. She would number plate watch. They would communicate to her, so if she got a bad number plate when she was at the wheel, that would be a problem. Meals were always difficult, especially if we were eating out. She has an inability to sit still in public, and meals are a trigger point. If the food doesn't come quickly, she feels something must be happening to it and gets quite animated. She would accuse close family members of being in on 'the plot.'"

Alex says he always found it easy to make friends, but he struggled to find deeper connections with people. He gets emotional at the thought of this. "What I struggled with sometimes was taking friendship further. Mum estranges everyone in her life—especially family." Alex would make a friend at school, and eventually a playdate would be fixed. But his mother would become obsessed with the idea that Alex and his new friend and their family needed to know "the truth" about an evil plot or whatever paranoid thought she was having. She would record her own voice on a cassette tape, then drive to the playdate and play the tape for the other parents.

I ask Alex what impact all this might have had on him. Like me, he had to act as a parent of sorts, conscious of managing his mother in a way other small children would never have to do. "My dad did prepare us really well, saying Mum is different and she needs more support." And it seems Alex had an early instinct to try to "fix" his mother. "One of my earliest memories was gently challenging Mum's paranoia about shiny surfaces. I went round the whole house and pointed to all different cassette players and their shiny tape heads. And I said, 'Look, Mum.' I was maybe five or six, and I pulled apart a cassette tape to show her. 'There's no listening device here.' That didn't work, and it was my first inkling that there was no way of getting through to her on that particular point. But I did learn there were ways that you can support her and manage her, and she does actually have insight of when she's moving into a space where she is being unusual.

"Mossy surfaces are still a problem to her, because she thinks of it as 'thought dust.' And even to this day, if she thinks there is moss on the roof of the house, me and my siblings have to go up there with improvised harnesses and scrub it all. Which we choose to do to support her, so she isn't sectioned [committed]. So, you're getting a sense now of how we work as a family to support her. It's not carte blanche—I have been close to having her sectioned [committed]. But maybe we are unusual, I don't know, in how we mobilize together and give her a lot of license."

As I speak to Alex, I'm moved by how he and his siblings have taken on the challenge of looking after their mother, making sure she can still live as full and as independent a life as possible. The picture he paints of him and his siblings being the net his mother needs, should she fall, is touching. Even while managing their own families and careers, they have essentially become Monica's medication. I ask him if he ever worries that this might enable her conspiracies or worsen her symptoms. Alex says his mother was put on antipsychotic medication twenty years ago, but calls the experience "awful." "I know medication works, and this is just us, but we feel that medication works at too high a price for Mum," he says.

"I put myself in her shoes. She genuinely thinks this stuff is happening. And if you were really thinking that, to be able to manage that fear and anger and all of those emotions the way she has done is truly remarkable, and testament to her power as an individual." Alex's father, who was the principal caretaker for their mother, died two years ago of Lewy body dementia. "For four years he deteriorated and started having delusions and hallucinations himself. There was a fascinating moment when Mum went from the 'cared for' to the caretaker. We were really worried, but she was fine. I really want to give a lot of credit to her, for managing her own illness."

It strikes me how much her children mean to Monica, and how much her sanity depends on them. So often, those with schizophrenia or other serious mental illnesses are separated from their families, from their own children. Alex's family has their own particular circumstances, and his mother's diagnosis is unique to her, but his family has found a way to support their mum without the intervention of the state or clinical services. While talking to Alex, I do find myself wondering whether my father's condition might have been better managed if he'd had more of a role in my life, and vice versa.

Every five or so years, Alex's mother has some kind of crisis, but importantly, he feels she has real insight into her condition. On one occasion, she decided on a fast—no food or water for forty days. Alex describes bargaining with her about at least drinking nutrient smoothies to stop her from getting very sick. He picked up the phone and dialed nine twice and told her he would press it a third time (the UK equivalent to 911), at which point she agreed to take the drink. The result was that Monica completed her fast with this concession. On another occasion, Monica became obsessed with the idea that there was an apartment in Copenhagen that Emperor Hirohito had given her. "We managed it once with humor. We said, 'That's completely ridiculous, isn't it, Mum?' And she laughed and she got it." But then the delusion returned, and Alex's sister decided to take Monica to Copenhagen to find the apartment. Of course, there was no apartment. But they played along. "We were very gentle in the disappointment that Mum felt. We brought her back, and we were very loving and caring about it. Obviously, we didn't mock her, but she said, 'Okay, you were right.' But since then, when she's had similar delusions, we invoke that and she's, like, 'Ah, okay.' There's a real level of rationality to her world, if you let her explore it safely."

Alex is committed to the idea that family is the tonic for Monica's condition, and that this idea should carry on to the next generation. Alex has explained to his two children that their grandmother "sees the world differently, and very vibrantly, but it can be a very scary place for her, too." He says she is a fantastic grandmother. "She is really wired into them, really loving and caring, really wants to spend time with them. It's effortless for her, so they have a really strong and beautiful connection."

Alex gets very animated when he discusses how important it is to get to know people with a mental illness like his mother's. "Schizophrenia has such a gravitational pull. Everything gets called schizophrenia. But Mum is a forceful character. So, for example, if you're annoying her, she'll let you know. And the number of times I'll hear someone say, 'Oh, that's because she's a nutter.' NO! It's who she is. When you've spent the time we have with our mum, you're much better equipped to understand where the personality ends and the illness begins."

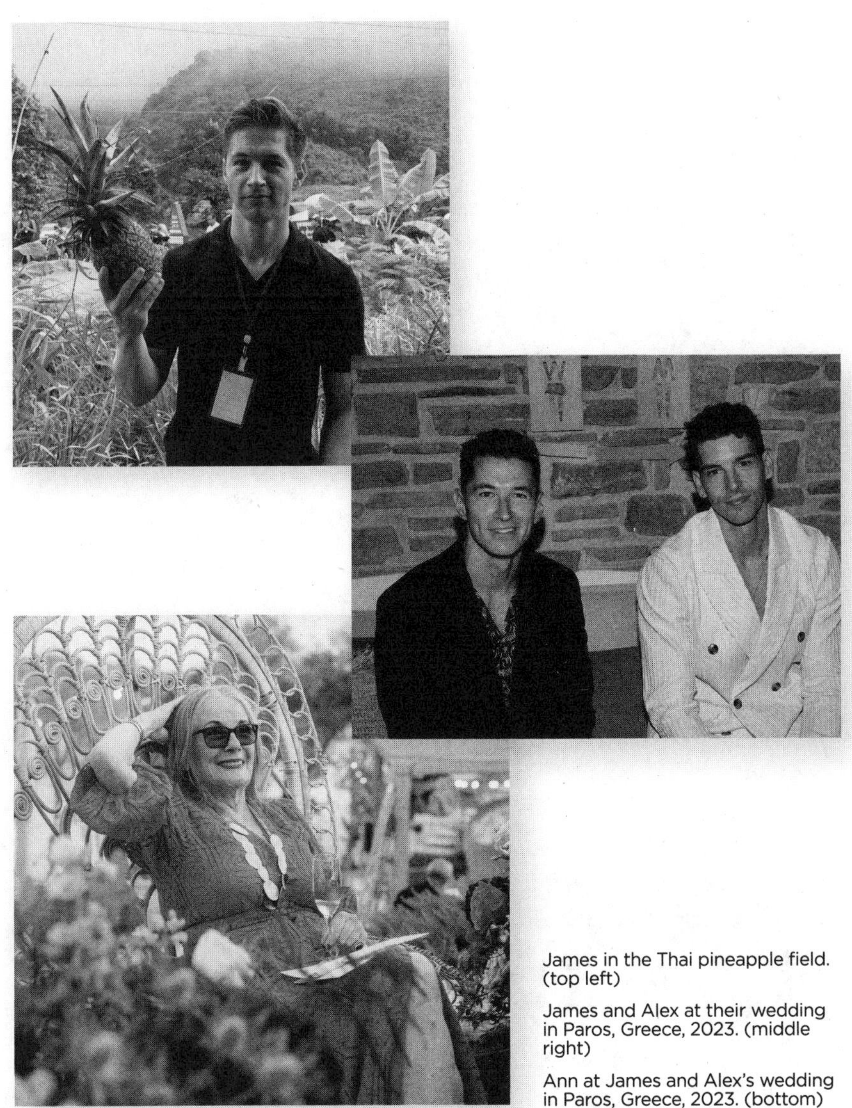

James in the Thai pineapple field. (top left)

James and Alex at their wedding in Paros, Greece, 2023. (middle right)

Ann at James and Alex's wedding in Paros, Greece, 2023. (bottom)

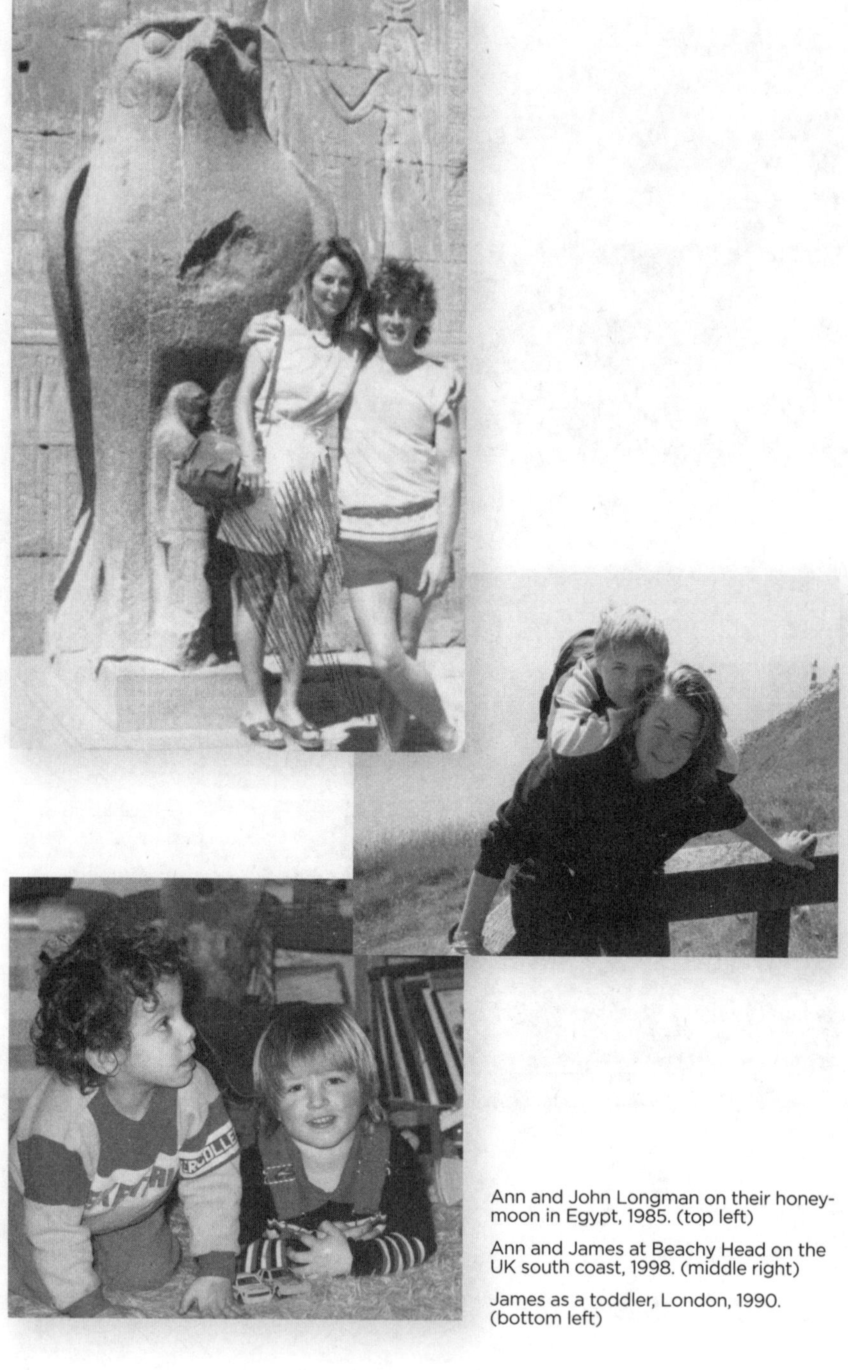

Ann and John Longman on their honeymoon in Egypt, 1985. (top left)

Ann and James at Beachy Head on the UK south coast, 1998. (middle right)

James as a toddler, London, 1990. (bottom left)

CHAPTER 7

IN MY MOTHER'S WORDS

I did not go easy to motherhood. I faced it as soldiers face their enemies, girded and braced, sword up against the coming blows. Yet all my preparations were not enough.

—MADELINE MILLER, *CIRCE*

As I grew up, I started to really think about families and ask myself why mine seemed so different and so damaged. Two feelings defined my younger and teenage years: shame and anger. I'd lost my dad, and the only person close to me was unpredictable at best. I compared myself to all my friends at school and their seemingly blissful lives. I heard about ski trips and family adventures and siblings' birthdays and thirtieth wedding anniversaries. I wanted it all. As I grew closer to these friends,

I'd be invited to take part in their events, and so increasingly on school holidays I'd stay with other families instead of going home. But there was a sadness in this, too. I felt that in a room of vibrant color and activity, I was a lonely black-and-white portrait. I wanted to join in, to accept all of their love and warmth and make it mine.

Now, one of my favorite places to be in the world is on the sofa at Alex's family home in the English countryside, doing a crossword with his dogs on my lap—I'm so lucky to have married into a family like his. But I do still have moments when the color drains, when it is hard to fully engage. I can be in the thick of it one minute, surrounded by people I love and who love me, and the next, all I want to do is be alone in a quiet room and lie down for hours. Everyone gets overwhelmed. Everyone needs a break from their family. But this feeling is more like a fissure reopening. Like a tectonic plate, deep beneath the surface, cracking back to life. It's like I've never truly been part of anything, and all the stuff I've piled into my life—my job, my relationships, all of it—has just been dirt sitting on top of this crack. And when it opens, all that falls into the fire, and I float off into oblivion.

And this is because in the back of my mind, constantly, day and night, my father is sitting there. His solitude is what I carry with me all the time. I feel he's in my bones somehow. Or, to be more precise, his solitary nature is in my bones. And over the years, my mother's constant worries about "the Longman curse" have concentrated that sensation. Because, despite all the drama of our lives, I love her. She is my mother. I know in an objective sense that what she says isn't always right or true. But I don't *feel* that way. I can know something rationally, but still feel completely differently. The love you have for family is not always rational; it's not meant to be. And so, for good or for bad, I am inextricably bound to my mother and her opinions about me.

I opened this book with a story about receiving hurtful messages from my mother. These are messages I've shared with friends and colleagues over the years. The advice is always to block her. I can go for weeks or months without speaking to her after receiving messages like this, but during that time, guilt over her situation builds up, and I eventually unblock her. It has taken me many years to realize our relationship is not normal. The first time I went to Alex's family home, we had a great day with his parents and sisters—and, of course, the dogs. I felt happy and welcome. But that night, Alex said to me, "So today, you swore a bit in front of my folks. I'm not angry or anything, but try not to do that." I was instantly mortified. I felt I'd embarrassed myself and ruined whatever relationships I was going to form with his family. But that wasn't the case. He wasn't angry. Alex was simply explaining a boundary to me, something I realized I'd never really had before. With my mother, anything goes. I've seen her in the most desperate situations, often feeling like I had to be the parent. Between us, nothing is off-limits. Our roles are not defined.

You are no doubt wondering how I can write all this while hoping to continue a relationship with my mother. Well, the answer is that she knows exactly what I'm writing, and has seen it all before publication. Nothing I have written is intended to hurt her, and she knows this. It is just my life as I have lived it and remember it. But in the spirit of sharing, she has also written what she remembers of my father, and what living with him was like for her. These are things that, in the thirty-seven years of my life, she has never before told me. Or at least, never sat down to really think about and explain in a meaningful way. I told you this book would be a process of rediscovering my father. Well, these are my mother's recollections of him. I have condensed and abbreviated in parts, but otherwise, this is her voice.

Your father and I met in 1975 at a South Kensington party given by my flatmate's parents. A somewhat shy—but sociable—31-year-old John had just returned from a monastic life with the Maharishi on a Swiss mountain. He burst out of his shell and asked me to dance. And that was it. We spent the evening philosophizing about the advantages of dipping into the "normal life" he had so brutally abandoned for ten years.

We dated for about six months. A miraculous twist of fate had landed me a job as an interpreter at the Mayfair head office of a mining company. Whilst John—prompted by your mother—had converted his Camberwell School of Art graduation certificate to a BA degree. This was to help maximize his chances of finding work as a graphic designer in the big bad world of advertising as well as in the more specialized—but limited—world of fine art. He happily lived an impecunious artist's life in a decent flat share, but, in the smallest room, not much bigger than his single bed! I guess his nimble movements (unforgettably characterized by his acrobatic cycling in London traffic with paintings tied to his body, whilst smoking a roll-up!) enabled him to indulge in his artwork on a cramped easel surrounded by random canvases and a few books.

Much talking was done in our relationship—always in friendly discussion—as we were both obsessed with exploring "why we are here." Through these intimate moments, John found the Catholic approach to the "big questions" appealing. He loved monastic plainchant, for instance, and was captivated by sacred music and the smell of incense. Not that he didn't also love Cream with Eric Clapton's mesmerizing guitar playing. And especially the Doors. As for classical music, Chopin was his favorite.

Your father would often pick me up from the office at Stanhope

Gate, invariably dressed in jeans and a tight-fitting blazer. His prematurely gray hair dyed brown to (in his view) mask his age. No doubt his fear of growing old before finding his direction consumed him. His appearance was a not unpleasant curiosity among my pinstripe-suited colleagues, whose dress code never ventured outside the '70s formal wear of London's executives. But there was something about his aura which meant he never looked out of place. One day, he uncharacteristically took me to a local Mayfair pub after work.

It wasn't crowded, and we sat at a small table by the window. Suddenly, he broke into his famous grin and said, "Can I ask you a question? Will you marry me?"

The activity that ensued swept us into a delirium triggered by the multicultural scope of our respective connections. His parents were over the moon, and mine broadcast the good news to relatives and friends on every continent.

Invitations were dispatched among the frenzy. We were to be married at the Carmelite church in Kensington in September 1978. My bosses had generously offered the handsome, paneled, Baroque Boardroom with its glorious painted ceiling for the reception. Even the office caterers were lined up for the intended gastronomic feast. By the end of August, everything was in place. Both families reveled in their feverishness. John—the humble artist—would even wear his father's morning suit. And his Scottish grandmother's engagement ring had been adjusted by the Queen's jewelers—Garrards of Regent Street no less! My parents had had a miraculous escape from civil war in Lebanon. It was to be a very special affair.

Then came the titanic blow. A month before the big day,

during a carefree coffee at our usual greasy spoon, your father's complexion suddenly turned sallow as if his entire blood supply had drained from his body. Suddenly, I was thrust into a parallel universe.

"I can't do it," he said. "Can't do what?" I replied. "The wedding's off." All I can recall at that point is the scratching of his chair on the lino as he swiftly removed himself from the cafe. Throwing back an anxious murmur as he opened the door, he exclaimed, "Honey, please go and see your friends, you'll need them."

I don't know if I paid for the coffee. I must have done. But I did go straight to my friends' house. They were both doctors expecting their first child. They knew your father well. It was a logical first port of call.

John's father was heartbroken and blamed his son's behavior on the effect of ten years of excessive amounts of meditation which he said had "disturbed his mind" and torn the family apart. Principally ashamed, his embarrassed mother coldly conceded that "there was no going back—the wedding is definitely cancelled." Of course, I returned the ring to her—as it was a family heirloom.

How could I imagine that 6 years later, I would see that ring again?

A sweet letter signed "John" came through the post on a fine day in the mid-1980s. "Wonder if you've found Mr. Right yet? If not, maybe you'll answer this? After what we had together, it would be a pity not to. So much water has gone under the bridge. . . . I've grown up a bit. . . ."

But it wasn't a simple case of "male development." Your father had voluntarily been "in and out of the 'bin,' " as he called psychiatric care. His parents had practically disowned him since his TM period with the Maharishi—seen as an unacceptable rebellion—followed by the embarrassing drama of a cancelled wedding. This endeared him more to me, as it proved his sincerity and resolve to continue a beneficial, meaningful forensic investigation of his mind and soul—and significantly, his purpose.

Your grandfather had shot himself in the family garden, having ceased to tolerate unbearable pain and isolation caused by terminal prostate cancer. Beric James had been a lonely, sensitive soul. But no one had paid much attention to this hard-working man.

It was never difficult to detect that the boys must have suffered emotional deprivation in childhood. There were many glaring examples of this throughout my association with Beric James's family. Of course, their untreated wounds were destined to bleed profusely on facing the responsibilities of adulthood.

Your grandmother's already married younger son had been unable to earn a living, following diagnosis with schizophrenia on dropping out of Exeter University. They lived a paradoxically comfortable hippy life, with middle-class luxuries provided by the family. Tony Longman indulged his talent for carpentry at his Somerset house, complete with a large work shed, lush garden, and two dogs. His academic wife held various teaching posts in the locality. They were anchored, secure and content, with the full support of medics and family.

The very opposite of itinerant artist John who, in his mid/late-thirties, remained a loose cannon on his intense search for a direction. Material needs were superfluous unless directly related to tools enabling him to perform his art. Paints, notebooks, canvases. However, it troubled him that the purpose of fine art seemed to be embellishment rather than absolute necessity. Earning a living should form an intrinsic part of one's karma, he felt, inextricably related to every cell of one's being. He did not just want a "job" to put bread on the table. This was the essence of John's philosophy which appealed to me. Money for its own sake could not be satisfying. There had to be a way to fuse the social inevitabilities of this world with personal pursuits which brought contentment whilst guaranteeing safe living.

Your father's nonchalant approach to the mundane pursuits was wholly fatalistic, and dependent on intuition and spontaneity. He would cross the road without looking, for example.

Material things had changed during the intervening years. But our minds had matured, or at least we thought they had. After all, we were best friends. John had been dumped by a nice English girl who had grown tired of his lifestyle and "incurable emotional crippling" as she put it. I had not found "the one" in my relationship with a Polish gentleman.

One sunny day your father appeared on my doorstep with a small package. "This is yours," he said as he delicately placed it in my outstretched hands. It was the ring!

So, this time, the wedding went through as planned on a modest scale at my parents' local Catholic church in Eastbourne—somewhat to John's widowed mother's disappointment.

From September 1984 until March 1985, John's mood had not faltered. His activity was focused. He looked for work as a graphic designer rather than languishing for hours in the customary, daily, boiling hot baths before incarceration in his artistic den. Your father's job as a graphic designer with an advertising agency was scheduled for May/June 1985.

The honeymoon to visit my family in Cairo was a roaring success. Random friends and family competed to entertain us. This amused John greatly. Without exception they found my husband "sympathique." The reciprocated appreciation was such that John expressed a desire to live there! He loved the atmosphere of every aspect of the place: the constant distant din in the sometimes-dusty air; the incomparable blue sky which fell at one's feet; the opiate smells of the jacaranda contrasted by the odors of overladen donkeys.

We took a boat up the Nile—a simple felucca, not one of those fancy, air-conditioned ferries! Even though we slept on deck, floodlit only by the lavish desert starlight (along with fifty equally enthusiastic backpackers!). All this enthralled this English artist who'd lived a sheltered existence in the comforts of the Green Belt or the confines of a mountain monastery. Maybe I should have initiated a move from Notting Hill to the land of the Pharaohs? How would that have influenced the outcome of our lives?

The return to the reality of inexorable mundane living in a demanding modern city was not too daunting at first. Your father enjoyed the novelty of graphic design for a while along with spreading the news of an exceptionally memorable honeymoon. Then the sense of futility of advertising crept in. He was disappointed. It is unmanageable disappointment which breaks the spirit. The hot baths became longer, and he resigned from his work.

John was a talented artist, but he had trouble believing in himself—in being proactive. A turbulent domestic background had intensified John's yearning for the perfect family, and especially for the perfect occupation in the bewildering spectrum of the art world.

Your father felt deep frustration that everything could not be on his terms alone. Persuading him to accept commissions in trompe-l'oeil frescos, and painting portraits from photographs, required all the faith and diplomacy I could muster. The result was a home routine played out in seismic silence which thickened the air almost beyond its breathable limit. Then came the pregnancy. The joy of all joys: you were on the way. You were to be a Christmas baby.

Such a life-changing diversion had the effect of exhilarating your father rather than provoking further unease. We were both as innocent as the fledgling couples who attended pre-natal classes. However, his ecstasy was not sufficient to arouse empathy for the demands of a rapidly expanding torso on a forty-year-old woman. When I asked him to meet me from work at the bus stop, he curtly replied, "You're an adult, aren't you?" His thoughts on gender equality rested on the notion that all adults were capable of protecting themselves as they chose. Personal choice was the key. Reason—or even pure kindness—did not enter the equation. He could not grasp the nuances.

The national conversation on human emotion stayed away from the levels of psychological discourse it freely exposes now. In fact, it was almost taboo. The words "mental health" were anathema—especially in polite society. Problems relating to the mind did not belong in the general physiological treatment of the individual. People were either neurotic or psychotic. Neurotic ones were given tablets and told to "get on with it." Psychotic ones were heavily sedated in psychiatric hospitals. This explains John's frequent attendance of "the bin" and the sadly fragmented character of his life. Your father was the subject of a most extensive exploration of personality, by medics, experts, and associated agents. His healthy physical presentation was misleading. Even they had trouble making sense of human behavior with the still crude guidance available in a constantly evolving specialty.

The long pregnancy created a buzz which your quiet father embraced with total acceptance and renewed vigor. Far from being nervous, he did not show a single sign of fear of fatherhood. He took an active part in all the fun, even using his keen carpentry skills to decorate our home and build a cot fit for a king. The prenatal classes had been superbly entertaining. And the 40-year-old "primigravida's" (Elderly first-time mother! Elderly, meaning anyone over 28!) delirium was complemented by enough random reassurance. Management of our day-to-day living was left entirely to me, as always. We had nothing to row about. So, we never did. Confrontation of any description was something John avoided. When his mood needed lightening, he would go for long solitary walks in nearby Holland Park or Kensington Gardens.

John was well integrated in the euphoria surrounding your birth, in spite of his natural solitude. A false alarm took us to the hospital a little early, and we had a Christmas party with the new mums and dads in an abandoned staff banquet hall, instead of an induced delivery. The seasonally festive ambience created by overworked but cheerful midwives dressed as fairies and obstetricians dressed as Santa Claus permeated the air to such an extent, it was difficult to believe we were in a hospital rather than in an amusement park! Despite supreme medical efforts, your later to be exhibited stubbornness had started its apprenticeship in the womb! Not joining those crazy guys today, you must have thought.

Assisted by forceps (and probably a shipyard-caliber towrope!), an earthquake regurgitated a huge, bonnie baby boy and a placenta "the size of a tree root," according to John! I wouldn't know, I was out of it.

All I remember of that gory scenario was your father chanting "Zeusy, Zeusy" (your nickname, an anglicized version of the Arabic, "ya noussi," my favorite term of endearment), as he placed you in my arms, some three hours after the birth. He looked pale but mellow in his wonderment, as if he had well shared the bonding in what was for me a mystical experience. Most importantly, he hadn't fainted!

It was not long before the activity surrounding the needs of a demanding tiny person entered the arena of unreasonable competition. Not because being a father didn't thrill John. But rather because the alteration of our lifestyle exceeded by far John's perceived expectations. Those tenacious imps gradually gnawed at his mind until the call of the wild could no longer be resisted.

One evening in February 1987 your father did not return from his walk. Mozart, the cat, was on guard at the foot of the bed, whiskers at 90 degrees. Your frequent night feeds were absorbing time until I switched on the little black-and-white TV. The BBC was breaking news with the announcement of a ferry disaster in the Channel. The Herald of Free Enterprise *was sinking on its way out of the Belgian port of Zeebrugge because the car deck doors had not been properly sealed. This disaster punctuated my own, which was unravelling in spooky parallel that night. Your father was nowhere to be seen. Fortunately, the shock had not caused my milk to dry up. So, your Michelin-starred restaurant remained open, and you nonchalantly seized the day.*

The usual enquiries—friends, hospitals, police, etc.—yielded nothing. It was not until sunrise that I received a phone call. It was from a remote village in the West Midlands. "Mrs. Longman, we have your husband." Mozart yawned with his enquiring look, but you were too busy to react. My relief was matched only by the knowledge that my precious newborn did not seem perturbed by the drama that was unfolding. John was alive but shivering from the effects of hypothermia. The Good Samaritans had given him a hot bath, a change of clothes, and industrial quantities of cups of tea. His rescue had been a miracle. Instead of walking to Hyde Park that evening, an urge overcame him to get in the car and drive continuously until he reached the Headquarters of Maharishi Yogi's British branch. It mattered not that he didn't know its precise location, or how to get there. His instinct would be a reliable navigator. It mattered not that it was snowing heavily. It mattered not that all he was wearing was a light jacket and black jeans or that all he had in his threadbare pocket was cigarette papers and tobacco. The dashboard would provide the light. What else could he need?!

Paradoxically, smoking actually saved your father's life. On returning home from the theater, a couple noticed a tiny, flickering light in a mound of what looked like a car buried in snow. Concerned, they decided to investigate. It was John—stuck in a snow drift with a roll-up glued to his frozen lips.

Our married life seemed to be heading towards a precipice.

Your father's struggle with normality continued to build unwanted opposition to sharing a space which intruded—even mildly—on his high voltage agenda. The hot baths grew more frequent. The walks around the area grew longer. Already scant shopping expeditions became sterile. Medics remained baffled. Mobile phones had not yet left experimental levels in 1987. I had to constantly ensure that one of the house phones was within reach, in between nappy change, as well as be near a red, public phone box when out and about with you. The tension was palpable, even in the fresh air. Thankfully, as well as my French lullabies, often shared by a doting grandmaman, the many excursions into the delights of Portobello Road and Kensington Gardens kept you entertained by admiring onlookers. You never cried.

And then came his suicide attempt. We walked into the emergency room as if we were attending a routine meeting. John was vertical, fully clothed and though subdued, quite lucid. You were clasped to my body like a clam. The paramedics calmly described the situation to the hospital team. Suddenly, I felt my head spin and sail into a semi-conscious whirl. "Life-threatening paracetamol poisoning" was what I was gently told. It slowly took effect over time. This explained your father's deceptively normal presentation. John was nevertheless critically ill. "We are looking to find a bed in the Liver Unit at King's, as we do not have the facilities required for—"

At that point, the consultant's solemnly delivered explanation disappeared into the ether. It felt as if my brain was splattering, not in my head, but somewhere in a horror movie projected on the wall. Only the day before we had been the very picture of domestic bliss. Your father had proudly shown a work-in-progress portrait to our dinner guests. Interesting conversation had been stimulated by his exposition of a newly-found painting style. And there was little leftover food.

"We'll do our utmost to ensure that your husband gets the best possible treatment. Have the nurse bring you a cup of tea. What a beautiful baby." Again, voices faded as John was scurried into a cubicle and a drip instantly plunged into his hand. Surely all they had to do was pump out his stomach, I thought. Isn't that how swallowed poison is dealt with? Mercifully, your gurgling remained joyful throughout....

A heavy paracetamol overdose taken the night before has a complex trajectory. It was already in John's system and attacking the liver. It was difficult to gauge your father's physical as well as mental pain. He seemed so detached. This lack of outward signs became unspeakably worrying. I wanted to dive into his mind and scrub the grime that had soiled his happiness. But how? Was there anything I could do?!... All became progressively blurred as I clung on to my baby. It didn't make sense. Your father did not look seriously ill.

"Why?" I asked. "I wanted to see what it's like on the other side," John replied dispassionately, as one might murmur whilst passing the salt over lunch. Those words are seared on my heart until the day it stops beating.

You and I stayed in intense vigil at John's bedside for two weeks, whilst he deteriorated slowly, turning progressively yellow with excreted body fluids becoming a darker shade of brown. Until those fluids became a paler shade of yellow. Guardian angels worked overtime. The pending request for a bed at King's was cancelled and I later took your father home—pale and deflated—but alive!

In his usual contradictory way, John was relieved that his irresponsible experiment with mortality had failed. John's strict regime was marked on the board, telephone cables were extended, and supervision of your father's movements intensified whilst guarding the freedom he cherished. You were oblivious to all this. There was never a feeling of being trapped in an atmosphere loaded with adversity. Everyone—including my attentive mother—maintained their sense of humor. And I thanked every Saint in paradise that you were not old enough to remember. Living together, though, was no longer possible.

"Mummy, Mummy, have I got a daddy?" You asked me this when you were very young. John did see his "babe in arms" when he visited. It was only when you began to speak that he showed an active interest. You don't remember your pre-nursery years of course, but you did have a daddy. He no longer lived in the same house not because we didn't get on as a family, but because he was fighting a bloody war with himself. His solution was to treat his crippling injuries "far from the madding crowd." This could only lead to a catastrophic implosion. And it did. When you were a small child who repeatedly nagged me to see his "daddy," I picked you up, showering you with kisses, saying, "You have a daddy, darling. He often comes to see us. But because he is a painter, he lives around the corner in his studio, so as not to make a mess in the house."

The eclectic mix of creative people and traders meant that my many forays into the colorful territory of Portobello Market with a baby's pushchair, looking for John—who would regularly go missing from his new abode—became a norm. I felt responsible for your father. Despite the nagging advice from many to leave him be and get on with my life, they were not aware of the reality and of how I felt I had to deal with that reality. I was an accomplice in his search, and I could not let him down. I was not an aggrieved wife weaving her way through the detritus of a vegetable market with an innocent baby and revenge on her mind. No one could possibly know the real, laidback John who was part of their fabric or the true motives of an abandoned wife and mother.

John had not responded to the indefatigable attempts at getting him back home where he belonged. Where he did not realize that he knew he wanted to be. All thoughts of protecting a child from a potentially "dangerous" father were quelled by the abiding desire to introduce a son to his absent, natural father. It was his right. And diving deep into my inner waters, I knew that your father's unmistakable qualities could be unearthed. John had the experience of a maturing mind in his four-year long period of mental acrobatics, ruminations, and extramarital adventures. This would require boundless fine judgement, tenacity, and—above all—infinite, unconditional love.

I could perhaps move from stage one of my "maternal protection policy": selective intermittent contact with John when his mood was deemed normal. Naturally, I continued to be concerned for his welfare whether he was living with us or not. And he knew that I would never deny him access to the baby. Always in my presence of course. Besides, juggling many, multicolored balls was not only my destiny, but also a feature of my intrinsic character; compulsive problem-solving, determined to try "fixing" your father. And I had taken Catholic marriage vows—which are indissoluble unless an annulment is sought. Something I refused to do as it would "nullify" your existence. That makes me a widow and a single mother.

My compulsive mirth and generally positive demeanor could misleadingly cover up the silent terror which had defined my life with John. But I did plunder every personal level of creativity and tentative learning, to try to be a "father" as well as a tender mother to my most cherished son. I also subscribed to the belief that "it takes a village to raise a child." Stretching your horizons and enriching all good experience was foremost in my aspirations. As it had been for your father who had depended on me to introduce him to discovery beyond the boundaries of his intense, inwardly focused mind.

John was not dangerous per se. His unpredictability made him dangerous. He always presented a most gentlemanly, charismatic posture to the outside world. My family liked him. Other than my deeply engaged and affectionate mother, no one could know how "quietly" cruel he could become when the green-eyed monster devoured his soul. Or when the mundane clashed with his expectations and misinterpretations of a baffling existence which seemed normal—even if not entirely pleasant—to other inhabitants of the shared world.

Just about everything my mother has written here I learn for the first time as I enter her words into this book. I didn't know how she met my father, or how my father proposed. I didn't know about his efforts to work in graphic design and advertising. I didn't know I had spent my first three hours of life with my father while my mother was recovering from giving birth. And I didn't know I was at the hospital when my father was admitted for a suicide attempt.

Reading my mother's words, I'm incredibly moved at her obvious commitment to him. My parents have always been two very separate people to me, the complete opposite from one another. He was calm, often withdrawn, and docile. She was fiery, emotional, and sometimes unpredictable. In these pages, she has shown me how much of a team they were, how they shared similar philosophies. When my father was well, she was his soulmate. She hasn't explained very much to me in person, other than to say she suffered. But for the first time, I truly understand how hard it must have been for her, and how much she loved him. Why else would he come back to her after so much time apart, after he was "in the bin," as he called it, if he did not love her deeply? And why would she have spent so much time trying to help him, if she didn't harbor those same feelings?

I understand now just how much pain his illness must have caused her. Perhaps when she writes to me *You're sick like your father*, she's referring to her own pain rather than the illness itself. Perhaps she is so deeply scarred by the experience that all upset, all sadness, all disappointment puts her back in that place mentally, like a reflex. I'm not sure. I'm also struck by how much like my mother I am when it comes to my own search for family. All she ever wanted was to provide a good, safe home for me. To create the family ideal that I looked for in my school years. She, too, wanted packed Christmas dinner tables, roaring fires, happy families. But she didn't get those things.

She explains very clearly how much she wanted to "fix" my dad. How she was convinced a "normal" family life was what he wanted. But it is clear to me from his medical records that a life like that was almost impossible. She could not fix him, because it was never in her power to do so. But I guess when we love someone, we feel we have to keep trying. It must have been infuriating for her to learn he'd decided to stop taking his medication. I can see in the medical notes how much time and energy she spent speaking to his doctors, trying to get him help. When he decided he didn't want the help, it must have felt like a monumental rejection.

For many years, I've been desperate to learn more about my dad. I set out to write this book in the hope that I could build him out into a real person, rather than the mysterious hero of my imagination. Through reading my mother's side of the story, I realize I've never really known her that well, either. Or, at least, her in relation to the most momentous event in either of our lives. All my focus has been in trying to get to grips with who my father was. But now, I also have a much clearer picture of who she was then, and who she is now.

Shame, and how it pervades our lives, is a theme of this book. With Kim, whose mother ended her life, I discussed the shame of our family situations, and our relationship to that shame over time. "You grow up thinking you live in a normal family—and then, at a certain age, you start to realize, 'Maybe I'm not so normal,'" she told me.

It's this realization that is profoundly shame-inducing. Kim says of her mother, "I did find it easier to love her from afar," and I have felt exactly the same about my mother. But because this is a parent I'm talking about, these thoughts send me into a spiral of guilt from which I'm unable to extricate myself. I feel sadness for her situation, and I want to help. But I'm also torn because I want to protect myself, just as my mother tried her hardest to protect me from my father's illness. Her account of her time with him makes that very clear. But it seems to me that after he died, her efforts to "fix" continued, and I suppose I was the one she had to fix.

This book will never end if I try to address every kind of psychological dynamic at play in families. Alex Bushill showed me how families can overcome some of the hurdles of mental illness in the way he and his siblings care for his mother, Monica. I also want you to meet thirty-two-year-old Alaina, from Montgomery, Alabama. Her bipolar disorder went undiagnosed for years. But then her mother was also diagnosed with the same condition, and much of what had not made sense before became clearer.

From an early age, Alaina says, something drew her to work in medicine and psychology. Ambitious and determined, she excelled through school and college, until she started working on a PhD in public policy. Suddenly, everything changed.

"In retrospect, I can see that I did have symptoms growing up, and I just wasn't aware. I struggled a lot with social anxiety and bouts of depression." It was the end of 2016, and Alaina says her sleep patterns changed radically. "I just wasn't sleeping at all, but I was still feeling energized, somehow. I felt invincible. I was heavily involved with my church, with my studies, and had an active social life and was just racing to keep up with all those things. I started getting racing thoughts, and my speech sped up."

And then, in January, a severe psychotic episode hit like an earthquake in her life. "It was like a switch," she says. "One moment I was here in the world with everyone else, and the next I wasn't. I was at home by myself and then got into my car. I was driving while I was hallucinating." She says she started feeling paranoid and having both visual and auditory delusions. "It's almost like living a dream. This was downtown Atlanta. It was dark. I remember parking and walking the streets. I was in the middle of traffic at one point."

Luckily, she ended up not far from a hospital, and a worker saw her in the street and realized something was up. "I went to the emergency room and then the psychiatric ward. I wasn't telling them who I was, because I was so paranoid. So, I was missing. My family didn't know where I was." It was only after a few days of medication that Alaina says she started coming back to herself. After about a week in the psychiatric ward, Alaina was allowed home.

"It was a very hard time," she says. "I had to move home and essentially start over. I felt very ashamed about it. I couldn't tell anyone for years. Not my friends. I spoke about it a little with my family, but I got very isolated and severely depressed, as I didn't know what I was going to do with my life. I'm so used to achieving and accomplishing things, and excelling. My PhD program dominated my mind at the time. I felt I'd failed. I felt people would think I was crazy if I told them what had happened. I felt if I shared that piece of myself with other people, they would treat me differently."

Alaina was misdiagnosed after the episode. Doctors told her it had been a stress-induced attack, and that it was unlikely to happen again. It was only after more psychiatric help from different mental health professionals that she was diagnosed with bipolar disorder and given the proper medications. "That was the first person who sat me down and asked me about my history," she recalls. "I just went to the right place, and the right person was there. Honestly, I felt relieved. I knew it was more than just stress. But of course, I'm not a professional. I felt relief that I had a label that I could call it, even though everyone experiences it differently. I could learn more about the disorder and, in doing so, learn more about myself."

She says her experience in the psychiatric ward opened her eyes to the reality of mental illness. "What was most interesting was the variety of people there. Not everyone is there for the same reason. You meet people across the spectrum of needs. I don't think people realize how different everyone is. I think people think it's all straitjackets and tie-downs. It's not like that at all."

It was then that Alaina's mother realized she needed professional help, too. "It wasn't until I had experienced all my stuff that she started noticing similar symptoms in herself." Until then, Alaina's mother having a similar condition wasn't on anyone's radar—they had simply attributed her symptoms to her personality. Her mother began reading more, learning more, and attending therapy. Eventually, she was also diagnosed with bipolar disorder.

A second episode hit Alaina in late 2022, and made her aware of a pattern. Not long after having her baby, she was back in the hospital with a psychotic episode. There had been physical challenges with the pregnancy, she was feeling stressed, and she had not been taking her medication. She came home from running errands and began speaking incoherently to her husband. "My husband was confused because he'd never seen this before. I had delusions, I thought I was God or thought other people were God. My emotions were all over the place. I was calm and collected at one moment. And then I'd cry my eyes out. I thought I was hearing or thinking things. Next thing I remember is waking up on a stretcher in the ER."

Of her mother, Alaina says, "We are very close. I wouldn't say the diagnosis brought us closer, but it explained a lot of things. From childhood and into adulthood. It was, like, 'Oh, okay, that makes sense now.'" Alaina and her mother now blog about their shared diagnosis and provide a platform for others with the condition. "I did a lot of hiding. Personally, sharing and not hiding from it have really helped in my recovery."

Alaina and her husband want to try for another child, but given the psychosis her first pregnancy triggered, she's hesitant. "I guess I need a better plan going into it this time. The tricky thing is certain medications are not advised to take during pregnancy. There's a lack of research about what they would do. That is something that scares me. I've been told the more relapses you have, the harder it is to recover, and they can become more spontaneous. So that scares me, too." Alaina also thinks a lot about her daughter's genetics. "If she does have bipolar [disorder]," she tells me, "it'll make me a better parent because of my own experiences. I think I'll know what to look for and how to help her regulate her emotions. And if I start early, I can help her work through that."

In talking to Alaina, I wonder how I would have coped with my depression had my dad been alive to talk to about it. His condition was different and far more serious, but he also experienced low moods. Unable to really discuss my struggles with my mother, I've always missed what I hope would have been an understanding ear. The situation I found myself in with her after my dad died, as full of love as it was, was very difficult for me, and I think in no small part contributed to the depression I would encounter years later. It filled up my jam jar, which was already laden with the rocks of my genetic susceptibility, and at various points throughout my life, when other things have brought me down, my jar has spilled over. I could, like Alastair Campbell, adapt rings to fit over the jar so I can take on more water. And I do: I exercise, I speak to my friends, I'm trying to develop a working life that fulfills me and gives me purpose. But the idea of putting more and more rings on my jar is also terrifying: watching the water rise, having to find new and creative ways to prevent it from spilling over. What if instead there was a way to shrink those rocks, somehow? To make them take up less space in my jam jar?

James with a childhood friend on the beach in Eastbourne, 1994. (top left)

Ann and John, 1996. (right)

James and Gabrielle (Sawaya) Claridge, 1996. (top)

Gabrielle and a young Ann Claridge, Libya, early 1950s. (right)

CHAPTER 8

EPIGENETICS

History does not repeat itself. But it rhymes.

—ATTRIBUTED TO MARK TWAIN

So, to recap: My father ended his life. His father ended his. And I have a difficult relationship with my mother. Not a great outlook, is it?

On even an anecdotal level, you don't have to be a rocket scientist to guess I might find life tough sometimes. But just writing it off as a few bad genes and some batty relatives isn't enough for me. I've already explained what I've learned about genetic susceptibility. I've given you an insight into my environment growing up. But I'm also interested in how those environments can impact us on a biological level, and how those changes can not only affect us, but be inherited.

In her book *The Epigenetics Revolution,* Nessa Carey shows how quickly our understanding of "inherited" illness is changing. Once we take away the less than 2 percent of our total DNA that is responsible for our physical traits, such as eye and hair color, we're left with the "junk

DNA" that is responsible for many of the emotional, behavioral, and personality traits we inherit. And it turns out it's far more important than previously thought. In the last ten years, there have been some incredibly exciting discoveries about what that 98 percent is actually doing. And that, in a word, is *epigenetics.*

"Epi" is derived from the Greek word meaning *over*, or *above*. In practice, it means that there are chemicals that sit "on" our genome and control how those genes behave. If the genes are the hardware of our system, epigenetics is the software. (One scientist, Joseph Bellanti, coined the memorable phrase, "Genes load the gun and epigenetics pulls the trigger.") Nessa Carey is a former forensic scientist who investigated crimes with London's Metropolitan Police. She has a real gift for taking complicated topics and making them more understandable for wider audiences.

"Whenever two genetically identical individuals are nonidentical in some way we can measure," says Carey, "this is called epigenetics. When a change in environment has biological consequences that last long after the event itself has faded into distant memory, we are seeing an epigenetic effect in action."

While genes are set for life, what happens at an epigenetic level can come and go over time. Bring that DNA ladderlike structure back into your mind. There are a number of epigenetic processes that can turn genes along the strands "on" or "off." One of them is DNA methylation—when a chemical group is added to certain places along the DNA, thus blocking the proteins that would normally attach there to read the code. In other words, the chemical groups get in the way of the gene being "read" by the body, and mutes that particular gene or expression. Another process is called histone modification. Histones are the proteins around which DNA wraps itself. When histones are packed tightly together within a DNA strand, the strand of DNA cannot be read easily; when histones are loosely packed, more of the DNA strand is exposed, and can therefore be read. By tightening and loosening that DNA strand, the histone modification process turns genes "on" or "off." Moreover, twin studies have shown that two genetically identical babies can diverge in gene expression more and more as they get older. This isn't some magical effect of time, but an epigenetic process. Age is one of the major contributors to the DNA strand becoming unfurled, allowing more of that strand to be read by the body.

In other words, I may have the same genetic predisposition or risk of schizophrenia as my father, but epigenetic processes might have switched *off* the effect of those genes. It works a little like a dimmer switch: My dad's switch might have been turned right up, whereas mine might have been turned down. To illustrate this phenomenon, Nessa Carey uses the example of the Shakespeare play *Romeo and Juliet*. If DNA is the script as Shakespeare wrote it, epigenetics is the interpretation of that script by a specific group of actors. They can't change the actual words, but they can change how they are expressed.

It's also possible that new versions of that interpretation can be copied and passed down. Carey gives the more specific example of Baz Luhrmann's adaptation of the play: *Romeo + Juliet*. Luhrmann gives Leonardo DiCaprio a copy of the script with all his notes written on it—for certain words to be whispered and others shouted, for instance. DiCaprio then gives Claire Danes a copy with *his* notes added, perhaps building detail into what Luhrmann had instructed. All of a sudden, you have two different versions of the same script, with different notes and annotations, which in turn can be copied multiple times to give to all the other members of the crew. Those crew members then write their notes on their copies—lighting cues, let's say. The original script has not changed—all the words remain the same—but Luhrmann's annotations,

DiCaprio's notes, and the crew's lighting cues have changed how the play is performed.

In much the same way, my father (Baz Luhrmann, in this example) had a specific DNA code that could not be changed, but his environment might have changed how the code was expressed at crucial times in his life, or in his early development. What turned his dimmer switch up? What kept mine down? Those are the big questions.

UK mental health organization Mind put me in touch with all kinds of people for this book as I tried to make sense of the science by sharing the experiences of ordinary people. Among them is twenty-eight-year-old Olivia, who lives in Surrey. Olivia saw her family story repeated through the generations, each experience annotated like a Baz Luhrmann script, each annotation seeming to emphasize, rather than dampen, the instructions written out.

Olivia and her younger sister lived with their parents until they separated when she was sixteen. After developing eating disorders and depression in her teens, and a series of suicide attempts when she was at university, she was diagnosed with depression and borderline personality disorder. Borderline personality disorder is the most commonly recognized personality disorder in the UK and can cause emotional instability, disturbed patterns of thinking or perceptions, impulsive behavior, and intense but unstable relationships. The mental illnesses I have discussed in this book so far are distinct from personality disorders, which can result in personality traits becoming rigid and unchangeable. By contrast, mood disorders involve constant or frequent changes in emotional disposition. There is, of course, a lot of overlap, too, and as we've seen, diagnoses for these myriad disorders or mental illnesses can be difficult. But as one person described it for Mind, "Borderline personality disorder is like the emotional version of being a burn victim.

Everything hurts more than it seems to for everyone else, and any 'thick skin' you're supposed to have just isn't there."

Olivia's childhood was shaped by a mother with the same condition. "She wasn't diagnosed until I was sixteen or seventeen, so there were a lot of unaddressed mental health issues as I was growing up. I wouldn't say I was abused, but I'd definitely say I was attacked by her on a lot of occasions." She says her mother would react to small issues that seemed relatively minor but that she was unable to process. She would then fly into a rage, and Olivia would take the brunt of it. "I don't think I ever developed a proper connection with her," she says.

"It wasn't a very happy childhood. I was in a parent role from quite a young age, managing her outbursts." She feels a lot of her self-harm and suicidal behavior was learned. "There were many instances when I was a child that she assaulted me. The most traumatic was when she started strangling me, but then realized what she was doing as she was doing it." Olivia describes her stricken mother putting her in the car and driving them both to a mental health crisis center. "I've just strangled my child, please help me," Olivia's mother told them. But they didn't. She was told she had anger management issues.

Olivia's upbringing was so traumatic that she first attempted suicide when she was just twelve years old. "Mum and I would have an argument, and she wouldn't be able to control her anger and would end up attacking me in some way. I remember quite spontaneously going to the medicine box and swallowing everything in there." But she never told her parents what she'd done. "I was just very sick for the next few days, and my parents just thought I had a bug. I don't think I realized the significance of what I'd done until I got older."

Like me, Olivia says she feels torn between anger and loyalty toward her mother. "If she wasn't my mum, I would have cut her out," she says.

"I did actually, fairly recently, for a full year. I couldn't recover properly, so I needed a full break."

Judging by these accounts, Olivia's dimmer switch was turned right up from a very young age. I ask her where she feels her own diagnosis came from. Is it genetic, or was her childhood so chaotic that these issues were bound to affect her? "Both my grandmother and my great-grandmother had very similar behaviors," she replies. Her grandmother was depressive and had problems with alcohol. So much so that when she was pregnant, she drank a bottle of liquor and threw herself down the stairs.

"The experiences I dealt with maybe triggered my genetic predisposition," she says. Her sister, on the other hand, was less exposed to the difficulties in the household. She was younger at the time her mother was most unpredictable, and Olivia made efforts to protect her. Later, she went to live with their father. Olivia says her sister has not developed depression or borderline personality disorder. Whether or not her genetic predisposition was the same as Olivia's, the events in her life have not led to severe mental illness.

"My mum recognizes the problems I have," says Olivia. "She feels guilty about my diagnosis. She has a sense that she's 'given' me something."

Olivia now works as a mental health trainer for companies, training staff in how to manage mental illness at work—putting her personal experiences to professional use. She describes her relationship with her mother as "fairly surface," but now that her mother has the proper medication and better support, her mother is in a better place.

"I know I don't have a functioning parent now," she says. "I've just kind of accepted that isn't a relationship I can have. I accept what I've got, and I make the best of it. It feels like a loss. In recent years, I've come to terms with the fact that she's not a mother. There's a grief for the mother I wanted and didn't have."

As you know, I have felt this same grief for the family I wanted and did not have. But what strikes me during my conversation with Olivia, and having read my mother's letter to me about her life with my father, is how much I was actually guarded from my father's illness. While Olivia experienced her mother's condition up close, with no one to stand between it and her, I had my mother. No, she was not perfect. But the outcome could have been far worse had I been more exposed to my father's illness: had my mother not sent me away to a school where I could be protected; had she not decided to put my well-being above her own. Maybe it was my mother's protective measures that kept my genetic dimmer switch down, blocking genetic coding that would otherwise have been read. The more I learn, the more I'm starting to believe I avoided schizophrenia partly because, at a crucial time in my early life—when the impact would have been most severe—I was kept away from the truth of my father's illness.

Because this book is about hope, I also wanted to share with you stories of families who have found positivity in their shared diagnoses. Like some of the others who I've spoken to, Eleanor Segall finds sharing her story has helped her cope with her condition. She is a blogger and mental health activist, and the author of *Bring Me to Light*. The title of her book says a lot about her outlook—she talks to me on Zoom from her London home, and, despite the heaviness of our conversations, her demeanor is light and giggly. Raised in an Orthodox Jewish family just outside London, Eleanor was diagnosed with bipolar disorder when she was sixteen. Her father, Michael, had been diagnosed with the same condition just four years earlier.

"I really think what you're trying to do is amazing," Eleanor says. "And I've spoken to my father and he's totally happy for me to talk about our experiences." Her father's bipolar disorder went undiagnosed from when she was about three, when his symptoms first appeared, until she was about twelve. "During that time, he had three major manic episodes. The depression caused him to stay at home in bed and not work. My mum became the breadwinner. They tried to shield me from all of that, but I did start to get anxiety from about the age of four, which I attribute to maybe my dad not being around and not being well."

Things came to a head when Eleanor was twelve. "We were getting ready for school and my mum found him in the bathroom with a pile of aspirin, counting them out, contemplating taking his own life. Thank God she found him. She said to him, 'I don't think you want to be doing that, do you?' She looked him in the eye, and he said, 'No,' dropped them, and ran to bed."

Eleanor says he'd struggled with these bouts of mania for nearly a decade, but it had never been identified by doctors. As is so common, her father's symptoms were attributed to his personality—just his natural, outgoing temperament.

I ask Eleanor what his manic episodes looked like. Like me, she can't remember a lot because she says her mother shielded her so much from it all. "He would go out partying till the early hours and said he felt amazing. It was true mania. He didn't get any psychosis, he was just up all night, talking really quickly. He would have been about thirty-three when he first started getting these symptoms."

Eleanor says even though her mother stopped her from seeing the consequences of the illness, her parents did discuss with their children the battles their father was fighting. "They were very open with the fact that my dad needed medication," she says, "and that my dad needed help. I didn't fully grasp at twelve what bipolar [disorder] does. But three years later, I became ill myself." Eleanor started to feel incredibly anxious and increasingly withdrawn and depressed. She was given six weeks off school, during which time she says she just cried under a blanket at home until she was sent to a child psychologist. They diagnosed her with depression and gave her antidepressants, and her anxiety began to dissipate.

"Then, three months later, when I turned sixteen, I had my first manic episode." Eleanor was in Israel on vacation when her behavior started to change. "I started having racing thoughts, I couldn't control my energy." She says she became sexually uninhibited and was overly touchy with people. "I'd be hugging people randomly, just being a bit inappropriate." Her behavior was completely out of character and the tour organizers knew something was up, although Eleanor herself didn't think there was a problem. Her father flew out to get her. She was furious. "I didn't think anything was wrong with me. I just thought I was having a good time."

Eleanor's episode lasted six to eight weeks. By the time she came out of psychosis, there was still no diagnosis. Initial assessments didn't find anything wrong; it was only later that she would be diagnosed. "I was hospitalized later that year with a mixed psychotic depressive episode, which was very scary," she says. "It was a voluntary admission, but that was when I was first diagnosed with bipolar [disorder]."

She was given mood stabilizers. But at sixteen, she couldn't take stronger medication, which she says is what she really needed. Her drugs were tweaked over the years, but the episodes only got worse, and reached their climax when she was twenty-four. "I'd had a deep suicidal depression," she says. "I was self-harming. I was telling everyone the whole time because I didn't want to take my life. I was given strong antidepressants. But I think that then triggered a psychosis, because the mood stabilizers had stopped working." She suspects the antidepressant medication tipped her into mania. "I was still taking my meds, and I was thinking, 'Why do I feel so bad?' I didn't get it. I was scared."

It's important to note here that properly medicating different mental illnesses is a major goal of genetic research. As we have seen, misdiagnosis is very common—particularly with women, and especially when psychosis plays a role, as it can for those with bipolar disorder or schizophrenia. Because different symptoms appear at different times, it is easy for a physician to only observe one dynamic of a person's condition. Understanding more about our genetics may mean people like Eleanor are better diagnosed in the future, and the medications they receive better tailored to their needs.

As for many people who experience bipolar disorder, Eleanor's thoughts were characterized by making grand, unrealistic plans out of the blue. "I was on the way to work, and I suddenly thought, 'I'm going to reunite my whole family from all over the world. I'm going to reunite one hundred people. And then, that evening, I went to the Strand in London and started talking to homeless people with the idea that I would open a homeless shelter." During her episodes, Eleanor didn't become a danger to other people. Instead, she became a very vulnerable person—vulnerable to others who would take advantage of her. She says she was sexually assaulted by "someone who knew I couldn't consent to anything but didn't care."

Alaina in the last chapter and now Eleanor describe similar symptoms in their bipolar disorder: a combination of depressive lows and magnificent highs. "You change when you're manic," explains Eleanor. "You become this really hyper, exuberant, over-the-top character." One person described it to UK organization Mind as "an emotional amplifier: when my mood is high, I feel far quicker, funnier, smarter, and livelier than anyone; when my mood is low, I take on the suffering of the whole world."

But through all of it, Eleanor didn't think anything was wrong, what she describes as being "so ill that I didn't think I was ill." Her family had to devise a plan to get her checked in to the hospital. They pretended her mother was sick and needed Eleanor to accompany her to the emergency room. When they arrived, it became clear to Eleanor that medical staff were trying to help her, not her mother. "I was so ill that when the nurse was giving me medication, I thought I was going to be poisoned. I didn't trust anybody. It's a horrible, traumatizing experience, being sectioned [committed], because everyone is telling you you're ill, but you don't think you are. I felt my family was conspiring against me. Security was keeping me in certain rooms. I was very frightened."

This was the first time Eleanor was administered lithium, which she now attributes to keeping her episode-free for nine years. "It worked for my dad, and it worked for me," she says brightly. Lithium is a mood stabilizer and contained in many antipsychotic drugs used to treat people with bipolar disorder and schizophrenia. It was part of my father's treatment, too, but he complained it dulled his creativity. There was perhaps also a level of paranoia at play with my father's condition (not the case with Eleanor's dad) that made him wary of medication, of the control he felt others would have over him. My uncle Tony, his brother, who also had schizophrenia and also took lithium, had very little energy most of the time. His wife was careful to make sure he always took his medications. Whenever I was with him, I would wonder to myself whether my dad, if he were still alive, would have been destined to live in the same slow, ponderous way.

I ask Eleanor if she feels the medication she takes dulls her mind the way my father said it dulled his. "It's a strong drug," she says. "I have to look after myself. I have to be aware of my salt levels, for instance." (Lithium-based medication can cause sodium depletion, because salt works to break down the toxicity of the lithium.) But Eleanor is used to her new reality. "Because I have the role model of my dad taking it and being well, I know taking it works. I'm definitely a different person to the one I was before taking it. But it hasn't dulled things for me the way it can do for others. It's kept my mood on an even keel. But it certainly is hard knowing you've got to be medicated for the rest of your life."

Eleanor is certain bipolar disorder runs in her family. "It's not just my dad. I have other family members who have been diagnosed. I have family in the US with the same diagnosis, as well as my grandmother's sister who was on lithium—but that was back in the 1950s, so we're not sure what it was exactly." There is a tendency toward secrecy in the Jewish community, she tells me, and the idea of a "corrupted" family is particularly problematic for more orthodox groups. "They cannot come out and say 'I have this illness,' because it will ruin their marriage prospects and their standing in the community. We don't live in that community, but there was still a sense of shame. I didn't want people to know that I was a teenager with bipolar[disorder]. Back then, no one talked about it. If you told someone you were bipolar, they'd run a mile from you."

After all the ups and downs, Eleanor says she now has a positive relationship with her parents. "I'm really lucky that I have very supportive parents," she says. "And because of my father's mental health, he understood that I needed treatment and support. We always check in with each other. My dad will sometimes say to me, 'Oh, I'm getting a bit hyper manic today.' He's reclaimed a part of him that he had to hide for a long time. It's brought us closer. He just gets it, he knows. If you're low, he understands. When I went through my really bad phase ten years ago, he was there and knew what to say and how to act and how to be around me. Sometimes, people without the illness don't exactly know how you want to be treated."

Eleanor met her husband, Rob, in 2016, and says they clicked straight away. She calls for him from the other room, and a man with thick brown hair and a kind smile emerges. He waves. "On the second date we started talking about mental health," says Eleanor, "because he has family members with some of these issues. And I thought to myself, 'Do I tell him? It's a big deal.' And then, on the third date, I told you, didn't I?" she says, turning to him. "And he was so supportive and caring and loving. It was so different to what I expected." I can see how much Rob's understanding means to Eleanor. He doesn't stay long before waving his goodbye. But their partnership is clear.

Children are in the couple's future, and they have already met with a perinatal psychiatrist to discuss their concerns. "If you have a child naturally, it can put a strain on your mind as well as your body. And I'm worried about taking lithium during pregnancy, so there are things we need to be conscious of." Meeting with a perinatal psychiatrist is a chance for women on medication for a mental illness to better understand how it may affect their baby, and how they may need to reduce certain medications. While there, Eleanor was also advised to visit a parent and baby unit to relieve some of the anxiety she feels about going into a hospital. For many people with mental illness, hospitals can mean traumatic experiences in psychiatric care. The perinatal psychiatrist told Eleanor that making these visits part of her plan would reduce the risk of bipolar relapse around the birth.

Eleanor says it does bother her to think of passing bipolar disorder on somehow, even if there's only a 10 percent chance of doing so when one parent has the condition. "I hope they don't get it, and I hope I don't see the pattern repeat. But if they did, I'd be the best person to be able to help. And so would my dad."

Olivia and Eleanor both had a parent with a mental illness, and they both eventually developed that same illness. Both of them experienced stressors in childhood that might have activated whatever predisposition they might have had. Olivia was exposed at a far younger age than Eleanor, and she saw up close her mother's difficulties. Eleanor says she was shielded, to a certain extent, and that when her own symptoms emerged, her family was prepared to navigate them together. The love and understanding her family showed her from a young age may explain why Eleanor has been able to move on with her life. I'm especially struck by how Eleanor's mother responded to her father's diagnosis, and then how both parents responded to hers. They were able to not dwell on a family pattern repeating itself, but to focus instead on the benefit of a shared experience. This might have had some kind of epigenetic impact—"dimmed" the genetic coding of her condition—in a way Olivia might not have experienced. Of course, I'm not performing epigenetic tests on everyone I interview. But their examples serve a wider point: While genetic predisposition can set us on a path, it does not mean we are destined to walk it forever.

Developmental biology explores how stressors in childhood can activate genetic predisposition. Cell biologist, lecturer, and author Bruce Lipton pioneered research on cloned human stem cells that laid the groundwork for epigenetics. He grew thousands of stem cells, all of them in a laboratory version of blood called a culture medium. He placed three sets of genetically identical cells in three petri dishes, but each in a different culture medium—a different environment. He discovered that, amazingly, they developed into entirely different cells. The cells in dish one became muscle, those in dish two became bone, and those in the third became fat. The finding was incredibly important: The environment dictated the genetic activity of the cells. And if the environment's chemicals altered how the genes functioned, then identifying the chemicals was the key.

Lipton calls the brain the body's chemist. It dispenses those chemicals into the blood, changing the environment for the body's cells. His goal was to work out how these chemicals are generated and triggered in the brain, and therefore how our biology and our psychology interact. Much of his work focused on the stress experienced by pregnant mothers and the impact it had on their children. He concluded that a mother's emotions—like fear, anger, love, and hope—can biochemically alter the genetic expression of her baby by releasing "signal" molecules into the blood. Certain molecules attach to the DNA of the baby, and though they may not change the genes themselves, they can alter how much they are expressed: Physiological changes have been observed in the development of babies' nervous systems, as well as in their cardiovascular, respiratory, and digestive functions. In short, the life stressors of expectant mothers can be "passed on" to their unborn children and affect their physical health.

This work has inspired a generation of science that seeks to understand inherited stress or trauma. Remember, DNA is not being changed per se; it's about how the genes are made to function. Rachel Yehuda is a professor of psychiatry and neuroscience at the Icahn School of Medicine at Mount Sinai. Her research is focused on finding the source of epigenetic markers and how they can be imposed in utero, on the child's DNA. In short: When and how did that epigenetic marker first become attached to the gene? Most fascinating for me is that Yehuda's work suggests not only how trauma might originate biologically, but how the human body *also* arms us with special defenses that it knows we might need.

In "How Trauma and Resilience Cross Generations," Yehuda discusses one of her early studies, which looked at levels of cortisol—the stress hormone—in certain groups. She focused on combat veterans from Vietnam who demonstrated symptoms of post-traumatic stress disorder (PTSD). Counterintuitively, she found that they had *lower* cortisol levels. This was interesting because in people with mental disorders or depressive symptoms, cortisol levels are usually found to be higher than what is considered typical. The study of PTSD was in its early days at the time; the consensus view was that it followed similar patterns to other mental illnesses. But Yehuda's research showed instead that PTSD disrupts cortisol production rather than only sustaining high levels of it.

Yehuda continued to explore the biology of PTSD, this time with Holocaust victims in the area of Cleveland, where she grew up. Again, she found the same thing: lower cortisol levels than were expected. Yehuda then extended her study to the children of those survivors and found that they were three times more likely to experience PTSD than the children of similar Jewish parents who were *not* Holocaust survivors. And when she tested their cortisol levels, she found the same thing: hormonal abnormalities and lower cortisol production. There was some kind of biological marker that was being inherited.

Yehuda went on to study pregnant women who were at or around the World Trade Center on 9/11 who went on to develop PTSD—and also found that they had delivered children with low levels of cortisol. Trauma seemed to be traveling from mothers to children, in the form of a complete deregulation of stress response systems. All this pointed to an epigenetic change that was occurring in response to the development of PTSD.

When Yehuda looked into the genetic makeup of her 9/11 study participants, she found sixteen genes that expressed differently in those who developed PTSD after 9/11 compared with women who were present but did not. That means in sixteen areas of that strand of DNA, a molecule had attached—just like it did for Bruce Lipton's pregnant mothers—and changed the way that gene expressed itself. When she cross-referenced her findings with her findings on the families of Holocaust survivors, she found these changes evident on the same bit of genetic code. Even though the children had never seen the horrors of the Holocaust, their genetic makeups reflected the impact. This seemed to show that traumatic events can be physically stored such that they survive cell division and reproduction, and reverberate through the generations.

I think it's vital to say here: Nothing my mother experienced before she had me, or that I have experienced, comes close to the subject matter Yehuda and others have been studying. But it's by assessing the most extreme cases that scientists can start to find patterns that may help a broader group of people. Yehuda also places a great deal of emphasis on personal experience; none of her Holocaust subjects with PTSD had recurring nightmares or flashbacks of what had happened to *others*, or particular reactions to the full scale of the horror. Their recollections were entirely personal. All our experiences are relative, Yehuda determined, and understanding that offers us insight into why depression or other mental health conditions can affect each of us in different ways.

So, you can carry a genetic predisposition to depression, as Professor Lewis has shown, and the effects of the environment your parents experienced can *also* be passed down, like Dr. Yehuda demonstrates. Combine this with the environment *you* experience—the suicide of one parent and difficulties with the other, for example—and the possibilities for mental health issues seem to grow. You might think all this is terribly sad, that these inherited traumas and childhood problems lock us in some kind of genetic prison from which there is no escape. I prefer to think about it in a different way: The knowledge that my body may react differently because of my biology allows me to see that it is not my "fault."

Our admirable efforts to build a more tolerant and accepting society have perhaps blurred the lines between mental health and mental illness. Instagram posts now tell us everything from mindfulness to kombucha can suddenly make us better. To me, this feels like de-sciencing serious debate about mental illness. I've also seen a lot of discussion online condemning those who suggest biological markers exist, for fear of entrenching stigma. I totally disagree. Meditate and eat clean if you like, but get to grips with your own biology—our shared biology—and perhaps you'll find a clarity you didn't know you had, which might even enable you to protect yourself from whatever family patterns of mental illness you might observe. To use that jam jar analogy again, it may not be possible to turn the jar over and knock those rocks out. The genes I have, I'm stuck with. But understanding epigenetics makes me feel like I have the power to make them take up less space. Maybe I can shrink those rocks after all.

It is worth repeating that the studies I've explored here are controversial, and you'll find entire bodies of literature that seek to undermine their findings. One skeptic, Margaret Lock at McGill University, says epigeneticists are too reductionist, seeking to quantify trauma or the environment as measurable quantities, or what she calls "the molecularization of the environment." Epigenetic tags and the changes they elicit are more easily traceable for purely physical conditions like cardiovascular disease or cancer, but many point to the vagaries of mental health or trauma inheritance as cause for doubt. Others say that because their science is so new, the work of researchers like Rachel Yehuda cannot be used as definitive evidence for patterns that exist in all of us. There are also those like John Read who say science is as vulnerable to trends as any other industry, and that since the discovery of the genome, there has been an obsession with finding genetic reasons for all of our illnesses. Geneticists look for answers in our genes, he says, because the pharmaceutical establishment needs new drugs to market and sell, or because funding for their work depends on it. Still others point to distinct socioeconomic trends and cultural realities that genetic explanations do not take into consideration. For example, according to the journal *Science,* "Within a given location, those with the lowest incomes are typically 1.5 to 3 times more likely than the rich to experience depression or anxiety."

I'm sure this book will have its critics. But as with most things, there is room for more than one explanation to be valid at the same time. Genetic explanations don't claim absolute truth, but readily accept that there is much we do not know. And all science has to start somewhere. Yehuda's work suggests there does seem to be an intergenerational component to trauma, and that genetics seem to play a role. It strikes me as worthwhile to know that if we improve the environments of our children, they can inherit epigenetic markers that may mean a *better* quality of life. Put simply, knowing my history, and doing what I can to make myself the "best" possible version of me, makes me hopeful that my own children are destined for healthy, fulfilling lives. That I can somehow attach dimmer switches to my genetic transmissions.

Many people with serious mental illness in their family have wondered about these questions. I asked Eleanor if knowing about a genetic link would benefit her or make her feel stigmatized. "I'd like to know," she said. "Because I can see it so clearly in my family. I have like eight relatives with this diagnosis, and not just this. There's depression, anxiety, and OCD. It would be a breakthrough. With things like cancers and heart disease, there's a lot more known about the genetic link. But with something like this, it's so much harder—but still good to know." A better understanding of bipolar disorder and depression, for example, would have perhaps helped Eleanor avoid a manic episode brought on by her antidepressants. This isn't just theory—it's these real-world situations that genetic research is trying to help solve.

Kim, who we met in the last chapter, spoke to me about her mother's schizophrenia. I asked if she found knowing about the genetics of mental illness useful. "Is any of this useful? Does it make you sad to know there's something in your DNA which is forcing this on you?"

"For me it's good," she said. "You have to work with it. It's like having no leg, you've got to work around it. It's a reality you have to deal with."

If I sit in the sun with no cream for even just ten minutes, I turn a rather vicious shade of pink. If my husband, Alex, does the same, he'll get a nice tan. It's a biological reaction to the sun that neither of us did anything to earn nor can do anything to change. But the knowledge that this is bound to happen will at least ensure I sit under a parasol to avoid getting burnt. Knowing how our bodies work and respond to their environments does not diminish who we are. It makes us stronger.

James and Gabrielle at his first communion, London, 1995.

James and Alex at their wedding in Paros, Greece, 2023. (top)

Painting by John of the flat he shared with Lizzie, early 1970s. (middle left)

Painting of John when he was twenty-one by his mother, Nancy. (middle right)

James and Lizzie in Hackney, East London, 2021. (bottom)

CHAPTER 9

VOICES FROM THE PAST

What had Deidameia thought would happen, I wondered, when she had her women dance for me? Had she really thought I would not know him? I could recognize him by touch alone, by smell, I would know him blind, by the way his breaths came and his feet struck the earth. I would know him in death, at the end of the world.

—MADELINE MILLER, *THE SONG OF ACHILLES*

During the coronavirus pandemic, while most of the world was on lockdown, I was one of the few still able to travel. From the earliest days of a mystery illness striking those small villages in Italy, to sweeping emergency lockdowns across Europe, to the sudden and widespread deaths in the Indigenous communities of the Amazon rainforest, I spent two years on the road, witnessing this worldwide experience.

Meanwhile, in a locked-down London, my father's first proper girlfriend found that the stillness afforded her the chance to reminisce about my dad.

Lizzie had messaged me years earlier. She'd heard a radio report of mine when I was at the BBC in Beirut, recognized the name Longman, and, after a quick Google search, realized who I was. She'd emailed me not long before I left the BBC. I remember being overjoyed at receiving her message, but I didn't have the chance to reply before I left the company, at which point my email was disconnected! She became a voice from my father's past who I longed to hear from again but had no idea how to track down.

But then, while traveling through Frankfurt on my way back from reporting on how well Greece had managed the first wave of the pandemic, I received another email.

Lizzie's memories of my dad opened up a whole new world of understanding for me. With my grandmother gone, I have almost no one to talk to about his early days. I remember him only as my forty-something-year-old father who was sometimes well but sometimes sick. I remember his silver hair and his smoke-smelling shirts. But I never knew anything about his younger days. I never knew anything about my dad at the age I am now. No one had really told me anything about his student life, or his life before my mum and me.

With one email, Lizzie shone a light on a huge, shaded part of his world.

In her letter, she describes their revolutionary art school days, his family life, and the early days of his illness—all details I knew nothing about. And in one incredibly important way, she provided another lens through which to understand his illness: the possible influence of the intense meditation that was part of his life with the Transcendental Meditation movement, and how in trying to access his subconscious, he might have unleashed his genetic predisposition to schizophrenia.

For a time, I wondered how best to include what she wrote in this book. Then I thought, *Why not just include most of her message?* It paints a far better picture of my father than I ever could. And you'll see in her writing that Lizzie shares the same self-effacing humility of my father. I can see why they were close.

Hello James,

I was thinking about John this morning and thought maybe you would like to know a bit about the years I was close to him.

We met at Camberwell in 1968, we were both doing fine art. He had come from Guildford Art School after dropping out from law and I was from Shropshire, my dad was a country vet and I had just moved down to London. You can imagine art school in the '60s. We were both from fairly traditional, conservative backgrounds but by then I was doing my best to be as nonconformist as I could, and John had begun to grow his hair, but he still wore a tweed jacket.

We arrived just after the 1968 sit-ins and general solidarity with students from the Sorbonne and French workers, and were a bunch of completely inexperienced privileged kids on grants, or in our case parental support, who were playing the game of revolution.

I shared a flat with Sarah. John, like a lot of men, was really attracted to Sarah, but she had a long-term boyfriend. So eventually, as second best, he hooked up with me.

Two things happened fairly early on during our time at Camberwell: one was that we threw over the established structure and instead of regular life drawing and painting we erected cubicles. I remember John as being very instrumental in this and lugging around large pieces of chipboard as we partitioned ourselves for some revolutionary reason.

We also dispensed with any formal teaching and were suddenly faced with the yawning chasm of having to make up our own creative agenda. Possibly as a reaction to the terrifying freedom we had imposed on ourselves, John and I both signed up to learn meditation. One of our tutors, Geoffrey, had been in India with the Beatles at the ashram of Maharishi Mehesh Yogi in Rishikesh, and one of our fellow students was also involved with Transcendental Meditation. Her mother had recently died, and I was struck by her composure. So off we both went to become initiated.

This became a big part of our lives and as I look back, I feel I now understand and am in a better position to explain the underlying reasons and problems that underpinned this decision. I'll come on to that later. For now, we spent most weekends going to Brighton in John's famous Mini, he was one of the few people who owned a car. There Geoffrey would regale us with stories of the Beatles, the Beach Boys, Donovan, and Maharishi the great Guru. He could imitate all the voices and certainly did, we would listen in awe for hours on end. A woman called Millie, in whose flat we spent the days, made us peculiar vegetarian food with jasmine tea.

We became more and more preoccupied with this Eastern world and less engaged in our own reality. Had I been more perceptive and less naïve I might have seen the signs earlier that would later manifest as his illness. John would often work all night and be consumed with excitement about an idea—this is important, his ideas were the driving force of his whole being.

He hated getting up and would languish in bed for most of the day, take very long baths, and we would often arrive at college as everyone else was leaving for the night. We saw a lot of films. You might be wondering why but I adored him so much I just did what he did. We developed a lot of running characters with whom we used to amuse ourselves, he was often a lathe operator, I can't remember who I became.

We had a black-and-white television and Monty Python had just arrived. We also liked the Marx Brothers, I think that came more from me. We saw a lot of bands and Hyde Park had a festival for the first time. We bought our clothes in Kensington Market, white sailor trousers we dyed in the bath, and naturally we became sort of macrobiotic but with cornflakes, toast, and marmalade, John's favorite food.

We lived in a series of horrible rat-infested flats in Southeast London until eventually we acquired a Victorian four-floor empty shell which had been used by rough sleepers and didn't have either a bathroom or kitchen. We set about doing it up ourselves. We amazed the neighbors with displays of enormous strength as we both lugged dustbin-loads of rubble out and up the steps. We looked fey but we worked like dogs. We had nice neighbors who were delighted someone was taking the place on. The wife was a lecturer at the RCA and the husband earned the money, they had small boys we would babysit for.

We went to Austria on a big European meditation course and left another John, recently arrived from the West Indies, to sort out the bathroom and kitchen while we were away. He lived with his wife and six kids in a couple of rooms and was glad of the work and I imagine he came pretty cheap. Unfortunately, when we came back from the mountains, geraniums, and the gathering of two thousand hippies—which was our first encounter with Maharishi—John had ripped out the beautiful cast iron fireplaces, the moulding, and any original features he felt were not modern enough. The totters [junk dealer] had taken them away so that was that, except we had a very basic bathroom and kitchen not exactly fitted but a cooker and sink downstairs and a bath and loo upstairs.

You hung a picture of the front room of this house when you moved into your new house, my daughter's boyfriend follows you on Twitter and showed me. We painted a lot of the floors yellow and I'm horrified to tell you I painted the hall purple with lime green stairs.

We mixed our own paint from the powdered pigment. John had a phase of hanging canvas across whole rooms and most of us had become abstract artists of one sort or another. I did small paintings based on an exhibition of tantric art we had seen and used a lot of gold paint. David Hockney once gave me a prize for one of these drawings.

This was our second year. In the third year we decided to become meditation teachers and started a course at weekends. We visited your grandparents Nancy and Jimmy at Parklands and I insisted on taking our cat whenever we went. Jimmy and the family in general seemed to attract bad luck, he fell off the roof and damaged his back and one weekend there was a terrific crash as the kitchen cupboards fell on him as he was reaching for something. He was quite distant with John, and they had a pretty formal relationship, he often seemed to be annoyed and we tended to tiptoe around him. Nancy adored John and he was very like her in many ways. He also idealized her family, poor Jimmy didn't have anyone, his mother was divorced and was a shadowy figure who may have died by then, I never met her. He [John] loved Scottish Uncle Sandy and [Rosie]. He also hero worshipped his (at that time Rhodesian) cousins who he considered to be real men, another of his particular perceptions as he felt he wasn't in that bracket, being a stockbroker's son from Surrey and an artist rather than doing a proper job.

This remained with him as long as I knew him. He had the same feelings about my family although compared to life in Surrey I thought of mine as bumpkins, although they were also farmers and did real work.

We spent the long summer holidays at my parents' as at that time we lived in a large house by the Wrekin near the River Severn which meandered a short walk away through fields and woods. My parents were generous and liked having us to stay even though we lounged about as if we were on holiday from boarding school. There weren't many of us at Camberwell who had been to boarding school. It was easy to get jobs then and I worked in a children's zoo and for the Evening News *and waitressed, I don't think John had to work as he had the famous trust fund.*

He was embarrassed about his wealth and completely disinterested in owning anything, he couldn't give away stuff fast enough. Our house in Nunhead was owned by some very dodgy characters in Walthamstow which unlike now was properly old-time east end then, full of villains. John had to meet them to negotiate and because of the state it was in we were or rather he was offered the house for £2000 or we could lease it with a year's free rent by some terrifying men, one with his hand wrapped in a bandage.

Needless to say, John chose to rent, he wasn't going to become a property owner while as usual he was madly trying to dispense with his belongings. It would be worth a lot today. Nancy gave us beautiful furniture so on our bare floors, some yellow, we had a few antiques, a weed-infested long garden in which we put canvas to sit on and the most basic of appliances.

Two of our fellow students moved in, another John lived in the basement and made lutes, and maybe a Paul upstairs. John and I had the ground and first floors. The rooms were large and spacious and mostly empty. Eventually I let two young girls live in our spare room. They were Rod Stewart's groupies, it was fairly sordid what they got up to, but we didn't see much of them.

We read a lot of Black literature purchased from Railton Road and generally felt angry about racial injustice and capitalism. We were a mixture of earnest and wildly unrealistic, unable to take anything seriously for very long. One of John's favorite images was to compare the tip of a screwdriver to the universe, he liked the big picture better than the detail.

So finally, Camberwell came to an end and I planned to go to an art teacher's training college, Bretton Hall in Yorkshire and John decided he was going to finish becoming a meditation teacher and would go to Majorca where Maharishi was running a course. I got a place at Bretton but decided I would, as usual, follow John. So a few weeks later I set off, my first flight abroad on my own.

I got mixed up with the 24-hour clock and missed it. Fortunately, in those days I just got put on the next one and arrived in Majorca in the dead of night. During the taxi ride I suffered acute indecision and kept changing my mind about going, not going, going, until the taxi driver stopped the taxi and asked if I had a boyfriend there? Eventually we decided I may as well go on, so I did. I signed up to become a member of the kitchen staff as I had no money so would earn my course that way. People thought we were brother and sister, perhaps we were. We finished each other's sentences.

This is getting too long now, there's so much to tell you, we drifted apart in Majorca, but we remained friends as close as ever. The craziness of that time is another whole story and how he came back and taught meditation in Leeds in a maroon suit. Then Maharishi asked 108 people with private means to work with or rather for him in Switzerland and he [John] horrified Jimmy and Nancy by deciding to go and taking his famous trust fund with him.

By then I had returned from India with my own complicated family life, a small baby, and a young Indian husband. John came to Shropshire and told me he had imagined we were Adam and Eve as he began to hallucinate in Switzerland and I still felt the old strong connection which was really confusing.

We always had the connection and he stayed with me not long before he died. There were occasions when Nancy and Tony asked me if I could persuade him to go to hospital when he was acutely ill and I was often the only one who could persuade him, but when he was there he had terrifying experiences. Once he felt he was being skinned alive and I realized that it was real for him and he was experiencing hell, it wasn't anywhere else. He used to converse with my thoughts as if I had spoken out loud. He came to hospital to visit me on the day I had an abortion and when I came round from the anesthetic, discovered that Anna (Boo) my five-year-old daughter had been rushed to hospital having had an epileptic seizure at school. That night I was in the abyss and John came. He was probably my closest friend and I think of him most days.

The way we meditated led to an addiction to the experience, the dopamine which was really no different from a drug but possibly more dangerous. To get out of that addiction is very difficult and it needs someone with no agenda to help you do that.

I hope you don't find this too disturbing, there is so much more I can tell you about John and the years I knew him before you were born and the difficult times later when we were still able to share our thoughts with each other.

He was a beautiful, detached, confused, generous soul who was too sensitive for the world and became lost and couldn't find the way back. I hope he is safe now.

Anyway, just put me down as a dotty old woman who is spending a lot of time alone and reliving the past. I have pictures by both John and Nancy in London in my abandoned flat which I could photograph when I return, or you would be welcome to come and see for yourself one day.

I hope wherever you are that you are safe and I very much admired your film about inherited mental illness. You are so very like your dad.

Love Lizzie

I can't read this letter without crying. Those final words, *You are so very like your dad*, make me so happy, because all I see in Lizzie's words is his big heart. The picture she paints of their lives at art school is exactly what I'd imagined but had no way of knowing was true. For the first time, I'm seeing my father as the man he was underneath his illness. The politically astute, occasionally rebellious, but ultimately relatively conforming young man who was being given opportunities to break boundaries for the first time in his life. When I think of my father and his illness now, it can be quite bleak. These pages have injected something very simple into the image I have of him: fun. And I can't help but contrast it with my own experience of university, when I found myself experiencing my first bout of sadness. John Longman was, however, something of a carefree hippie, making friendships that would last a lifetime. I feel so happy that he knew Lizzie and Sarah and this ragtag bunch of freethinkers.

The letter has given him a hinterland in my mind, a place where I can root him, rather than keep him as this drifting specter who I knew only as a charming but ultimately lonely man. The Beach Boys, the Marx Brothers, Monty Python, and the Beatles, all the competing and complementary richness of the 1960s infuse my father with color and life. And although I knew none of the detail of what Lizzie wrote, somehow it all makes complete sense to me. She has almost summoned my father back to life. Her letter convinced me I have to meet her.

So, when lockdown finished, I went to see Lizzie. I sat in the Uber with my heart racing the whole journey. Meeting people who knew my father and were close to him is as close as I can get to him. It's as though I'm traveling back through time to unlock new knowledge of him.

I knocked at the door of Lizzie's east London house, and a lady with a pile of white-gray hair and a huge smile opened the door. With bright pink floral trousers and an equally loud canvas bag, she was the artistic bohemian I had imagined, and in whom I could see much of my father. We hugged immediately. The connection my father gave us meant we weren't strangers, and I could tell it had already affected her, seeing my dad in me on her doorstep. She invited me in with a smile, apologizing for the mess. There were boxes everywhere, half filled with the life she was packing up. "I'm moving to Wales," she said, turning to head upstairs. "So I've got to get all this stuff sorted." My heart dropped a little as I realized this one connection to my father was moving away. Sensing my disappointment, perhaps, Lizzie added, "But I've got some of your dad's paintings to show you." She was smiling at me from the top of the stairs.

I could tell showing me my father's paintings made Lizzie feel closer to him, just like it did for me. She told me that the painting I described here earlier, of a chair sitting in the soft light of large windows, in fact depicts the apartment they shared when they were in art school. I had not known this before she wrote to me, and I was overwhelmed at seeing so much more of his work. One of the paintings was the view from our apartment in Notting Hill down to the street below. Technically, it isn't very good—the proportions are a bit off, and I don't quite know what to make of the thick gray paint of the pub on the corner. But everything she has to offer is a masterpiece to me. The best of them is a painting he did when they were students staying with her parents. It's a waterscape of the River Severn in oil. Greens and blues fill the small canvas with a dreamlike quality. It continues to amaze me that he would only have been about twenty or twenty-one when he painted these. The river painting is now on my kitchen wall, next to a portrait of him that my grandmother painted.

Lizzie's house was near Hackney Marshes, a huge green space in the east of the city. We walked around it for hours. It was a sunny September day, and we followed the canal through the park and watched other groups of Londoners making the most of the last of summer. "You are very like him," she said to me. "Your nose. And your eyes. You have the same look about you." Lizzie may have been a hippie, but she's quite matter-of-fact in her delivery. She doesn't dwell on emotion or sentiment. It seemed to me that she was relaying her observations as pieces of fact, rather than whimsical musings. This made it that much more powerful to hear.

"We were just all searching for something," she said. "Art school was all about exploring and working out who we were. I think I guessed he was searching a little harder than everyone else. But I never saw anything like a mental illness. That just wasn't something we'd even recognize then. Honestly, I just wanted to be with him all the time. He was magnetic."

We stopped at a café by a lock and found a small table in the sunshine. Life spun all around us: Families gathering around cups of tea in paper cups; children nagging parents for bits of cake; dogs winding their way through tables to find other people's crumbs. But I felt suspended in this other world that Lizzie had created for me. I felt as though she'd rendered us invisible, as though she were a wizard from an age ago and I her present-day student who she'd come to instruct. I felt close to him in a way I had never experienced before, sharing the same summer air as the person who so loved my father in his most formative days. It felt almost as though he might come bounding out of the café door at any moment, three cups of coffee gripped precariously in one hand, roll-up cigarette sticking out of the corner of his mouth as he squinted through its faint smoke. And we three could sit there, shimmering in this parallel universe, unnoticed and indifferent to the mortals around us. I must have been an alien to her, from a time well beyond the one she'd shared with him. And yet I could feel her look at me and remember him.

James and John Longman, London, 1996.

CHAPTER 10

INFLAMMATION TECHNOLOGY AND HEALING THE BRAIN: IS IT POSSIBLE?

Our capacity to destroy one another is matched by our capacity to heal one another.

—BESSEL VAN DER KOLK, *THE BODY KEEPS THE SCORE*

Our genetic coding is one thing; how these markers translate in real life is another. So let's dive inside the brain. It is, as Bruce Lipton told us, the body's chemist. Neuroscience has made huge leaps forward over the last few years, discovering what chemicals the brain dispenses into the bloodstream and our central nervous system, and how those chemicals are generated. While geneticists and behavioral psychologists may be divided on the causes of mental illness, they agree that the brain is where the effects are felt.

As I noted earlier, mental illness is broadly a symptom-led diagnosis. You tell the doctor how you feel, and you are diagnosed. But you don't do that with something like cancer. You don't say *I feel a bit short of breath* and suddenly get told you have lung disease. Doctors look inside you for proof.

We are a long way away from that being possible for our mental health. But researchers hope it will one day become a reality. And how exciting is that? For me, moving away from the idea that depression is purely a thought illness, and understanding it as a biological one, is very helpful. In a practical sense, better brain science means better and more tailored medication. Skeptics argue that "biologizing" mental illness feeds a kind of societal hypochondria through which we rely too much on medication. They say Western countries are already too heavily dependent on the drugs manufactured by major pharmaceutical companies who seek to profit off our illnesses. While I'm all for holistic treatments, I can tell you something very clearly: Antidepressants work. However, "biologizing" my mental health isn't just about medication. It's about discovering what processes are transpiring inside me, and then figuring out how I can undo or work with them. I find that discovery empowering.

Donna Jackson Nakazawa explains the material ways our brains can change in her book *Childhood Disrupted.* Worryingly for me, perhaps, she writes, "Cutting-edge research tells us that what doesn't kill you doesn't necessarily make you stronger. Far more often, the opposite is true: the early chronic unpredictable stressors, losses, and adversities we face as children shape our biology in ways that predetermine our adult health."

Oh dear. Her work is based on that groundbreaking public health research study I mentioned earlier: the Adverse Childhood Experiences study. The study measured ten types of adversity and revealed the mechanical bodily changes that occur in adulthood as a result of these psychological stresses in childhood. At least two of the adversity types apply to me: the suicide of a parent, and the abuse of alcohol by a parent.

"We all know that when we are stressed," writes Nakazawa, "chemicals and hormones can flush our body and increase levels of inflammation. That's why stressful events in life are correlated with the likelihood of getting a cold or having a heart attack." Inflammation is a key part of our immune system. It occurs when cells, proteins, and tissues are recruited by the body to fight bacteria, viruses, or other foreign bodies. The chemicals generated in this process are called cytokines, and they provoke the inflammatory response.

When everything is working as it should, these chemicals leave our body afterward. But when a child experiences a trauma or repeated stress, and these chemicals are repeatedly shot into their system, epigenetic changes start to take place. Chemical markers attach themselves to specific genes that regulate the activity of stress hormone receptors in the brain. They "mute" these genes, leaving the child less able to endure any kind of stress—however small—for the rest of their lives. This is the same epigenetic process underlying the changes observed by Rachel Yehuda in her Holocaust study. A chronic inability to turn off the stress response leads to higher levels of inflammation and a compromised immune system.

The link between the immune system and mental illness is only now becoming clear. In *The Inflamed Mind*, Dr. Edward Bullmore goes into great detail about the relationship between our psychological health and our immune system. It's an area of science called neuroimmunology, in which a physical inflammation of the brain has been seen to take place in those who are depressed. The cells and antibodies that circulate in the bloodstream to create our immune system are also able to access the brain. These are hormones that create powerful inflammatory effects. And it can be a vicious cycle. An elevated inflammatory response leads to an increased sensitivity to stress, which in turn generates more of those stress hormones, which in turn inflame the brain. And thus, the cycle continues.

Where once inflammation was considered a positive immune response, chronic inflammation is increasingly associated with serious disease. Neuroinflammation in particular is becoming increasingly associated with cognitive decline, especially in Alzheimer's disease. In his own work, Bullmore builds on these connections, citing multiple examples that demonstrate the link between inflammation and depression. A 2014 study of 15,000 schoolchildren in England, for instance, found that children who were not depressed but slightly inflamed at the age of nine were significantly more likely to be depressed ten years later. Another, which tested over 73,000 people in Copenhagen, found increased levels of inflammation generating stress hormones in the blood of those who identified as depressed. Bullmore says the probability that this could have occurred by chance is less than one in a trillion.

Inflammation doesn't just cause hormones to attack the brain. "When nerve cells are inflamed," says Bullmore, "the connections or synapses between them are less capable of learning patterns of information, and that inflammation reduces the supply of serotonin as a transmitter between nerve cells."

The historical study of schizophrenia is particularly fascinating in light of this. Emil Kraepelin was a nineteenth-century pioneer of the scientific understanding of the condition. Contemporary Victorian understandings of "mania" and "melancholy" had all placed the illness in the mind, as purely psychological damage of some kind. But Kraepelin called schizophrenia an "auto-intoxication," or self-poisoning, of the brain *by* the body. His theory came well before modern understandings of the immune system but sounds awfully close to what we understand now as a malfunctioning immune response: an immune system that is not properly regulated, oversupplying stress hormones and causing chronic illness.

Incredibly, decades later, Dr. Cathryn Lewis and others working to identify specific genes for schizophrenia have found that the most important genetic variants are located in the part of the human genome known to be important to the immune system and autoimmunity. Now, I know Dr. Lewis herself will be the first to say this is very early science and warn against extrapolation. But it *is* extraordinary to think that a predisposition to schizophrenia—a condition so completely associated with the mind—may have its genetic code intermingled with the code for our immune system and our overall physical health. It forces us to rethink how our biology and our psychology intertwine.

Let's (briefly, I promise) zoom in on the genes. Each of us has twenty-three pairs of chromosomes in each cell of our body. They carry our DNA and transform it into proteins, which in turn carry out the instructions—"make eyes blue," for example. Our chromosomes are numbered. According to a 2017 study, the part of the human genome with the strongest association to schizophrenia—which, notably, also codes for our immune system—is Chromosome 6.

This chromosome codes for a group of nearly sixty proteins in the blood or on the surface of cells. They include nine major protein groups, labeled C1 to C9, and their jobs are to identify foreign pathogens (broadly speaking, these are organisms that produce disease) in the bloodstream and tag them for destruction. Recent groundbreaking research has found that schizophrenia patients have unusually high levels of C4. This group of proteins is specifically involved in "synaptic pruning"—essentially, the body's process of clearing out excess synapses, or connections that the brain no longer needs. But in schizophrenia patients, C4 proteins work too well, leading to over-pruning and possibly to the wrong brain synapses being killed, just like an autoimmune reaction. And this whole process usually takes place when a person is in their late teens or early twenties—the same age range when schizophrenia symptoms usually begin. These are the earliest pieces of research suggesting we might eventually think about schizophrenia in the same way we think about autoimmune conditions like lupus or multiple sclerosis.

We began this book with the idea of a split genetic and environmental predisposition to mental illness. We examined which genes were at play and investigated the role of the environment. We then saw that rather than two separate processes that "add up" to a mental illness, genes and the environment should be understood in combination: Environmental factors trigger epigenetic changes that not only affect us, but might be passed on to our children. Now, we've seen how the immune system seems to play a central role in that epigenetic process. The immune system—and the inflammation it triggers—appears to be a potential link between our genetic predispositions and the environmental factors we encounter in our lives.

One area of study takes the word *environment* literally, finding a link between air pollution and schizophrenia. A 2011 study found that many of the genes altered in schizophrenia overlap with those affected by exposure to toxic fumes in the atmosphere. Specifically, air pollution has been found to alter the immune cells of the central nervous system—called microglia—which play an important role in brain development and injury repair. Air pollution also seems to alter cell communication, essentially by interrupting the electric circuits by which cells communicate. As it turns out, these are the very same processes that seem to not function properly in those with schizophrenia.

Gut health is another major area of study right now that demonstrates possible links to schizophrenia. Tim Spector is a professor of genetics and world leader on the microbiome—the collection of all the microbes, like bacteria, fungi, and viruses, that naturally live on and in our bodies. He says we should take the microbiome as seriously, and treat it with as much care, as we would an organ in the body. Crucially, while genetics plays a part in the health of our microbiome, it's an area we have the power to actively change for the better. Even in identical twins, he says, only about 34 percent of the microbiome is the same. Eating the kinds of food that generate "good" bacteria is the key to a healthy microbiome.

This is relevant to us here because the microbiome has been found to influence the development and maintenance of the immune and nervous systems. It's even been called the gut-brain axis. One 1997 study found a link between irritable bowel syndrome (IBS)—an inflammatory response—and schizophrenia. It found 19 percent of those studied who had schizophrenia also had IBS, compared to just 2.5 percent in the general population. The microglia—those immunity cells—are overproduced, leading to gut inflammation and brain inflammation. This shows a correlation between poor gut health and poor mental health, and perhaps how our immune systems link the two.

In fact, 90 percent of serotonin, which we tend to associate with brain chemicals, is actually made in the gut. Changes to the gut microbiome driven by inflammation can also alter the production of serotonin, which we know is disrupted in mental illness. A microbiome that is not well looked after can also begin to affect the blood-brain barrier, which is the network of blood vessels and tissue in our central nervous system that prevents harmful substances from reaching the brain. Crucially, microbiome health in expectant mothers has a major impact on the unborn child and how their own gut-brain axis is primed for later life.

From the earliest moments of our childhoods, right through to the present day, our bodies are responding and recording our actions—and what we had for lunch. Understanding how, as Nakazawa puts it, "your biography becomes your biology" is in my view vital to overcoming serious mental illness. Much of the research focus has been on schizophrenia, as there are clearer genetic patterns for scientists to work with. But, as we've seen, all three major mental illnesses discussed in this book do share genetic variants. And Tim Spector, for example, says gut health can be restored with better foods in just three days—even after a lifetime of bad habits. And other scientists agree: "We can reverse the effects of early toxic stress on our biology," says Nakazawa. The implications for clinical diagnosis and better help for patients—and for better mental health for all of us—are huge: A focus on the immune system, rather than inflammation-*inducing* medication, could revolutionize our mental health solutions.

Rodents have been used in the testing of early life stress for decades, often through the use of what researchers call "maternal separation": Groups of newborn mice are separated from their mothers for an average of three hours a day over a two-week period in order to mimic early life neglect or abuse in humans. Some studies also manufacture neglect through the reduction or disruption of their nesting capabilities. The rodents then grow up to display depressive or anxious behaviors. They do not move for large parts of the day; they separate themselves from others; they choose not to mate. Some of these rodents then have their environments "enriched," their cages adapted to enable increased social interaction and physical activity. It is these rodents in whom depressive behaviors fade, while those whose environments are not changed continue to show depressive symptoms.

Rodent tests are not perfect. All kinds of variables—from the strain of rats or mice used to the need to differentiate different types of neglect more specifically—can influence outcomes. But many of these tests indicate how malleable the brain can be, and how what happens to us in childhood can be overcome in adulthood. Edward Bullmore says, "We can move on from the old polarized view of depression as all in the mind, or all in the brain, to see it rooted also in the body; to see depression instead as a response of the whole organism or human self to the challenges of survival in a hostile world."

So how do we reverse these trends, if that's what they are? How do we de-flame our brains, detoxify our genes? If mice can do it, can we?

We have touched on serotonin a number of times in this book. After identifying its importance in stabilizing mood, scientists later found that it's not just the amount of serotonin that makes a difference to mood, but how it affects the neurons in the brain. And that effect will differ in different people, which is why many do not find SSRIs helpful in lifting their mood. What causes this difference? The answer, as you will have guessed, is in our genes and in our environments. The rebalancing of a chemical in the brain is a treatment—of sorts—but not a prevention. Prevention is inside us.

If you're interested in genetics, you will likely have heard of David Sinclair. He is a professor of genetics at Harvard Medical School and a pioneer on the study of aging. In 2014, *Time* named him one of the one hundred most influential people in the world. Since then, he's had a number of breakthroughs in what he calls his mission to "increase lifespan." Sinclair argues that illnesses and diseases that affect humans—everything from diabetes to Alzheimer's to heart disease—are all linked by one common feature: age. It is as we get older, he says, that these illnesses become more likely. By that logic, if the signs of aging can be reversed, then the chances of illness can be lowered.

Finding the secret to eternal life sounds like the plot for a movie. But Sinclair has shown that biological age *can* actually be reversed—it's just a matter of reversing processes on a cellular level. To illustrate the workings of a cell, Sinclair uses the analogy of a cassette tape. DNA is packed tightly into the cell and is only unwrapped slowly so that different parts of the code can be read or activated over time. But as we get older, that process becomes more unwieldy, like the tape on a cassette coming loose. Certain genes are eventually misread, causing those cells to lose their identity: Skin and hair start to thin; bones become weaker and less able to carry muscle.

These are, of course, the usual signs of aging. But the aging process can also mean that certain genes in our genetic code that may otherwise stay bound up and unread get unspooled and activated. Basically, our epigenetic process gets confused, and our body starts to read all the genetic predispositions to disease. According to Sinclair, there are ways to bind that DNA back up more tightly—a bit like taking a pencil and jamming it into the cassette to wind the tape back into place. Rather than treating each disease separately, finding ways to rebalance the chemicals in our genetic makeup and reverse the signs of aging might improve our chances of staying disease-free. Sinclair has proposed many strategies to accomplish this, ranging from diet to supplements to certain types of exercise.

Sinclair is a proponent of intermittent fasting—he says an optimal fast is sixteen hours—and of high-intensity interval training. Now, I'm sharing this with you in the knowledge that there are all kinds of self-help, dieting, healthy living, and exercise books out there. This is not intended to be one of them. But Sinclair's strategies have really spoken to me, and I've found interval training in particular seems to keep my mood up. However, this is not about training and feeling better in just a few days or weeks, and I'm certainly not suggesting you will stay clear of genetic predispositions to disease by doing the odd CrossFit class. It *is* about knowing enough to implement a long-term strategy of habits, built up over many years, that might help activate biological mechanisms that keep you healthy.

That knowledge is power, and therefore has a restorative quality to it, is a central premise of Rachel Yehuda's work. But she goes a step further: She says if our genes can learn sadness, then so too can they learn happiness. She has found that epigenetic changes occur not just in trauma but in psychotherapy, and that healing can essentially be inherited as well. In jam jar terms, it is not just about reducing the amount of water you take on but shrinking those stones at the bottom of the jar. They may still be there, but perhaps they'll take up less space.

And for healing to happen, surely the brain is a good place to start?

I first came across the work of Dr. Roland Zahn at King's College London in 2016, when I made the short documentary on my father and inherited mental illnesses for the BBC. Like a lot of research in the fields of neuroscience and psychotherapy, his studies have found root in Freud, who said guilt was an integral part of feeling depressed. But the connection precedes even Freud. The Greeks made Oizys the goddess of depression and grief. She was the daughter of Nyx, the night. And tellingly, it was her twin brother, Momus, who was the god of mockery and, by extension, blame.

I think a lot of people who have felt down can attest to feelings of self-blame or guilt at some stage. Some with truly chronic illnesses may not have the energy to feel any connection to the outside world. But in many, guilt is pervasive. It certainly has been for me. "If you look at how people respond to a death," says Zahn, "self-blame seems to play a distinctive role when you compare people who develop depression with those who just go through the normal stages of grieving."

Zahn's work focuses on the parts of the brain that generate these feelings of guilt and agency perception: the section toward the front of the brain (the anterior subgenual cingulate cortex), and the section underneath the right temple (the anterior superior temporal cortex). He found that in people with depression, synapses in these parts of the brain are weak, often misfire, or don't connect properly. His aim, in response, has been to increase the connectivity between these two areas, and thus reestablish a "normal" correlation between agency and guilt.

"In the brain is where biology and psychology meet, because the brain changes in response to your learning experience," he says. "And that's why the changes we've found in people with depression, I think they're reversible because the connectivity in the brain is a learning signal. So, it should be possible to relearn that." But how? Well, the answer may sound more holistic than scientific. But in reality, it is a mixture of both.

Back in 2016, I went under Zahn's brain scanner, an fMRI machine that maps the brain and monitors the connectivity between the anterior subgenual cingulate cortex and the anterior superior temporal cortex. As I lay under it, I was asked to think of scenarios that made me feel guilty. It sounds artificial—and it is—but the brain can't lie. Sure enough, my brain sensed guilt when I told it to. I lay there and thought about not visiting my grandmother Nancy enough before she died, not doing enough to help my mother, not being a good enough friend. And the doctors monitoring in the other room could see that my brain had an overactive guilt reflex—usual in people with depression.

On a screen inside the machine was a bar graph. I was tasked with decreasing the level on the graph by visualizing my guilt being reduced. The researchers had developed hundreds of different mantras for test patients to repeat for whatever guilt scenario they had imagined: "Your actions wouldn't have made a difference." "Lots of other people feel this way." But it was one phrase, repeated over and over in the minds of patients, that worked the best: "I forgive myself."

The researchers explained to me that this is because there is no answer to this mantra. If you say to yourself, for example, "Lots of people don't visit their grandparents in hospital," you may feel less guilty. But there's always a response: that your relationship was extra special, or that they were sicker than others and therefore needed your visits more. The guilty mind finds a way to rationalize its own guilt.

But with self-forgiveness, there is no response, no inner voice saying "yes, but..." Dr. Zahn's work proves this on a biological level. Over 70 percent of respondents in his trial demonstrated improved connectivity in their brain and a recalibrated management of guilt, just by repeating the phrase "I forgive myself."

It was a very strange sensation to lie there saying that phrase. I felt stupid. I felt it would definitely not work. Honestly, I felt like it wasn't science. I also felt really self-conscious, trying to find meaning in these three words in a lab full of strangers. But then it dawned on me: I had been to many therapists over the years who had all suggested variations of the same mantra. "Be kind to yourself." "Don't give yourself such a hard time." Friends have also offered this advice. I had often received it as a mere placation, something for them to say when most words seemed futile. But here, for the first time, I was being offered empirical proof that my brain was actually responding to these suggestions. I went into the lab next door to see the graphs for myself. I saw one part of my brain telling the other to feel less guilt. Just as Dr. Zahn had said, I could, in fact, teach my brain to relearn healthy patterns.

One of the people I spoke with as part of my research was Dr. Jeffrey Borenstein, president and CEO of the Brain & Behavior Research Foundation (BBRF). The BBRF is the largest private funder of mental health research in the United States; over the last thirty-five years, it has raised over $400 million in funding for pilot brain research. "Often, people are very concerned about their genetic predisposition," Dr. Borenstein tells me. "But it's better to have any of these illnesses today than it was ten or even five years ago." Borenstein, like Sinclair, is interested in prevention rather than cures. "In the field of psychiatry, we haven't really focused on prevention. We do for heart disease—we tell people to eat better and exercise. We do for cancer—we do screenings. But we haven't had the means to do that with mental health. Until now. And it's very exciting.

"When I finished my residency in 1988, at that point in time in my training, we were taught that old brains cannot grow new cells, and 'old' was after the age of two," says Borenstein. "And we now know that's not true. Old brains do grow new cells, and at all ages. We know this for sure. Exercise is a very important part of that. When I'm speaking with patients, I may recommend talk therapy, medicine, and exercise. So the brain is malleable in a positive way, and especially for younger people because the brain is still developing through the mid-twenties."

One area of research the BBRF has funded is Dr. Robert Freedman's work on fetal brain development. Freedman is professor and chairman at the University of Colorado School of Medicine. He says, "Of the twenty thousand genes we humans have, more are devoted to building the brain than anything else. And more of them are active—about tenfold—before birth compared with after." Freedman's lab has been studying what neuroscientists call "inhibition," the process that calms signals between nerve cells. As we saw earlier, when a person experiences a trauma, stress hormones are excreted. In a healthy person, once the trauma or danger subsides, the hormones are no longer produced. But in people with schizophrenia, for example, that ability is compromised, and those signals can become overactive.

Yet we're learning of new ways to address this in those who might be susceptible to schizophrenia—as early as possible. Choline is a nutrient that helps regulate memory, muscle control, cell viability, and other functions. The body produces it naturally, but we need more of it in our diets to avoid a deficiency. Beef and chicken liver, eggs, fish, and some vegetables are rich with it. Expectant mothers have long been told to take choline supplements for the general well-being of their unborn child. Freedman's lab has identified a new, potentially life-changing mental health benefit of taking choline: It is vital for the development of biological inhibition.

"We've gone from learning ways in which the nervous system doesn't work in schizophrenia, to actually doing something to prevent it from happening," says Freedman. Now, expectant mothers are advised to take choline specifically if their families have a history of schizophrenia or other psychotic conditions. For those parents who worry about genetic predispositions, this research not only is hugely encouraging but could prevent schizophrenia in some people. Life changing in the truest sense of the term.

Stem cell research at the BBRF is contributing to our understanding of the brain and has the potential to improve treatments. Scientists are able to take a skin sample, turn it into stem cells, and turn those stem cells into brain cells, which are then grown in a petri dish. Borenstein tells me this process is currently being used to study the brains of people with schizophrenia compared to the brains of those without it. "Down the road," he says, "as a practicing psychiatrist, somebody will be able to come to me. I'll send their skin cells to a lab, and the lab will send me information that helps in diagnosis." He predicts that in the next few years, it may even be possible for doctors to recommend specific antidepressants based on readings of skin cells.

The BBRF has funded a number of treatments for depression that have gone on to be approved by the FDA. "One of the areas that we were early supporters of and is now widely used is transcranial magnetic stimulation," says Borenstein. In transcranial magnetic stimulation, magnets placed on the patient's head induce a very slight, precise electric circuit in the brain, reducing hyperactivity in the parts of the brain associated with depression. "This can treat depression in a few days instead of a few weeks," says Borenstein. "It also has the potential to be useful in obsessive compulsive disorder, and potentially in chemical dependency."

If the brain is the body's chemist, it is also the body's fuse box. The human brain has some 89 billion neurons, all communicating with one another in order to keep us operational. Brain waves send electrical signals, whose strength reflects how well the neurons are communicating, and in what capacity. The most prevalent brain waves are delta, theta, beta, and alpha. They vary in speed—measured in hertz—and each one has an associated use. Different areas of the brain can be evaluated based on which brain wave is more dominant at any point in time.

In August 1995, my father was referred for an EEG, or electroencephalogram, which is a test that measures these brain waves. Small electrodes

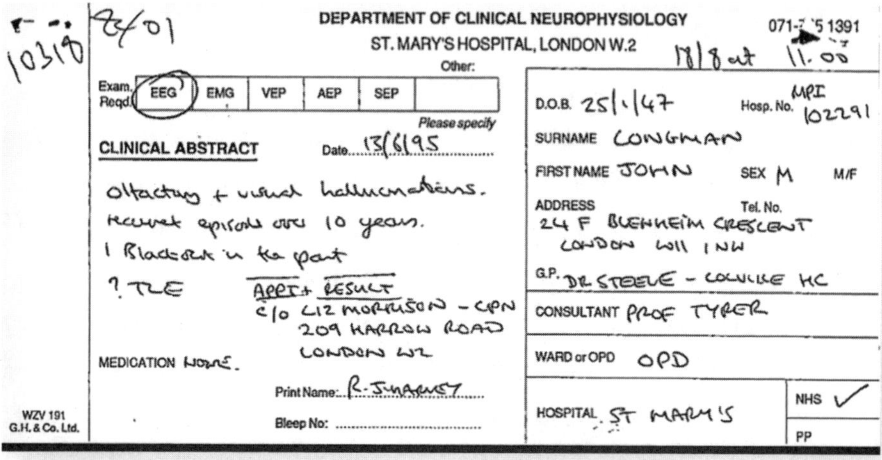

10319 28/01

DEPARTMENT OF CLINICAL NEUROPHYSIOLOGY
ST. MARY'S HOSPITAL, LONDON W.2
071-[illegible] 1391
18/8 at 11.00

Other:

Exam. Reqd. EEG | EMG | VEP | AEP | SEP

Please specify

CLINICAL ABSTRACT Date 13/6/95

Olfactory + visual hallucinations.
Recurrent episodes over 10 years.
1 Blackout in the past
? TLE

APPT + RESULT
c/o LIZ MORRISON – CPN
209 HARROW ROAD
LONDON W2

MEDICATION NONE.

Print Name: [illegible]

Bleep No:

WZV 191
G.H. & Co. Ltd.

D.O.B. 25/1/47 Hosp. No. MPI 102291

SURNAME LONGMAN

FIRST NAME JOHN SEX M M/F

ADDRESS Tel. No.
24 F BLENHEIM CRESCENT
LONDON W11 1NW

G.P. DR STEELE – COLVILLE HC

CONSULTANT PROF TYRER

WARD or OPD OPD

HOSPITAL ST MARY'S NHS ✓ PP

John Longman's medical notes

were placed all over his head. In his pre-appointment letter, he is asked to make sure his hair is clean so that the electrodes can stick properly. The notes explain his hallucinations—the visions he was seeing and the voices he was hearing. They mention at least one blackout. Doctors wanted to rule out other brain conditions such as seizures.

Delta is the slowest brain wave, and it is active when we are in deep sleep. We don't dream in this particular sleep state, but delta is working behind the scenes to restore brain function. If we wake up during deep sleep, we might be confused about where we are. The delta brain waves function to restore the hippocampus, which is needed for memory storage, as well as to promote the release of human growth hormones. If delta is detected when a person is conscious, it may mean serious brain injury or learning problems. Luckily, that was not the case with my father.

Theta is active in the dreamlike sleep state, often called REM sleep. Outside of sleep, theta waves can also be detected when you're daydreaming, meditating, or in deep reflection. It relaxes your body and connects you with your intuition and subconscious mind. Theta was "rarely" detected in my father's brain, likely because he was focused on the test.

Alpha waves are present in a relaxed state associated with focused visualizing or imagining, and the state my father was in for much of the test. Creative individuals tend to have a higher ratio of alpha brain waves, so it does make sense that it's the one his test most picked up on. While alpha promotes relaxation of the mind and boosts creative thinking, an excess of these waves in the frontal lobes of the brain can indicate ADHD or depressive symptoms.

Beta is a focused wavelength—the kind of brain wave that is activated when you give a talk or presentation or try to engage others. Problem solvers—those with logical patterns of thinking and high levels of focus—often have a lot of beta wavelengths pulsing through their brains. Extended periods of concentration, excess levels of stress, or focusing too hard for too long can elevate beta brain waves. (The subsequent rush of blood to the head that beta waves initiate can cause mild headaches.) I can see from his results that my father did not have a beta-orientated brain.

Resetting the electric circuitry of the brain, and helping to regulate the activity of these brain waves, is one method of treating mental illness. This is the focus of Professor Helen Mayberg's work. A professor of neurology and psychiatry at Mount Sinai, Mayberg has mapped depression in the brain and pioneered precision surgical treatments for neuropsychiatric disorders. In a 2015 TED Talk, Mayberg said a better understanding of how brain circuits work and mapping markers for depression is important, but she also said, "There's something about the pain of a major depression that's unlike anything. That, to me, has always been the part that's hardest to explain, hardest to localize. Because in many ways, everything else is a derivative of what happens when you have that negative experience. So the question is, where is that?"

Through her research, Mayberg discovered a part of the brain called

Brodmann area 25, where cells seem to regulate emotion, anxiety, motivation, and even sleep. This is the same part of the brain Dr. Zahn's research and his fMRI scanner has focused on. Like Zahn, she found it hyperactive in patients with depression and believed that administering electric shocks to this part of the brain could calm that hyperactivity down, settling the brain waves into more regular patterns. This is a much more precise version of electroconvulsive therapy (ECT), which remains part of modern-day treatments for severe mental illness.

My father's medical notes reveal he underwent ECT in his twenties. I'll be honest—reading this really upset me. My mind was flooded with images of mad scientists attaching electrodes to his head and slamming down a lever to crank up the voltage. In fact, early treatments *did* use high doses of electricity without anesthesia, and they led to memory loss and even fractured bones. As a result, in our collective imagination, we tend to view ECT as an archaic procedure performed in cold, dark asylums. Things have, happily, changed. Patients are sedated, and only small currents are passed through their brains to trigger brief seizures.

I hope my father's treatment did not cause him pain. He would have been eligible only if his medications were not working properly, and I think he was someone who wanted to try everything to see what worked. If he could rewire his brain, and not be reliant on the drugs that he felt sapped his energy and muted his creativity, then trying ECT might have seemed like an attractive path. He didn't do it again, though. Which tells me perhaps it wasn't a happy experience.

Mayberg's procedure is a kind of bespoke, twenty-first-century electroshock therapy in which patients have holes drilled into their heads and electrodes attached to the part of the brain she identified—Brodmann area 25—to provide stimulation. The drilling holes bit does take my imagination back to that dark asylum, but this is cutting-edge technology. Her

CLINICAL NEUROPHYSIOLOGY
St Mary's Hospital, London W2 1NY
Telephone 0171 725 1391

REPORT FOR: EEG (ROUTINE)

Surname:	LONGMAN	Procedure No:	33768
Forename/s:	JOHN	Appointment:	18-Aug-1995/11.00am
Address:	24F Blenheim Cresc	Hosp/Doctor:	SMH/Prof P Tyrer
	Notting Hill	Hosp No/Origin:	MPI 102291/Outpatient
	LONDON	Req Received:	17-Jul-1995
	W11 1NW	Printed on/by:	07-Sep-1995/JoyS
DOB/Age:	25-Jan-1947 48yrs	MINDEX Ver/DOS:	n6.41/621337/010318

Relaxed and co-operative patient, although he had a persistent cough.

Alpha regular and well sustained rhythm at 8-9 Hz, 30-60 µV is seen posteriorly and attenuates normally on eye opening. This is symmetrical.

Beta small amounts, low voltage and diffuse.

Theta rare.

Hyperventilation - performance was good for 3 minutes. This does not induce any significant change.

Photic stimulation - no definite following responses.

Chief Technician - Z Cockbain

COMMENT:

Within normal limits. No focal/epileptiform features.

Dr Shelagh Smith FRCP
Consultant in Clinical Neurophysiology

John Longman's medical notes

results—still early—show a major change in patients for whom nothing else has worked. Her first patient reported an instant change. Awake and alert during the experiment, the patient, Mayberg says, "suddenly felt calm. What she was describing was a lifting of this void, this negativity that she was feeling for the past five years." The speed of the change was remarkable. As soon as the team turned the circuit off, the patient returned to her depressive state, and did not believe that she had briefly felt calm. The reactions Mayberg and her team observed in these tests, of the electric circuit having an almost immediate effect, showed just how malleable the brain can be. It may be that just like pacemakers for the heart, some brains of the future will be given microchips to keep their electric circuits functioning properly.

Physicians are also changing their approaches to certain drugs as attitudes toward depression and its related conditions evolve. Ketamine's use, for example, is being reevaluated. Though it has historically been used only as a tranquilizer in medical settings, new research is showing the impact it can have on treating depression. Borenstein is excited about the latest developments. "A version of ketamine which can be used as a nasal spray has recently been approved for refractory depression—or depression that doesn't respond to typical treatments. It lifts the signs of depression in two to four hours. Think how much of a difference that is making in people's lives."

What are often considered "party drugs" are having a significant impact on treatment, too. Rachel Yehuda's work has focused on psychedelics like MDMA, which she has found to be useful in managing trauma when it develops into post-traumatic stress disorder. Although now grouped in with the psychedelic revolution, MDMA is an entactogen, or a drug that promotes empathy, introspection, and interpersonal trust. Its early use in therapy was to help people open up and confront painful memories. Yehuda describes it as "medicine that gets you to face things that are usually more difficult to face." Healing from trauma, she explains, involves creating a new narrative about yourself in an effort to see what happened in a different light. For Yehuda, MDMA creates an opportunity for a kind of introspection that maximizes self-compassion and minimizes self-criticism while talking about trauma.

By the time you read this, there will doubtless be even more exciting leaps forward in the experimental treatment of depression, bipolar disorder, schizophrenia, and associated mental illnesses. It gives me hope to know that so much work is being done in this field, and that so much progress is being made. But that hope is diluted somewhat by the sense that in Britain, at least, care in the community for people like my father does not seem to be a priority. You'll recall that my father's doctor, Dr. Salkeld, lamented that if my father were alive today, he might not receive the same level of support from community social workers. It is a well-known fact that in the United States, more people with mental illness are in prison than in appropriate medical care. Science is doing its part to find treatments for these illnesses. Society seems to be doing far less to look after the people who live with them.

James at a junior school ball, 2000.

James and Liz Morrison, John's carer, London, 2023.

CHAPTER 11

GUARDIAN ANGELS

There are dark shadows on the earth, but its lights are stronger in the contrast.

—CHARLES DICKENS, *THE PICKWICK PAPERS*

Finding my father's medical records opened up a whole world of information. They have enriched my understanding of who he was and what his struggles were like. I felt such joy when that wonderful soul at the National Health Service sent them to me. But I could not have imagined their arguably more important consequence: being connected with two people intimately involved in his care.

One of the names repeated in the records is Liz Morrison. It's her notes I included earlier on—she's the care worker who describes receiving the news that my father had died. I felt I had to try to find her, even though the chances of that were slim at best. She could have been anywhere. I thought to start with Social Work England, which is the governing body and quality controller for social workers in England, but they told me they didn't even exist when Liz was working. Had I tried the hospital where my father would have been treated? Well, the health-care system has gone through so much restructuring since my dad was alive, I wasn't even sure what hospital that was. I sent more emails into the ether and waited.

Miraculously, a few weeks later came a response. Someone somewhere had forwarded an email to someone else, and by some mystic process of communication known only to the NHS, Liz was found. I envisioned the scene in *101 Dalmatians* in which every dog across the land—from inner-city mutt to countryside collie—joins forces to howl a message over hundreds of miles to find help. Well, not only had Liz been located, but I was told she was keen to speak to me. And not only *that*—she was my neighbor! My countrywide howl had managed to find a woman who lives a mile or so away from me, in west London. It turns out Liz is still working as a mental health support worker not far from where she would see my dad, and after exchanging a few text messages (*I can't wait to meet you!* ♥) we arrange for her to come over.

When Liz knocks on my door, I open it to find a lady with big, shiny green eyes, blond hair tied into a ponytail, a wide smile, and a backpack—she's just come from work. She was attending to a patient, one of the many hundreds she has now helped in her more than three decades of supporting those with mental illness. She's got a raspy smoker's voice, a north London accent, and an easygoing manner. I can tell she and my father would have got on. Complete strangers, we stand on my doorstep and hug. It feels almost as if I'm meeting a family member I didn't know about. I show her into the kitchen, and right away she sees my grandmother's painting of my father. "That's the denim." She smiles, pointing to his collar. She remembers his denim shirt and jeans, which characterize my memories of him, too. I give her the medical records, along with the notes she wrote nearly thirty years ago. She settles down to read while I make tea. Liz began helping my father in June of 1995, about fifteen months before he died. "Wow," she says, reading through each one. "It's pretty amazing to read this after so long." She reads aloud one observation she'd made: "'The thought of taking something helps him more than the medication itself.' You see, that's what it was with him. He didn't like the meds.

"It was a long time ago, James, but I've always spoken about the man in Ladbroke Grove. And then this email popped up, and it triggered a memory." With so many patients over so many years, I didn't imagine Liz would remember much about him. "We had a connection," she says. "There was something about him. He had an aura. I really felt for him. He was on and off I think with your mum. And then there was you. I'd just had a baby and I felt touched by his situation, I felt sad for him because of the boy—because of you." As a young mother herself, Liz felt drawn to helping my father, wanted him to have a meaningful relationship with my mother and me. Incredibly, she also remembers meeting me as a toddler, coming up to the flat in Notting Hill. "There was an older woman there, attending to you," she says. That would have been my grand-maman, Gabrielle.

Liz was only twenty-eight at the time. I ask her if she ever felt strange helping a man who was more than fifteen years older. "I've always felt I had an old soul," she says. "I didn't think of age." Liz is from an Irish Catholic family who relocated to north London just before she was born. Raised with a strict sense of both family values and work ethics, she got her first job at just sixteen, as an operator at British Telecom. But it was helping people that she felt was her calling. As she tells it, she just knew it was something she wanted to do. So she went into support work. Not long after, she was assigned to my dad.

"He was very trendy," she says, laughing. "He had that hippie Notting Hill vibe—he fit right in. I remember him as charming, and funny. I remember him really happy to see me, you know? Properly happy. We were close. We used to like to sit in the back of Café Rouge for coffee, right round the corner from his flat. If we could go outside in the sun, we would. So we could smoke. We used to walk around Portobello Market—I loved that area." Her voice is wistful. "There were all kinds of coffee shops and places to go with patients. There were also charity shops along the King's Road I took him to, to see if he could get volunteer work. He was an intelligent man, and he was stuck. I was just trying to bring him out of himself."

I ask her if he felt lonely. I don't want to picture him in this way, but I know creating a fuller, more detailed idea of who he was is what's most important. "I think so," she says. She describes the other side of his character: more withdrawn, more prone to isolation and introspection. She'd meet him at his flat, which she says had candles and art everywhere, a mystic vibe with hues of pink and red. But it would sometimes be totally dark. "There was a heaviness over it. You could feel the energy, that he was sad. Like a cocoon, almost.

"In some ways, I have the luxury of being a support worker, rather than a psychiatric nurse. That's clinical, it's about risk assessments and managing up. But I can just be Liz. And I think your dad liked that." He didn't like taking his medication, and he didn't like to think of himself as sick. Liz was able to connect with him on a human level, to just be "a buddy," as she calls it. They would speak about art and about what he felt he wanted from life. It was a chance for him to speak to a professional, but not about medical needs: things like his psychosis, or his mood, or his medication. He was able to share with her instead his feelings about his life, and often his feelings about me. "I think he missed the relationship with your mum," Liz says. "But I think deep down, he knew it wasn't working."

And then she tells me something that makes me cry. "I remember I drove him past your school once," she says. "He wanted to show me. I got the sense he was very proud that you were going to such a good school. He wanted to be close to you. I think he was very sad over not being with you." This was my prep school in west London—I would have been about six or seven at the time. She drove him past the school to make him feel closer to me. My eyes fill with tears at the thought of it. It is not the big picture that hits me hardest when I think about my father. Not his illness or even his death. It is these small moments, these slim beams of light that shine and reveal his memory even now.

Liz continues to read out moments from her notes that move her. "'Claims to feel like a misfit,'" she says. "Ugh. It's so sad what these mental illnesses can do." And then, "'He's meeting up with you and looking forward to it.' That's nice." She smiles warmly at me. The notes are a journey through Liz's own history, too. She comes across a name from her past. "Ah—this psychiatrist, mentioned here," she says, showing me. "He was such a lovely man. But he ended his life. I think a couple of years after your dad."

Liz wanted to give my dad hope, and a life away from his illness. She found an art studio where he could spend time. "He loved it," she says, "but so many of these places have closed down." She finds an incident in the notes she remembers well. "I called the police on your dad, to break the door in. I was so worried, I thought he was in there and he'd done something to himself." My dad had been at a friend's house at the time and was really angry this had happened.

She remembers getting the call that he had died. "Gosh, it brings a lot to the surface, reading this. Processing it is hard. It was a devastating situation. I knew the potential there. He looked forward to seeing me, I got that from him. I think he realized that I really did care. I listened to his views on things when we had conversations, but I wasn't there to judge him. If you can give someone a little bit of a glimmer, rather than tell them to do this or do that. Just do something small to open things up. That's how I work."

Meeting Liz is an extraordinary gift. When I think about my father suffering, I think about him on his own. His last moments of psychosis and suicide must have been terrifying, and it hurts to think of him in that state. But I know now that he had people looking after him. Sitting with Liz in my kitchen—with his paintings on the wall behind us—is a wonderful full-circle moment, and an amazing opportunity to thank the person who kept him well. "When I read the email that you were looking for me, I was so happy. I was ecstatic. It just made me so happy, I was in tears. I thought, 'Can you imagine how he must feel that he's found me?'" Alex comes home halfway through our chat. She gives him a big hug, too. She does feel like family.

"There is a passion about this job," Liz tells us. "It's got to be in you. To make people feel good is second to none." I ask her how things have changed since she was helping my dad. "They've closed down a lot of facilities, day centers, things like that," she says.

In the mid-1990s, the UK government changed the way mental illness would be treated. Psychiatric facilities—many of them Victorian-era asylums—were shut down in an effort to integrate people back into society. The plan was called Care in the Community, and it continues to this day. The problem is that in the intervening years, much of the help on offer has been slowly scaled back or cut completely to save money.

What were once local centers that people like my dad could use—like the Denbigh in Notting Hill and the Diorama near Great Portland Street—have been shut down completely, presumably viewed as expendable, nonurgent luxuries.

A lot of care has now been recentralized, but the level and variety of that care remains much less extensive. If he were alive today, rather than going to the rehabilitation center on the Harrow Road just around the corner from his flat, my dad would now have to travel to a big hospital to meet with a psychiatric nurse. There is no longer a day hospital for someone like him to visit, or art therapy classes for him to attend. The notes show me he had a doctor who he could see regularly and at short notice. There were regular psychiatric assessments, immediate referrals for brain scans and medication renewal. And he had Liz to guide him. Anyone who has tried even to book an appointment with a doctor in London recently will tell you that all sounds like a distant dream.

It's not clear to me why British politicians thought the Care in the Community model would work. They needed only to have looked at the United States, where a similar system was implemented in the 1970s, to see how chronic underfunding can leave many vulnerable people even more exposed. When New York was plagued by blackouts and riots, and the glamour of the 1960s Big Apple had evaporated, state officials emptied psychiatric units into the streets, also suggesting that localized support would work better than institutionalized care. It is estimated that by the early 1980s, between a third and half of all of the city's homeless people were those ejected from mental health facilities.

Perhaps nowhere in the United States more clearly demonstrates the vast gulf between the haves and the have-nots than San Francisco. According to a 2022 study, 16 percent of the city's homeless have a severe mental illness. That vulnerability can also lead to substance abuse—the study found 35 percent had both a psychiatric condition and an addiction to drugs. It is a tragedy on a global scale that some of the wealthiest places on earth still leave so many behind.

Thankfully, the NHS is much more than its bureaucratic systems. Meeting Liz has given me hope that those with mental illness can still count on people like her. She still sees her patients—some twenty or so—regularly, in much less clinical, more healing environments. "I love to take people to the park," she says. "I can continue, because I'm not a clinical nurse. I can have that human connection, which I love."

She's excited to show me a recent change in how the service may operate. Rummaging through her bag, she pulls out a handbook from a course she's just completed. It's based on a Finnish approach called peer-supported open dialogue in which meetings with patients are carried out with family members. "Patients and their families often see it as a hierarchy, like them and us," Liz explains. "This breaks that down." It's a program that helps to make interactions with patients more human and more collaborative. "I mean, I've done this all my life, but I love it because it means I have even more permission to be the person I've been all my life." It's nice to hear the NHS is taking part in these treatment trials and courses to make helping those with mental illness easier for patients and their families.

It's toward the end of our conversation that I realize much of Liz's humanity seems to stem from a tragedy of her own. A year after my dad died, Liz gave birth to a little girl, Claire. When she was just eighteen months old, Claire was diagnosed with leukemia. "I suddenly found myself in this very strange cancer world, with these sick kids. It was all so scary." She reaches back into her bag and pulls out a framed photograph of a little blond girl with bright blue eyes. "That's Claire," she says. "She died four months after we found out about the cancer." The grief was almost paralyzing, but Liz channeled her emotions immediately. "I wanted to fundraise. I wrote to Richard Branson, Mohamed al-Fayed, anyone I thought would have money. I wanted to raise money for other kids on that ward."

And she did. She raised more than £8,000 for the department that had looked after her daughter. The fundraising had the added benefit of distracting her and her young family from their sadness. "When you've got grief like that in the house, it's silence. You don't even turn on the radio." Liz became pregnant again, and a year later, she gave birth to a little girl. "I had her on the year anniversary of Claire's death," she says, beaming. "Good things can come from sadness. Your dad would be so proud of you." Soon Liz has to head off to see another patient. Alex and I wave goodbye to her from our doorstep. Then he closes the door, and we stand hugging in the hall for a full minute. Later, I sit for a moment in the stillness of the kitchen and repeat Liz's words to myself. "He wanted to be close to you." She cannot know how much this means to me.

Revelations from my father's medical records didn't stop with Liz. Pat Leung was another name that came up repeatedly in the notes, but since she had retired, I wasn't sure I'd be able to find her. The hospital that had put me in touch with Liz had given me Pat's phone number, but I don't have much luck on my own—sensible people don't pick up random calls out of the blue! When I tell Liz, she dives right in with characteristic zeal and has a colleague drop a note through Pat's door. A week after asking Liz about her, I find myself once more in the surreal position of sitting in front of one of my father's caretakers.

I meet Pat at a coffee shop downstairs from my office. She has a musical Lancashire accent, and at once I can see the no-nonsense medical professional in her. She was a clinical nurse, and while she met with my dad in much the same way Liz had, her job was slightly different. She was assigned to assess his medical state, check that his drugs were working, and administer medication if needed. She was assigned to my dad the year before Liz, and passed him on to her when she moved to another hospital.

With her glasses perched on the end of her nose in matronly fashion, Pat scans the medical notes she wrote thirty years ago. Her handwriting is somewhat difficult for me to decipher, so I am glad of the chance to have her read it out. "Your father was in a research group," she says, looking up. I don't understand what she means. "The NHS wanted to understand what kind of help worked better." The idea, Pat explains, was to figure out whether a nurse or social worker with just fifteen patients—which they called an "intensive" caseload—would get better results than one with up to forty-two, which was standard. You should think of "intensive" from the patient's point of view, and how much time they get with their care worker, rather than from the care worker's perspective, for whom forty-two patients does sound intense! It seems obvious that the lighter caseload would mean more time with each patient, and therefore better results, but apparently the NHS needed proof this was indeed the case.

"He would have had to have agreed, and then you got divided into caseloads," Pat says. "Intensive or standard. The nursing teams were divided, too—we didn't know if we would get a standard or an intensive caseload. The research chose those with a history of being noncompliant, with more challenging behavior. They needed to be younger and resistant to medication." This is all completely new to me, and explains why even though he was in the standard group, my dad might have received a lot more attention than others with his condition at the time. Pat continues, "The problem that you have with things like that is we are all human. And with people who are struggling, it's hard to leave them be. Even on a normal caseload." I realize both Liz's and Pat's positions were funded by the research for a limited time. My father might only have been on the standard program, but he was very lucky to be part of this research. And of course, like so many committed caretakers, Liz and Pat worked overtime.

Pat sits back in her chair as the memories return to her. "He wouldn't eat," she says. "When things were stable, he would make me coffee in his flat. I remember big windows. But he would buy paint rather than food. He wasn't alone in that. People who have a focus and get fixated, they would do things like that. Everyone used to laugh about me saying I was the cupboard and fridge watcher. I would check to see what's fresh, what's not, things like that."

Pat says a lot of their conversations revolved around getting access to me. "Your mum saw your father every couple of weeks, but I don't think she always included you in the visits," she says. I ask her if he wanted me to be included, and immediately worry about the answer, panicking briefly that she will tell me what I fear most: that actually, he had not wanted to be part of my life. "Oh, yes," she says, sensing my concern and smiling at me. "He wanted to see you very much. It was down to your mum. She was worried about when his mood wasn't stable, how that would impact you. But he was really focused on that loss of you in his existence. So, when your mum saw him without you, that would be more painful for him."

In reading his medical records, I got the sense that fatherhood overwhelmed my dad, that he couldn't deal with me or what I represented. My mother has also said she had to force him to want to see me. I ask Pat what her sense of him was. Did he find fatherhood too much? "No," she says, emphatically. "What I recall was that he was very hurt that he couldn't see you. He understood that he was unwell and saw everyone trying to protect you. It's really difficult when someone has florid psychotic episodes, people tend to focus on what they see when they are very unwell. They forget that for a long period of time they're stable, they're living their life. They're trying to live in the world. Trying to just be. But the impact of that if you have children . . . Your marriage breaks down, you lose so much."

She comes across a moment in the notes when my father suddenly becomes unwell. "You were due to have your First Holy Communion at the weekend," she says. "There was a financial issue there." It seems my mum was asking his mother, Nancy, for money. Pat suggests that this push and pull, in and out of my life, was hard for my father to deal with. "It seemed that he's always there and people want things from him—your mother wanted things from him—but then he didn't get the reciprocal thing. Seeing you. And that is painful to live with. Bad enough you have a severe and enduring illness, but then you are almost punished for having that as well."

He seems to have spoken about me a lot with Pat and told her that he thought my mother was being too strict with me. "They had very different worldviews," I tell her. She was Catholic and had more regimented ideas about how I should be brought up. He was more skeptical of religion, more focused on the spiritual.

"He was quite good at telling me when he was feeling unwell," she says. "He wasn't floridly psychotic all the time, but when he became unwell and his mood dipped, he would tell me. He was very clear about when things were becoming unstable for him. But he wasn't always compliant with medication. Some of his illness was about perceptual shifts. If he'd been painting a lot—which seemed to calm him as well—he would say that things were moving in the paintings. He didn't feel he was in reality. He could get lost in that.

"I remember he would recover very quickly from psychotic episodes—sometimes in just a couple of days," Pat tells me. She often wondered if my father's illness was a mood disorder that was being churned up by his circumstances. "I can see sulpiride in these notes," she says. "That's for mood disorders. That's given to people who are manic depressive, really, who have a mood disorder. But again"—she laughs—"he was not compliant!" My sense, I tell her, is that he only took medication if he felt like he needed it. But by then it was too late—he was already entering psychosis. "Yes, exactly," says Pat. "But also, because he would recover quite quickly, he'd say, 'But I only took them for a few days!' Getting people to take these medications for a long time can be hard. They feel sluggish, he felt it would dull him. And it's true. It does. But then, what's the worst-case scenario? We don't want you to end up in hospital. We want you to function."

She eventually comes across the moment when she had to tell him she was leaving: "'Visited John at home today,'" she reads aloud. "'He was initially appropriate in speech content, but as the visit went on, he began speaking about philosophy, semantics, and searching for meanings. At times he made sense, but it was generally difficult to follow. He appears to be living in his own world without much of a grip on reality. He doesn't appear to be doing any painting at the moment and appears to be most of the time on his own.'" He doesn't seem to have taken the news that she was leaving well.

"Your dad understood what was going on in his mind. But the pushes and pulls of his life undermined it. If you've got no one to share that with, if you've got no close family or friends, you're alone. A lot of our standard cases, they were lonely, they were isolated. If people had children, often they would be kept from them. And in fact, that didn't help them at all. Not in my mind. I've got four of my own. We had our own pushes and pulls as well. So we sort of got it. If someone had told me I couldn't see my kids—well!"

Pat is a joy to speak to. Like Liz, she has dedicated her life to care. As a clinical nurse, she worked in psychiatric units before they were closed down in the mid-1990s. "I trained as a hairdresser, actually," she says, giggling. "But it was the 1970s, I needed work. I came down south to find it. And I dunno, there was just something about it. I just wanted to do mental health, really. It was just—can you make a difference to someone's life? Can you help them? Can you make the world not so devastating? Because it's not just devastating for the person—it's their families. It's an awful thing.

"Having an enduring mental illness is one of the most painful things in life. There was nobody to support these people. I would look after a lot of men—some as young as twenty, right up to forty or fifty. There was nobody to see their point of view. People don't understand you. You can be as unwell as anything behind closed doors, but what impacts you is you go out into the world, and somebody else notices, 'Oh, that person is a bit strange.' If you make a social disturbance when you go out into the world, you're going to get picked up."

Pat was right at the front line, working at Shenley Hospital outside London, when the order came down that it would be closed and patients would have to live in the outside world. Care in the Community had officially begun, and it was Pat's job to resocialize and rehabilitate people who'd spent a lifetime in an institution. "We did everything from teaching them to cook and clean. We had a ward of male and female patients, and we had a two-year plan to transfer them into community homes. So we'd do things like take them to the theater, to art galleries." She laughs at a memory. "I always remember one patient saying to me, 'Pat, you make us all have a hot shower and have our hair done before we go out to the theater, but some people in there, they absolutely stink!' I was dying!"

These were people who'd spent their entire lives in a hospital, and now they had to go out and live in society. I ask Pat if she felt at the time that Care in the Community was the right plan. "Well," she says, "the money should have followed the patients, but it often didn't. But we were lucky with the groups that we had. And I have to say, there are some people who cannot survive outside of a psychiatric community. Shenley was a community. And if we think statistically, every year we used to create a long-stay ward. They are people who need constant support and long-term care and will continue to be ill for the rest of their lives. And they were sent out. And I remember heartbreaking moments where after about six months, four patients—who were in a very well-supported house—would start coming back saying, 'People out there hate us. They call us names in the street. We stand out. We don't fit in.'"

One issue was that many of these patients had spent a lifetime in beautiful green countryside—Shenley was a psychiatric hospital with large grounds in Hertfordshire, a county to the east of London. But when they were sent "back," they found themselves in inner-city boroughs, a world away from the peace and quiet they needed. "Harlesden," says Pat, visibly exasperated. "How could you, when you've lived out in a leafy suburb for twenty years, go back to Harlesden, and the main road and the busy shops and things like that?" Eventually, the government did create smaller group homes for people like this. "We didn't need huge Victorian-era asylums. No. But there did need to be a lot more support." I tell Pat my father was in and out of what he called "the bin" for much of his life. "Someone like your father would have been terrified of being committed to an institution," she says. "So he did just enough to stay on the right side of it."

Pat has seen a lot in her long career, including in the early 1990s, right in the middle of the AIDS crisis, helping people with mental illness. "It was hard, to see young men dying. And they'd have a psychotic episode on top of it. The teams were all researching like mad trying to find some way to help. They were doing 3D scanning in the basements, and taking biometrics, and the scientists would be pointing at scans saying, 'Six months to live, three months to live.' They could pinpoint it, they just couldn't stop it. It was awful. And these young men kept dying. That was the saddest time. Just such a waste.

"I do remember one very young man—he was twenty-three—he hadn't told his parents. And he had full-blown AIDS. He was dying. I said, 'They need to know. Doesn't matter whatever you have, your parents need to know.' He said no. And he turned to me, he said, 'Pat, the worst is, I have loads of gay friends. And when I was in the AIDS unit, they'd all come and see me and cry over me. But since I've had a psychotic episode, now I'm here, they don't want to know me.' That was the most distressing thing for people—if they had a psychotic episode in the middle of it all. People were so cruel."

It was very soon after holding the hands of perhaps hundreds of dying men that Pat was moved to the research project and my father's case. All the love and tenderness she'd shown over the years would now be redirected to my father. I tell her how lucky I feel he was to have her. She had changed positions by the time of my father's death, but she has a vague recollection of being told he'd died. "Suicides in the team are really hard to take," she says. "Because you feel you've failed. I don't know what was going on at the time, but people need to have some hope, and what's going on in their lives can really hit them hard." I tell Pat that my dad probably liked her no-nonsense northern approach. She laughs. Like Liz, she says it was making sure he could continue seeing me that motivated her. "I used to say, 'Keep it together! If you want to see him, keep it together!'" she says. "You were the whole center for him."

James and Pat Leung, John's psychiatric nurse, London, 2023.

Frank, Sarah, and Lizzie meet James at his home, 2023.

CHAPTER 12

TRANSCENDENTAL MEDITATION AND DESTABILIZING A CHAOTIC MIND?

What if you slept,
And what if
In your sleep
You dreamed
And what if
In your dream
You went to heaven
And there plucked a strange
and beautiful flower
And what if
When you awoke
You had that flower in your hand
Ah, what then?

—SAMUEL TAYLOR COLERIDGE, "WHAT IF YOU SLEPT . . ."

While Liz and Pat knew my father toward the end of his life, my father's first girlfriend, Lizzie, knew him toward the beginning, and she was there when he had his first episode. Realizing how much meeting her had meant to me, Lizzie offered to introduce me to other art school friends who had known my father. And so, three years on from our walk in the park, Lizzie comes to my home with Sarah—who she mentioned in her letter—and Sarah's husband, Frank, who was part of their gang back then, too, for more trips down memory lane, and specifically to shed more light on the Transcendental Meditation movement they were part of. Sarah has a touch of pink through her hair, a smiley, expressive face, and artist's hands. Frank's big bushy mustache, pulled into points at each end, gives him the air of an Edwardian gentleman. The eccentric threesome shuffle along the hall into my kitchen and immediately gather around the painting of my father on the wall. "That was your grandmother's painting of him," says Lizzie, searching for the memory. "Yes, I remember. Nancy was rather good, wasn't she?"

I tell them I want to know more about Transcendental Meditation. Sarah explains that she was hugely skeptical of it, and it seems it became an issue that drove these friends apart at times over the years. But their friendship survived—and here they were together again, to explain it all to their best friend's son. Seeing all three in my kitchen together instantly makes me wonder what my dad would have been like in his seventies: no doubt part of this fun group of aging bohemian intellectuals, speaking about life through art without any pretension, just pure creative flair.

Lizzie and Sarah were eighteen in 1968 and had started their fine art course at Camberwell. They lived together in the apartment Lizzie mentions in her letter. My dad—who was a couple of years older after having tried law school and hating it—initially lived in a small basement nearby, but then ended up moving into the flat, too. "It was very crowded!" remembers Sarah. "But we had such fun parties."

Transcendental Meditation was an immediate attraction for this young, creative, and spiritual antiestablishment crowd. "There was a guy there who had been in India with the Maharishi and the Beatles," says Lizzie. This is Geoffrey, who she also mentioned in her letter. "John and I used to go and listen to him telling stories. We'd come from quite sort of 'English' backgrounds. We weren't really attracted to all the drugs that were going on—we were a bit stiff for that. But TM seemed like a safer alternative. We both got really into it."

I ask what Transcendental Meditation entails. Lizzie tells me it produces dopamine, which she believes causes an addiction. "If people don't meditate," she continues, "they become irritable, they get headaches."

Sarah brings out their yearbook. A binder with black-and-white photos, many of the people in them stylized in the way you might imagine an art student in the '60s might look: hair over the ears, long fringes, and turned-up collars. Among those in the photos is my father. In one of them, he is closing the trunk on his Classic Mini. "He was the only one who could drive!" Sarah laughs. "So he'd take us to all kinds of places. If you take a look at this book," she says, opening the page to a list of names, "virtually everyone was doing TM. It was just a thing people were doing—and some were even using it in their art." She describes their arrival to Camberwell as marking an inflection point, where an incredibly old-fashioned institution suddenly had an influx of alternative, politically minded young people. American expressionism was the artistic vogue, and student riots across the continent were raging. "They didn't teach us art history for two years, because they were frightened we might do something to them. It all followed the French sit-ins at the Sorbonne. So we thought there was something new to be discovered."

This new wave prompted these young students to throw out all they had learned before—everything that had got them to art school in the first place. No more polite still life drawings or picturesque landscapes. Now it was about avant-garde forms, breaking boundaries, and experiencing new highs, their meditations and spiritual exhortations lifting them to transcendental heights. As the group flicks through the yearbook in my kitchen, photographs spark memories. "Wasn't he that guy who lived in our basement and made lutes?" "Oh, that guy moved to Sweden and became a stand-up comedian." "She was wonderful—she did edible paintings!"

As far as anyone could tell, my dad's psychoses hadn't started by the time he was at art school. "He got manic," says Lizzie. "He'd be up all night."

"John always liked to be doing radical things," says Sarah. "He was always pushing. He always wanted to know. He wanted certainty about things. But that energy was very attractive. There were plenty of people who plodded along and just did paintings. John wasn't like that. He was always really seeking the truth. He'd get so excited. 'What's it all about?' he'd say. He was driven."

Since Lizzie was dating my dad, she spent time with my grandparents and saw the family together. In this way, too, she fills the gaps in his life for me. "He was a bit embarrassed about his wealthy, English, stockbroker background," she says. He'd attended Haileybury, a boarding school in the Hertfordshire countryside, and hated it. His brother, Tony, went to Charterhouse—another major public boarding school—and also hated it. "The brothers played at getting along," she says. "But they were never close.

"I think he felt he'd had such a restricted middle-class, boarding school background, he wanted to really break out. And yet he still wore tweed jackets, didn't he? And then he grew his hair and bought new clothes."

"Yes, things changed!" adds Sarah.

"He did go from being straight looking, to more kind of Renaissance-y. Long hair and velvet trousers," says Lizzie.

"There was a real coldness between John and his father," Lizzie continues. "He was quite a cold man, actually. Perhaps it was something about that generation. The war generation. Nancy was bubbly and sweet, and the perfect wife. Pastel-y, and cheerful. She was a bit like Judi Dench. And she came with a big Scottish clan, and John loved the Scottish family. Nancy absolutely adored John. She loved Tony, his brother, but John was her favorite. John was beautiful. He was sparky, artistic. Nancy didn't want to rock the boat. She was quite superficial in that way. She had a slightly Scottish, 'let's not dig' attitude. She had to deal with two sons with schizophrenia, and later a husband who killed himself. So she had a lot to deal with."

Lizzie is the only person I have met with an outsider's perspective on my father and his family when he was a young man. These observations mean so much to me, and I can see she is trying to remember more. Like the artist she is, she wants to add the color she knows I need. She tells me my grandfather Jimmy planned his death so my father would find him. "He knew John would find him. Nancy had gone off shopping, and he had this gun from his time in the Royal Navy. I remember John's reaction was seriously detached. He was almost nothing. I remember you saying to me at the time, Sarah, that it was like John didn't have enough skins. There was a terrible vulnerability to him. He could compartmentalize, and he could be very detached."

"I think that thing about having thinner skins made him very attractive," adds Sarah. "Much more open." I can see she is reaching for the best of him, away from the darker reality of his life. But she affirms something

I already feel: His illness was part of his depth, part of his magnetism. "When you're at art school, everyone is obsessed with building their status. But we were there to find out what life was about, and to explore and to grow up. And he was doing it more than most of us."

After art school, my father and Lizzie broke up, but they were both hooked on Transcendental Meditation. They remained good friends and went on training courses in Spain and the north of England to teach meditation. "We did what was called 'rounding,' which is meditating for hours and hours at a time. And if you do it for quite a long time, you're repressing a lot of stuff. So it's waiting to burst out. It was meant for a short time. The problem was becoming addicted and doing too much.

"The Maharishi had moved to Switzerland and was setting up something called 'The World Plan.' And he wanted 108 people who had their own money—self-sustaining—to go out and work for him. And John had his trust fund, and so off he went with a group of others. They were in the design team. And John had a slightly ambivalent attitude to it, but he did feel this was the answer to how to become enlightened. To find total peace and tranquility, etcetera."

And this was when he had his first major documented psychotic episode. As Lizzie says in her letter, he was found wandering around Lake Lucerne in his suit, barefoot. "All that money that he had he'd given to the movement. And then he found himself back home, trying to recover." There's a definite feeling in the group that my father was taken advantage of by the movement. He had been "chosen" as one of a select few, but when he needed them, those in the movement didn't seem to care.

"He wanted to find these places that had the truth, something that would give him an understanding of the world," says Sarah. "But that he chose something that would hurt him—it's so sad. And it wasn't just him." Sarah says there were lots of people in their year who got involved with groups that she says didn't have the best intentions.

It's clear that Lizzie and Sarah blame TM for my father's psychotic break. But given it has since become a form of meditation practiced by millions, I felt it best to reach out to the Transcendental Meditation movement in an official capacity, to try to get their take. I was able to connect with David Hughes, a spokesman for the Maharishi Foundation UK, who tells me he also spent time working as a TM student in Switzerland. Speaking from his personal perspective, he says, "I can completely understand why your father's friends feel the way they do about TM. But I can only give my personal impressions of a very positive and uplifting environment which was focused on promoting what we all felt to be a useful and accessible technique. I didn't meet your father," he continues, "but one person who met him there in the 1970s described him to me as a kind, charming, and cheerful man, and I am sure that had I met him, I would have liked and admired the talented and good-hearted person he obviously was." David couldn't find anyone who remembered my father's psychotic break, but he tells me TM teachers always stress they are not medical professionals, and he feels they would have been cautious of offering any advice. I tell him my dad's friends feel they took advantage of him and his money. "I really can't comment on the financial situation," he says. "But the only truly responsible course of action would have been to facilitate his return to the UK, and appropriately qualified experts, as soon as possible. I would sincerely hope this was done."

When I was younger, a friend of the family warned me away from Transcendental Meditation, saying it was his opinion it could unlock psychosis in me the way it had my father. My grandfather Jimmy was convinced TM caused my dad's schizophrenia, too, and Lizzie, Sarah, and

Frank are all deeply skeptical after witnessing a number of their friends develop mental illnesses after continued extreme meditation. So I have to ask: Are they right? What are the links between meditation, accessing deeper consciousness, and psychotic episodes?

Godfrey Pearlson is a professor of psychiatry at Yale University. Most of his career in psychiatric neuroscience has focused on the effects of psychedelics and other drugs on the brain. As a student at medical school in the UK during the 1960s, he says he also saw Transcendental Meditation up close. "A lot of my friends at medical school were into TM," he says. "So I know all about rounding." He tells me those who were inclined toward mystical experiences seemed to be drawn to the movement. "But they were drawn into it in a way that really didn't seem healthy. They left behind all of their prior friends who 'didn't get it.' They left behind former activities—they were seen as kind of shallow. At some point they left TM, or they were spat out. And they became disillusioned." This seems to have been Lizzie and my father's experience.

The cognitive processes triggered by meditation are not very well-known, says Pearlson; he warns that much of the science is in its infancy. It involves using fMRI scanners to monitor the brains of those in meditative states, then tracking their brains over time to see if any changes become permanent. Much of this research does not control for other processes that may be causing a heightened brain response. But this early science does suggest not only increased activity in some areas of the brain, but changes in structure.

A 2015 meta-analysis of fMRI meditation research found that "meditation practice induces functional and structural brain modifications, especially in areas involved in self-awareness and self-regulation, as well as in areas involved in attention, executive actions, and memory function." One study that looked specifically at the mindfulness practices of

Buddhist monks found the prefrontal cortex of their brains—the region responsible for high-cognitive functions such as self-control, memory, and emotional expression—was highly activated. Other research indicates that meditation can lead to an increase in alpha and theta brain waves—the electric pulses most closely associated with enhanced learning abilities and mental well-being, and which again activate the prefrontal cortex and frontal lobe. Meditation also leads to complex neurochemical changes in the brain: producing more dopamine and serotonin, as well as decreasing adrenaline and cortisol. All changes combine to give us the sense of happiness and relaxation meditation offers.

"There are, interestingly, differences in gray matter volumes in those people who meditate versus those who do not," says Pearlson. Some studies have found gray matter actually grows over time with sustained meditative practice. Still, Pearlson warns against overextrapolation. "No one has done a proper study to work out if that's causal. It may be that those with more gray matter tend to like to meditate."

So, in all these ways, meditation might help the brain. But there are also case reports of psychosis being triggered by meditative practice. Pearlson tells me that there *have* been documented cases of intensive meditation triggering not just a period of psychosis but an enduring mental illness. For example, according to a 2022 study in the *Irish Journal of Psychological Medicine*, psychotic disorders were found arising in association with meditative practices. It makes clear how difficult it is to attribute a causal relationship between the two, but as we've seen, schizophrenia is associated with disrupted connections in the prefrontal cortex, whereby this region cannot communicate properly with other parts of the brain. Since meditation also activates this region, there may be a risk of psychosis when the synapses misfire. Flooding the body with neurochemicals like serotonin or dopamine through meditation can destabilize an already compromised ability to generate the right chemicals in the right quantities. Meditation generates more of this activity, causing blood to rush to the frontal cortex and to activate the synaptic connections that may not have worked properly. My father's brain, already predisposed to this aberrant activity, was vulnerable to the effects of intensive meditation.

In most of the reported cases of psychosis induced by meditation, says Pearlson, the person was involved in intensive group meditation, just like my father. "Meditation does seem to be a stressor in people who are vulnerable to psychosis. Most of the case reports agree on this. The kinds of stressors that occur not when people are practicing meditation by themselves, but they happen during 'rounding.' People will be at an intensive retreat, undergoing a prolonged experience in a slightly disorientating environment—that's when psychosis seems to occur."

Pearlson compares this meditative psychosis to Jerusalem syndrome. "People go to Jerusalem," he explains, "and expect some sort of religious epiphany. They've read their Bibles, and they're going to this sacred place, which is the meeting place of various faiths, and they have huge expectations that this will be life-transforming. They get there, it's a bit disorientating and maybe not what they expected. And they develop a brief psychosis. And this is something that happens often enough that it has this moniker of Jerusalem syndrome."

Pearlson says intensive group meditation can have a similar effect. "Rounding, to my mind, is something like that. It's a vulnerable person, with a particular mental set, in a particular setting." In the world of psychedelic drugs, "set" and "setting" are established terms. Your "set" is how you're feeling in the moments before you take the drug: your expectations; if you had a bad day; whether you are feeling out of sorts. And your "setting" is literally where you are: Are you with a group of friends, feeling safe and comfortable? Are you alone, out on the street? Are you being confronted by another group of people, who seem aggressive? All of these variables, says Pearlson, will have an impact. "Set and setting apply as much to triggering psychosis as they do to what sort of trip you have."

The other thing to consider, says Pearlson, is "reverse causality. . . . If you have an at-risk nineteen-year-old, they may be drawn to meditation as a way to ward off psychotic experiences. And meditation has been observed to help people who have experienced psychosis. You should bear that in mind when you're thinking about your dad." One 2016 study found no link between mindfulness practice and an overall increase in psychotic traits, and further suggests that if done in the right way, meditation could have helped my dad. If schizophrenia means a shrinking cerebral cortex, and meditation can grow gray matter, perhaps it would have been an extraordinary help. I tell Pearlson that I suspect my father, through meditation, unleashed something that would plague him for the rest of his life. Jerusalem syndrome seems to come and go. His experience, if meditation is partially to blame, was life changing.

Lizzie talked about finding TM addictive. I ask Pearlson how this addiction might work. "The people that I've spoken to," he says, "have found it hard to separate the process of meditation from the experience of being in this social group of meditators." He talks about "love bombing"—when group leaders and other members shower new recruits in positivity, love, and affirmation. All kinds of movements are known to use this technique to recruit new members. "Some people describe that as addictive, and difficult to separate from the meditation itself," Pearlson says. "People miss the attention and the affection. It's tough to pull those apart."

Given "rounding" remains part of TM practice today, I ask David

Hughes how it works. "It is a series of simple yoga postures," he says, "followed by a few minutes of a breathing exercise, followed in turn by the standard twenty-minute TM meditation. People on a weekend retreat, for example, would repeat that sequence once, thus engaging in an extra session of meditation." David thinks that TM and other forms of meditation help those with psychiatric disorders, and that scientific studies support that view. I believe him. But I also get the impression the early days of TM may have been characterized by experimentation, and that my father's mental well-being may have been a casualty of this well-intentioned but also heady and spiritually intoxicating new world.

As our time together comes to a close, Lizzie, Sarah, and Frank all agree they see my father in me. "Your inquisitiveness about the world—that's very similar, in a way," says Sarah. "He was looking at it through art and in a spiritual way. And you're looking at it through journalism, you're investigating and you're finding things. That same energy is there." As usual, to hear somebody say that I am like my father moves me, and I can feel tears in my eyes again.

"He'd be so amazed by you," adds Lizzie. "You'd be the fulfillment of what he wanted to be." She gets emotional, too. "I literally think about him every day. And wish wherever he is that he's happy. When we were at the wake, I just felt like shouting, 'JOHN'S JUST DIED!' And I saw you. I didn't know you, but I thought, 'Oh, I want to give this boy something. I'll give him a camera!' And I wish I had. I had this idea that you'd be someone who'd look at the world, and you'd be observant. And you turned out a journalist. And I think that was rather perceptive of me!"

I realize speaking with these three just how much of my father I truly do have in me. But it's not his sadness or the depression that I occasionally feel that comes from him. I realize I have some of his best qualities.

His sense of humor. The silly voices and skits Lizzie says characterized her friendship with him—I do that all the time. It didn't ever cross my mind to sit in an office from nine to five. I wanted to explore and meet people. That was my dad, too. I feel his energy in the three free spirits sitting on my sofa now, and their memories conjure him, sitting beside them, one of the gang, who they'll never forget.

Katherine Stiff, best woman at James and Alex's wedding. (top left)

James in Milan, February 2021. (top right)

James in an ISIS prison in northeast Syria, 2019. (middle, top right)

James and producer Bruno Roeber, Ukraine, 2022. (middle left)

James and Kathy in Syria, 2007. (middle, bottom right)

James in Antarctica, 2018. (bottom left)

James in the Himalayas, 2018. (bottom right)

CHAPTER 13

WITNESSING HORROR AND BUILDING RESILIENCE

In a world of insecurity and ambition and ego, it's easy to be drawn in, to take chances with our lives, to believe that what we do and what people say about us is reason enough to gamble with death. Now, looking at your sleeping face, inches away from me, listening to your occasional sigh and gurgle, I wonder how I could have ever thought glory and prizes and praise were sweeter than life.

—FERGAL KEANE, "LETTER TO DANIEL"

I'm writing this now in a hotel, back in northern Syria. Well, the word *hotel* is a bit of an exaggeration. It's a group of rooms that occupy the second and third floors of a dangerously old building without proper heating or water. I have the overwhelming sense of a derelict old people's home. And every surface—bed, curtain, carpet, even tiled floor—has been so deeply saturated in smoke, I must now be on six secondhand packs a day. I've returned to Syria to take stock of a delicate situation left behind after Donald Trump's decision to pull out US troops.

Syria has an extremely special place in my heart. I first discovered it during my Arabic studies, when I spent the summer of 2007, between my first and second years at university, living in Damascus. I kept a journal during that trip—it's a leather-bound book full of the memories of a wide-eyed nineteen-year-old who had read William Dalrymple's *From the Holy Mountain* and had vague aspirations of being a travel writer.

Here's the first paragraph:

> *So here we go, day 1. I'm on the plane at last. Al-Italia, a great big flying green bus in the sky with lots of orange people on it. I'm supposed to be spending three months away! Not a clue where to start. One way ticket to Damascus. Arrival 2am. Brilliant. The plan is to find someone, ANYONE, at the airport and see if they can help me. Ah well. Farewell wishes from friends did wonders to cure any anxiety. "Don't get shot" seems to be the general theme.*

As I've read on, I've been reminded that the plane broke down in Milan, and that I spent the night listening to "All by Myself" by Celine Dion in the reception area of an incredibly rural Italian hotel before finally making it to Damascus.

When you think of Syria now, you'd be forgiven for thinking of war and violence, terrorism, and chaos. But the Syria I knew over those first few months, and in the years I lived there after that, was a dreamlike world of warm summer nights in stunning ancient courtyard restaurants, the smells of jasmine and black coffee, of cardamom and fragrant fruit. It was a time of awesome adventure, of days-long bus rides through the desert, all over the country, and to Lebanon, Egypt, and Jordan. It was a time when I was able to learn Arabic, but also better understand all the wonder and charm of the Middle East. It was a time of youthful excitement and endless scrapes with people who became lifelong friends. I feel an odd sense of warmth remembering it all now. When I have reported in Syria since, or met the many people who've lost their homes to the violence and found themselves dispersed all over the world, I always make sure they understand that I know what their country was, and how much I hope it can find its way back again.

That first summer, I stayed with the Georges family in the Damascus old town. They lived in a traditional house: an open courtyard with rooms sprouting off in all directions. I lived on the top floor and would sit up on the roof for hours in the evenings, staring out toward the sunset over the jungle of mismatched Damascus rooftops. The lady of the house, Madame Georges, was in her seventies and had different-colored hair most weeks. She was tiny and energetic, and always smiling. And she had a little dog named Bonnie, which in her accent sounded like *Bony*. It probably should have been neutered, because that dog could not go two minutes without trying to hump the nearest object. And as I was a new arrival, "Bony" was very keen on my legs. My arms. The side of my body. It didn't matter. Madame Georges was blissfully ignorant to his advances. And my Arabic wasn't very good when I arrived, so all I could understand were her attempts at French. One time, when I had terrible food poisoning, she stood outside the bathroom, and each time she heard me retch I could hear her shout, "Bravo, James!" When I finally emerged, ashen-faced and exhausted, Bony ran up to me and started humping my foot. "Bravo, Bony!" she shouted.

Her husband, Mr. Georges, was a large man with thick fingers and white hair and no teeth. He had something wrong with his foot, so in the three months I lived there I think I saw him standing maybe twice. Their son Jihad worked at a hotel, and their other son George worked in computers. "So, your name is George Georges?" I remember asking him, unsure if my Arabic had failed me yet again. "Yes," he said, not understanding my confusion at all. They had a framed photo of the pope on the wall, next to a photo of President Assad and another of Nasrallah, the Lebanese leader of Hezbollah. They were a Christian family, but this was one tiny way in which Syria distinguished itself from its neighbors: People from all faiths were able to live side by side in peace. In a dictatorship like Syria, though, putting a picture of Assad on the wall is also a good survival tactic.

When I decided to stay in Syria for the full year, I planned to live in a more modern part of town and rent my own place. I wanted a big space so that it could become a hub for my local friends, all of whom still lived with their parents. I remember the landlord was more than a little suspicious of me. "Jaasous," I could hear him saying to his son, through whom I'd found the apartment. It means *spy* in English. He found it strange that a young white kid wanted a four-bedroom flat opposite the Iranian embassy. I later learned that one of my neighbors was a senior member of the intelligence services. I should have guessed; his front door looked like the entrance to a vault. My friends and I often joked that the massive speakers on the walls in some of the rooms of my place were rudimentary microphones. Maybe they were.

My closest friend was my classmate, Katherine, who remains a best friend now. With her blond hair and electric-blue eyes, she stuck out even more than me. It was an alien-like experience: Almost every day, our otherness seemed to land us in ridiculous situations. A then-junior business minister had an office in my building, and I taught English to his son. We knew he was important because every time there was a power outage—a common occurrence in Syria—our building shone with light, like some blazing beacon in the darkness. You don't have to worry about power outages if you're a senior member of the Assad regime. He was a tall, suave man with dark eyes and black hair with silver running through it. Kathy and I often ran into him outside my building, getting out of his Mercedes while his driver handed him bags of expensive clothes. He liked to treat us. One time, he took us to a restaurant themed like a traditional English pub. There was green felt and exposed dark wood everywhere, a bar with beers lined up, and even a little corduroy trim lining the seats. But because they thought putting an *e* on everything automatically gave it a sense of old British authenticity, we arrived to find the sign outside read YE OLDE ENGLISH PUBE. Kathy and I could not stop laughing. And when we sat down at a table, which had been hastily arranged in the very middle of the packed pub, the minister ordered Mexican fajitas and chilled red wine for everyone and, with a quick clap of his hands, called on the entertainment to start. A man in a velour tracksuit with some rather evident plastic surgery began to sing Lionel Richie songs. Most days Kathy and I spent together we were faced with inexplicable situations like these, which made us laugh in that way that makes your belly hurt and your face ache.

Kathy and I were a funny double act. Our friendship was completely platonic, but at no point did I say anything about being gay. Reading through my journal from all those years ago, I can see I made no reference to men or women in those pages. I was hiding from myself. I felt safe with Kathy, and I think she felt safe with me. Our humor bonded us, especially in the Middle East, a world that can be difficult to navigate for both gay men and single women.

After my degree, I still had no idea what to do. I toyed with the idea of the intelligence services, which at the time had started to become much more transparent about their operations. There were adverts on the tube for applications to the security services, and it was spoken about openly at university. When I chose to study Arabic, a lot of people joked that I was training to become a spy. And I thought, *Why not have a go?* Some of us who had studied Arabic were contacted by a "central London agency," and I was asked to complete an online aptitude test, then had a series of phone calls. It never went any further, presumably because the math element of the tests cannot have gone well, and because if I was ever to become a spy, I don't think I could ever not tell anyone. Which they would have known. Because, you know. They're spies.

The only thing I really did know once I finished my degree was that I was in love with Syria. So I found a way to keep my focus there by opting for a master's degree at the London School of Economics. This was 2011, and by this time the protests that would start what became known as the Arab Spring were starting to boil over. I still had my student visa, and so decided to head back to a very different Damascus.

The city itself had not physically changed, but the charm and innocence of the place I'd known was starting to fade. The security services were much more visible. People eyed you in the street. The implied military presence from my student days had become more overt. The huge, gated government buildings in the center of town that had lain dormant now seemed much more active, with guards positioned outside. It had never been a secret to us that Syria was a dictatorship. From our earliest visits, we all knew about the violent potential of the Assad regime. We had studied the history and politics of the region, and my own family had had to leave more than one Arab country because of violent dictatorship. But Assad is not Syria. Those ancient cities were there thousands of years before his family, and they'll be there when he's gone. My student days had been spent in a somewhat naïve but wonderfully carefree haze; I had enjoyed the beauty and warmth of the Syrian people without paying too much attention to the murkier world of the country's political system.

But now, my job was to pay attention to it. I wanted to make my way to the protests that had started in some of the smaller towns toward the Lebanese border. Having spent so much time invested in all things Syrian, I had made a good group of Syrian friends in London, and through them was connected to a group of young activists. These were the people who'd keep me safe, and they were some of the bravest I've ever met. They'd seen what was happening in other Arab countries and wanted to emulate those calls for freedom. The government had responded with predictable force and hadn't granted visas to international journalists, and so the burgeoning movement really only had what we'd call "citizen journalists" to document what was going on. These young men and women were among them.

I had gone to Syria with the sole intention of writing my university thesis, but it soon became apparent that I was in a place a lot of journalists wanted to be but couldn't. After contacting a few newspapers in the UK, I had my instructions: Get to a protest and interview people. I had no burning desire or grand plans to "be" a journalist. But in that moment, I did feel a responsibility to share what was happening. Once I could see for myself how people were suffering, it felt like a normal human reaction to try and tell as many people about it as possible. A hopefully less naïve version of that instinct still drives me now.

However, we had a problem: I was a twenty-four-year-old white kid with blond(ish) hair, and was in no way going to be able to blend in. I'll always remember sitting in the back of a car one night not long after I'd returned, with the three activists around me discussing how best to hide me. I was doing my best to follow their Arabic, which they spoke very quickly under the soft orange glow of the car light. Suddenly, one of them threw a hoodie at me. "Wear this," he said. "Put the hood up." I did as I was told. "Not enough," he said. "Wear these." He handed me some sunglasses. He studied me for a moment. "One more thing," he said. And he passed me a surgical mask to put on my face. After adjusting it carefully, I looked up at the three of them staring back at me. A moment later, their serious faces cracked, and we all fell about laughing. I looked completely ridiculous. If they wanted attention, this was surely the way to get it. So I lost the shades and the mask, and went out with them.

We were in a small town. There were rows of two- and three-story houses laid out in a large grid, the uniformity disturbed by the gradient of the small hill it was on and the electricity lines that crisscrossed overhead. We climbed up the stairs of a small house, and I stood on the roof watching hundreds march past with signs and flags. They chanted repeatedly, "AlShaab, yuriid, iskaat al nitham!" *The people want the fall of the regime!* This was the first time I had the sensation of being somewhere that mattered, and it was incredibly exciting. It was also the first time I'd seen something for myself that until then I'd only seen reported on the news. There was a sense of taking part in a major event, rather than only being a spectator—although, of course, I was not one of the protesters. It felt good to be part of something, rather than watching from a distance.

I've since realized it's that feeling to which journalists can become addicted. And it's chasing that feeling that still fuels me now, in all kinds of places—from the Ukrainian front line to the scenes of terror attacks and everything in between. For a lot of people, it can become an unhealthy addiction, which they're prepared to take unhealthy risks to satisfy. But the advice I received from Dominic Waghorn, a journalist at the time at Sky News, I think has always kept me away from that danger: "No matter how dangerous the situation you're in is for you, it is much more dangerous for those helping you. Wherever you go in the world, whoever you speak to, know that involving them in any way can change their lives forever." I'm sure Dominic won't remember saying that to me, but I've always remembered it—and passed it on—because it's kept people at the heart of everything I do. Or at least, I hope it has. So as much as it was a thrill to be on that roof, what was much more important was how those marching were feeling. In some ways, it's a lesson that has guided writing this book. My own experiences are—occasionally—worth documenting. But only to serve a wider purpose, and always alongside the experiences of others in order to demonstrate a broader relevance.

The protest in Syria was later broken up by the security forces, who sprayed gunfire into the crowds. That night, I was taken to another house nearby. I could see every light was on in the building, and it was full of people, so many that they poured out into the street. I could hear crying. We went in and made our way through to the living room, where a man sat on the floor surrounded by his closest family. Everyone seemed to immediately understand why I was here, and I was ushered in to sit beside him. He had a bandage on his arm and shoulder and looked distraught. After a long hug and some brief discussion with the activist I was with, he started to describe what happened. "I was with my son in the street," he said. "And then the shooting started. I scooped him up into my arms and turned, but a bullet hit me in the back. I looked down and realized it had gone through me." And then he started to break down. "My son," he choked, through tears. A cell phone was thrust in front of me, and I looked in horror at the body of a young boy, his head split open.

Everyone in the room, including me, was crying by now. I felt shock, but also deep shame. In that moment I felt like a fraud, that this man not only had experienced the loss of a child in such circumstances but had then relived his trauma by explaining it to me. He needed a real journalist, not some kid. But he kept looking at me. "Tell someone," he said. "Just please tell someone what happened to my son." Everyone in the room was looking at me expectantly, as though it was now my turn. My turn to offer something that would make it better. I did not feel equipped in any way to do this. I didn't want to ask him questions, to make it worse. I just wanted to let him grieve with his family. I wanted to leave.

Gradually, those in the room lost interest in me and sank back into their grief. The man seemed exhausted from crying, as though retelling his story had taken what little energy remained. He'd had just enough left to tell me so I could pass it on. At the beginning of the war in Syria, everything was so closely controlled, the number of independent journalists inside the country so few, that verifiable information became almost a currency, a rare commodity that had to be protected at all costs. It felt like he'd handed me a precious parcel, which was now my duty to smuggle out of the country.

When the story ran in the foreign section of *The Times* the next day (heavily edited by someone on the news desk who could actually write), the guilt I felt dissipated slightly. I realized the power a job in journalism could have. I also realized I felt comfortable with sadness, and that a job that brought me close to it somehow felt right. That may sound like an odd thing to say, but I guess to me where there's feeling, there's meaning, and I wanted a job I cared about. Getting into Syria, meeting this man, writing his story, all of it was laden with emotions. With fear, yes. And huge sadness, of course. But I looked at this job in contrast to what I felt would be the mundane, emotionless world of a job behind a desk. (I have since realized, dear reader, that not every desk job is as horrible as I describe here. These are simply the feelings I had when I was twenty-four!) The final feeling I had was of a kind of redemption: a tiny feeling that for this one man, at least, the story of his son's life and death had been communicated, and that it might contribute to the world caring about the situation just a little longer.

I spent the rest of that year back and forth between Syria and London, trying to get commissions from newspapers and broadcasters. My student visa was still valid for a while, and I wanted to make the most of it. But every trip became more of a risk.

Later that summer, I was alone in the car with one activist, driving back to Damascus from a town in the north. There is one road that connects the capital with the north of the country, and all along it were checkpoints. Every few miles, we'd roll up to one of these desert posts to have our papers checked. The activist was an academic at a university, which carries a certain level of prestige in Syria. At each checkpoint, we were waved through quite quickly by the young conscripts who didn't know any better. Being an academic was a perfect cover for someone so key to the activities of the resistance.

But at one checkpoint about halfway back to the capital, our luck ran out. The soldier on guard wasn't a clueless conscript but a more senior military commander, and he could immediately sense something was wrong, with a foreign-looking kid this far outside of Damascus. The soldier was fat and sweaty, with thin hair combed optimistically over his shiny head. "Don't speak any Arabic," my activist friend said quickly out of the side of his mouth as we came to a stop. The soldier motioned to roll down the window and peered inside the car. "Come with me," he said to my friend. My friend did as he was told, and the two of them disappeared into a small shack by the side of the road. I was left alone in the car, with another soldier standing a few feet away. I sat in that boiling hot front seat, melting in fear and anticipation of what would come. My laptop was stuffed underneath me, full of images and videos of the protests I'd seen. I had notes on the people I'd met and the stories they'd told me. My phone, which was now burning a hole in my pocket, had the numbers of those who'd been helping me and messages the regime could use against them. I felt sick with panic, and an overwhelming sense of stupidity. Why had I put myself in this position? Why would I put my family through this?

I moved my hand slowly into my pocket to find my phone—an early iPhone—and looked down briefly to navigate to the camera reel. I found a way to slowly swipe to each image without looking, and delete. One by one, and looking dead ahead, I sat for what seemed like hours—but was only about twenty minutes—trying to erase any incriminating footage. As I look back now, it's clear to me that finding a way to send or store all this material, and not travel with it, would have been the sensible option. But I was clueless. And deleting these images would have made no difference if they'd decided to take the phone off me or search the car. I felt helpless but wanted to do something to help myself.

Finally, the two men emerged from the small building, and my friend walked with his head slightly bowed back to the car and got behind the wheel in silence. The soldier walked slowly around to my side, stuck his huge sweaty head into the car, and kissed me slowly and purposefully on the forehead. He pulled back, looked at me very closely, and said in Arabic, "Welcome," before tapping on the roof. We rolled away slowly, back down the dusty verge and onto the main road. The two of us sat in silence for a few minutes, until the activist turned to me and said, "You go back to London. Tonight."

I still don't know what was said in that room. Was the soldier asking for my details? Was he taking down those of my friend? Was my friend threatened? Was there violence? Whatever was said, it ensured I got out safely, and I am forever indebted to the activist who, by helping me, found himself in trouble. When I got back to Damascus, I spent a sleepless night in one of the group's safe houses, alert to any sounds on the stairs outside, before heading to Lebanon the next morning. I'd given a brief account of what happened to a family friend who was about my mother's age, and when she came to get me from the station, she scolded me like the child I was. "What were you thinking going there?! Are you crazy?" I guess I was, a bit. Or just young and with no real concept of the dangers I truly faced. But that was to be my last trip to Syria as a freelancer. The nausea I'd felt at that checkpoint stayed with me—and stays with me now—as a warning against heading into dangerous situations without planning properly. It is also a reminder of the danger so many people face, daily, all around the world. And a reminder of the relative comfort and security of my life.

And so, here I am again, in a region I love so much, but this time in my job as a foreign correspondent for ABC News. This morning we went to a refugee camp that some of the thousands who fled Turkey's invasion now call home. We met an elderly man, his face brown and creased, who held up a picture of his son, Sakhr. Sakhr was killed fighting for the Syrian Democratic Forces against the Turks back in October. He was my age. His father described getting a call from Sakhr's friend, saying he'd been hit. And the friend was with him, holding him as he bled to death. Sakhr's father told me he wasn't even able to stop and say goodbye to his son—because he was running for his own life—as the Turkish invasion intensified around him. Sakhr's body was never recovered. All this man has left is the tent provided by a charity, and his two other sons and their families. They all look after Marianne, Sakhr's baby daughter, who was only four months old when her father died in battle. They've left behind a family-run bakery—in business for forty years—as well as their homes and every single thing they owned.

This is the meaning of loss. This is also the meaning of resilience, which I'm powerfully struck by when I meet people in all kinds of devastating circumstances all over the world. Resilience is, in many ways, the flip side of depression.

Now, I should make clear at the outset: People like Sakhr's family will live with the trauma of his death for the rest of their lives. And many will experience mental illness. One 2020 study found that rates of depression, anxiety, and PTSD among Syrian refugees resettled in high-income Western countries are significantly higher than in the general population, with PTSD specifically up to ten times more likely. But whatever the impact of their experience, many of the people I have met have *also* demonstrated extraordinary resilience, even if they themselves may not be aware of it.

Something strange happens to me when I'm working in places like this. I find I'm able to connect enough to empathize—which is really the most important part of this job—but the often frenzied and rushed nature of our work means people's stories don't affect me too deeply in the moment. It's only later that I really think about what I've seen and heard. And then I wonder: How are these people surviving this? How can they have gone through so much for so long? How are they still able to put one foot in front of the other?

There are three people I've met during the course of my work who really get me thinking about these questions. In Grozny about five years ago, I followed the story of Amin, a young man who the Chechen authorities suspected of being gay. Chechnya has sadly become the archetype of unreconstructed misogyny and bigotry, most recently evinced in the rounding up and abuse—and sometimes murder—of LGBTQ+ people.

Amin was given up to the authorities by his own family and tortured for two weeks. He was waterboarded and electrocuted, and they even performed mock executions on him. But he survived. And when he was eventually released, he found the courage not just to escape, but to speak publicly about his experiences. Seeing that anonymous testimony of this barbarism was not changing things in his country, he decided to reveal his identity to the media. With us, and with other news organizations. Given those who escape Chechnya are often hunted down by the authorities, this is the kind of bravery that his tormentors can only dream of having.

The second is Mykola, who I met on a freezing cold March morning in Bucha, Ukraine. When Russian troops rolled into his town, a group of them came to his apartment building and demanded all the residents stand out in the yard. They told the men age fifty or under to step forward. They were shot on the spot. Mykola is fifty-three. He told me this holding up three fingers with a shaking hand. We stood just a few feet from the shallow graves in which he was forced to bury the other men. Planks of wood affixed with pictures of the Virgin Mary were jabbed into the barren earth to mark each one. Afterward, he and his neighbors took refuge in the basement of their apartment block. They would hear these groups of young men, the Russian troops, drunk on cheap spirits and power, squatting in their homes. One of them, apparently on a whim, threw a grenade into the stairwell of the basement, killing another of Mykola's friends. He was forced to pick up the pieces of his friend's body, put them in a bag, and bury him alongside the other murdered men.

I went back to see Mykola on a later visit to Ukraine. Summer had come. The area around his building was lush with greenery and flowers, and Mykola had started to put his life back together. He had retaken possession of his apartment, filled in the bullet holes in the walls, and reached out to the authorities for counseling, among other sources of help. He had been through literally unimaginable trauma, and yet we smiled and drank coffee together at his kitchen table. He was so happy to see me and the rest of my team, his blue eyes shining with joy at our return. Of course, this was just one day of many, and he will likely deal with the dark memories of that time for the rest of his life. He told us all about the difficulties he's had and the sadness he now experiences. But on the drive back to Kyiv, the team could only marvel at how he'd got on with life. It would be too much to say he had moved past his trauma, but he was enduring. Our own issues paled into insignificance when we met people like Mykola, and yet he had affected us all with his warmth and dignity.

The third person is a colleague. It can be rare to make close friends in your mid-thirties. So much of life has been settled, relationships fixed. But when Maggie Rulli arrived in London to join ABC News's foreign reporting team a few years ago, I knew I'd made a special friend. The thing about Maggie is that she is relentlessly happy. I hope she doesn't mind me saying it's become kind of a running joke at ABC, on both sides of the Atlantic. She is like a Labrador in human form. Her favorite flower is the sunflower, and that says so much about her: She's a beaming ray of light. This is not to say she isn't an intelligent, complex, deep-thinking individual. And, of course, she can get upset or angry. But her general disposition is one of joy. We've had chats about what I call her "happy gene," where she gets it from, and how I wish I had it. She doesn't seem to allow events to impact her in the way they can me. She has a form of resilience that I'm convinced is genetic. A capacity to overcome, and not dwell.

Now, I don't know if Amin or Mykola have a genetic predisposition to happiness. They are both clearly still dealing with the effects of life-altering hardship. Maggie has also, fortunately, not experienced any of the same traumas. But I do wonder if in their own ways, they have all been hardwired differently. I'd like to know: If there is a hereditary capacity for depression or other mental illness, is there a similar mechanism for people who can endure trauma, like Amin and Mykola? And for those who do not allow the everyday grievances of life to get them down, like Maggie?

The World Happiness Report 2022—yes, it exists—has sought to answer this question. Its work is based on the Minnesota twin study carried out between 1970 and 1984, during which identical and nonidentical twins were followed to assess their well-being. The report found that identical twins raised apart turned out to be more similar with regard to their well-being compared to nonidentical twins raised together. This finding was the first indication that genetic differences between people are a source of differences in happiness. Subsequent studies correlate and show—as is the case with mental illness—about 40 percent of the differences in happiness are accounted for by genetics, while the rest is environmental.

As we have seen, the interplay between our genes and the environment is complex and always changing. The World Happiness Report found that our genetic predisposition to happiness, like our genetic predisposition to mental illness, is activated by our environment. But if you have *more* of a predisposition, it's possible the environment may not need to work so hard. In short, Maggie is likely wired to become happy more easily than me. Researchers also pointed to a kind of positivity loop that those with these genetic predispositions may benefit from: If you inherit happiness from your parents, it's more likely you were raised in a happy environment. This means you not only have the juice inside you—you were probably showered in it growing up, too.

Researchers have gone further than just group tests to demonstrate probability. Those genome-wide association studies that helped scientists understand the heritability of depression also allowed millions of genetic variants to be measured for happiness. They led to the identification of three locations on the human genome associated with what researchers broadly define as well-being but which has been more closely described as life satisfaction and positive affect. The latest studies have produced the well-being spectrum: 148 variants total on these locations were found for life satisfaction, and 191 for positive affect. Brain mapping has found evidence for enrichment of genes differentially expressed in the subiculum, which is part of the hippocampus in the brain. As we saw from Eric Kandel's work and others', this is an area long thought important for the storage of memory.

A 2012 study by Jan-Emmanuel De Neve at the London School of Economics boiled things down even further, and perhaps got as close as anyone has come to finding a "happy gene." De Neve studied 2,500 Americans and revealed that two variants of a specific gene seem to impact how satisfied people were with their lives. The 5-HTT gene is involved in the transportation of serotonin in the brain and can be "long" or "short," which contributes to its ability to provide serotonin. De Neve found that among those tested who said that they were "very satisfied" with life, 35.4 percent had two "long" variants of the gene, while 19.1 percent had two "short" versions. Of those who were "dissatisfied" with life, 20 percent had two long versions of the gene, while 26.2 percent had two short versions. De Neve says that all things being equal, having one long version of the gene increased the likelihood of a person claiming satisfaction by 8.5 percent. And in those who had two long versions, it was 17.3 percent. Like all scientists in this field, he urged profound caution against overextrapolation. That standard, "all things being equal," is clearly not possible when measuring the experiences of humans in the world. In short, De Neve found *a* "happy gene." I'm making specific use of the word *a* and not *the* because, as we've seen, predispositions to certain moods are likely polygenic. That is, there isn't just one gene responsible. But I said it was as close as anyone has come to finding a happy gene because, unfortunately, subsequent genome-wide association studies, which tested far more people than those who took part in De Neve's study, did not identify 5-HTT or any of the other specific candidate genes for mood. Nevertheless, I include the study here because it demonstrates that gene expression is as important as the core function of a particular gene.

Another study of the same 5-HTT gene is also worth highlighting. Oncologist and author Siddhartha Mukherjee is one of the most thoughtful and deep-thinking medical professionals, and one who has sought clinical answers to his own sadness. He has considered the 5-HTT gene not as a marker of happiness, but of resilience. In *The Gene*, he highlights a 2010 study that took place in an impoverished rural community in Georgia in the USA. The Strong African American Families project randomly divided six hundred families with adolescent children into two groups. One group received seven weeks of intensive support that included education, counseling, and structured social interventions to prevent alcoholism and drug use. The control group received minimal support. Children in both groups then had their 5-HTT gene sequenced.

Like in De Neve's work, this study found stark differences between those with "long" and "short" versions of the 5-HTT gene. Those with the "short" version were more likely to turn to alcohol or drug abuse, skip class, and display antisocial behavior. This was something researchers had expected. But what the study also showed was that these very same children were the ones more likely to respond to interventions.

Mukherjee explains it: "The short variant encodes a hyperactive 'stress sensor' for psychic susceptibility, but also a sensor most likely to respond to an intervention that targets the susceptibility. The most brittle or fragile forms of psyche are most likely to be distorted by trauma-inducing environments—but are also most likely to be restored by targeted interventions.

"It is as if resilience itself has a genetic core: some humans are born resilient (but are less responsive to interventions), while others are born sensitive (but are more likely to respond to changes in their environments)."

Mukherjee traces the silver lining of our genetic code. Some of us may be born without as many tools to survive. But that very absence may spur us on to make the changes we need. In some ways, whether or not 5-HTT is the right gene to focus on is immaterial. The underlying principle still stands: A genetic predisposition does not doom you. And if the body takes with one hand, it may give back with the other.

Let's return to David Sinclair, the Harvard professor who says we can reverse our biological age. He makes the explicit link between our genes and our health and says that epigenetic expression—how our genes activate—can be controlled by our behaviors. Researchers started looking for "longevity genes" almost as soon as the human genome was mapped. A scientific route to eternal life seemed extremely attractive, not to mention lucrative. Billionaires with perhaps a little too much money and time now spend a lot of energy working out how they might live forever. I read a story the other day of one particular businessman who harvests plasma from his own children and forces his entire household to go to sleep at seven p.m., no matter what they may be in the middle of doing. Don't worry—I'm not nearly that extreme. But I do want to find ways to improve my genetic capacity to better overcome or endure trauma.

It all comes down to sirtuins, a family of seven proteins that contribute to a variety of biological processes concerned with antiaging, like metabolic regulation, stress responses, and cell regeneration. Working out ways to activate these proteins, says Sinclair, is the path to a healthier life. Our body needs help in clearing out dead cells in order to avoid major disease, and sirtuins, often called "the guardians of the genome," help in this process and can also reduce the rate at which cells divide. They are relevant to us here because they assist epigenetic processes, where genes have tags that can turn the genes' expression "on" or "off." Sirtuins provide the chemicals that move those tags around, and therefore help to control gene activation. In short, the more sirtuins you generate, the better your body will be able to control its epigenetic processes.

What Sinclair's work shows is how our genetic processes can be influenced by our behaviors. It shows how our bodies are able to respond on a genetic level—able to reinterpret our DNA—and keep us away from serious illness. And it shows me how it is within my power to keep my body, and therefore my mind, protected from triggering whatever predispositions I have. When viewed in this way, I am not "coping" with a history of mental illness—I am helping to break the cycle for a future generation. Sinclair's work primarily targets age-related illnesses like heart disease and cancer. But there is significant crossover into the world of psychiatric health because, as we've seen, our bodily immunity, our gut health, and our brains are all inextricably linked.

This book has hopefully demonstrated for you the new ways in which mental illness is being interpreted and treated, and in that sense it may have offered some help to those of you living with mental illness. But you may also have picked up this book hoping to help someone you know who is in crisis right now. I couldn't think of anyone more suited to helping with this than Joy Hibbins, the founder of UK organization Suicide Crisis Centre and an authority on suicide prevention and intervention. After a traumatic life event, Joy wanted to end her life and was admitted into psychiatric care. Afterward, she started Suicide Crisis Centre to help those who might be in the same position. There are few people more committed to ensuring those dealing with significant mental health crises are being cared for.

"There's so much advice to give," she says. "There's a history of bipolar disorder in my family, and I was diagnosed in 2015. I was in complete denial about it and couldn't see how it fit. Over time I did, and then I started to develop strategies to deal with it. Knowing that I was going to have future depressive episodes meant that I started to plan. I thought, 'If these are going to happen in the future, I want to think of strategies that are going to stop me from going that low.'" Joy says she encourages everyone to try to develop their own strategies that they can use when they notice depressive moments approaching.

"If you're supporting someone who is really depressed, it's important to remember that the person starts to think in a completely different way. They may start to think of themselves as completely worthless. So what friends and family can do is to not just remind the person of their positive qualities, but provide evidence of those qualities." If you are able to give the person tangible examples, says Joy, the person will not be able to dismiss them as merely kind words.

Joy also says it's important not to focus on the things a person has done in their life, but rather their innate personal qualities. "These are separate from anything they achieve in life. Because sometimes it's the achievements and the striving that become part of the struggle. And so, it's about ensuring that they know they have a value and a worth that transcends anything that they do."

One of the areas in which Joy is most interested is the suicides of people who apparently showed no signs of depression. This is a refrain you often hear when a person ends their life—especially young people: "They seemed so happy, I just can't believe it." I've lost count of the number of times I've heard or read that response. Joy calls this a "suppress and carry on" coping style, which can mean that the person with depression never has the opportunity to process adverse life events or ventilate the painful emotions those events can trigger. "They may be carrying the pain inside them for years. They may seem like independent or confident people, but sometimes that very independence was born of necessity. The self-reliance part of a coping mechanism developed in childhood means that by the time they reach adulthood, they have never learned to ask for help.

"Self-reliance is usually greatly admired and encouraged," continues Joy. "Being self-reliant can be a very positive quality—but not if you are so self-reliant that you never learn to seek help."

Joy works in a much more tenacious and proactive way than many psychiatric services. "Currently, in psychiatric services, there's very much a focus on patients taking the initiative. A phrase they like to use a lot is 'taking responsibility.' Particularly when individuals are frequently accessing services. You're expected to try and navigate your own way out of it. I struggle with that approach.

"We attend many inquests into suicides, and one of the things we've seen is that in many of these cases, clinicians were trying to encourage 'more responsibility.' But when you are in a suicidal crisis, almost always your thinking is entirely altered. So it is incredibly difficult to navigate your way out if your thinking is impaired.

"Another of the differences is the clinical distance," she says. "I don't say that as a criticism—it can be about self-protection or fears that the relationship may be misunderstood—but what I found when I was in care years ago was that clinical distance left me in that same detached place. When you are in a suicidal crisis, you find you are unconsciously detaching from everyone and everything around you. And that clinical distance just adds to that. And so what we do is work tenaciously to build a strong connection with our clients—a strong connection of trust where they know that we care about them, and we care about their survival. We can't be with them twenty-four hours a day, we can only spend perhaps an hour or a little more with them. But if you have that strong connection, it can hold them in the twenty-three hours you are not with them."

Joy has advised the UK government and health services on ways they can improve care. One of the most significant changes for which she advocates is more inpatient psychiatric care. "It's kind of out of step with current thinking, but I think for some people, a psychiatric hospital is the right place, and the most beneficial place. And I don't think governments understand this. There are so many media reports about failings in these institutions, and so pretty much all the focus is about how negative these places are. I think very differently, I think they are lifesaving. And a lot of patients actually want to be admitted.

"I was sectioned [committed], and I know it's horrible, because your liberty is being taken away. But once I'd adapted to my environment, I found it incredibly helpful. One of the most therapeutic aspects is the community that formed and supported each other. And it's not often talked about. That protected my life at that time. I look back quite fondly on it, actually. I think we need more psychiatric beds and more psychiatric hospitals. And that's not about creating a punitive environment. If you're going to make a transfer to Care in the Community, the provision needs to be really robust, and it just isn't. There's a lot of evidence that shows that more people die in the care of psychiatric teams in the community than die in the hospital." At this, I think of my father, for whom this was sadly the case.

Suicide Crisis Centre works in communities to support the UK's National Health Service, providing training to change the way patients are cared for. Joy wants to help the service return to the kind of ethos Liz and Pat, my dad's support worker and clinical nurse, seemed to embody when treating him. An ethos that gives clinicians permission to take their time and properly care for patients, without the looming pressures of a cash-strapped bureaucracy's depersonalizing targets, time limits, or red tape.

We hear virtually every day in the UK about a health service on its knees, or a mental health provision cut back to the bone. From the outside, it often feels like an insurmountable problem. I ask Joy if the challenge feels hopeless. Her positivity surprises me.

"I think one of the many things that gives me hope is the individuals that we meet in crisis every day. And what we know is that they are going to go out into the world and impact other people's lives in a positive way. And for the last decade, that's something that I have very much at the forefront of my mind. And I know that we are working in a way that is different and allowing our clients to survive." What's sad for Joy is the knowledge that some people may not find her service—or those like hers—in time. But she feels that goodness begets goodness, and her mission to help those in crisis is fueling a virtuous circle of kindness. As she changes more people's lives, the effects don't stop with them. And that gives her, and now me, hope. "It's about recognizing goodness in people. So many of our clients, as they come to the end of their time with us, say, 'I want to help people now.'

"The experience of trauma has made me unreasonably determined," Joy says. "It's this sense of wanting to overcome any barrier. It's hard to explain, but I don't think I would have been able to do that without experiencing that trauma. It's really changed me. I speak about kindness, and about how kindness is lifesaving. Small acts of kindness can help a person survive another hour. And that hour turns into another day. And gentleness—it's such an underrated quality. You never see a job advert asking for gentleness. But it's so important."

The love and care that Joy radiates is the kind I saw in Liz and Pat. They were so gentle with my father. But in reading the notes about his care, I'm struck by how much other people's ideas of what was good for him took over. And when they did, how sad he became. My mother tried so hard for him to be a father and husband, but in the end, he couldn't fulfill those roles in the ways that were expected. His mother was constantly calling his doctors, asking for their assistance. But I don't know if she took the time to find out what *he* wanted. And fundamentally, he wasn't getting the round-the-clock care someone like him might have needed. Despite the augmented support he received by being part of a research project, perhaps longer-term psychiatric care would have been in his best interests. Though I now feel much more informed about his situation, I'm still torn on this issue. Would I trade my father's freedoms for his life? And what would a life in permanent psychiatric care look like?

It sounds so strange writing this now, but I think had he never married or had me, he might have lived. I find that hard to square. His art, his solitude, his thoughts—they were part of his protection. When they failed him, he needed serious psychiatric interventions. Despite his condition, he did have insight, and knew what kept him safe. I'm sad that he couldn't sustain those things. But I'm grateful that so many people seem to have taken an active role in his care. Meeting Liz and Pat was an unexpected miracle. Their dedication to their work makes me so hopeful about a National Health Service in the UK that always seems to be in the news for the wrong reasons. They identified the things that kept my father happy: art, design, the outdoors. And they helped him do those things. I'm so grateful for their help, and for the hope they must have given him.

Other people I've spoken to for this book have all explained ways they keep themselves happy. Or happier, at least. Theo, who has lived with schizophrenic episodes all his life, finds water freeing. He swims regularly. He also values being able to help others when he is well. Feeling useful to others with his condition is its own tonic. Eleanor is lucky in having the support from her father. The repeating pattern of bipolar disorder in her family has actually helped her learn how to make sense of it, and their relationship is a stabilizing force for her. The same is true for Alaina and her mother. They and Olivia have turned their experiences into work. Olivia now helps others understand the signs of severe mental illness in the workplace and gives them the tools to intervene. In speaking to her, I could also see what we had in common: an understanding that even family sometimes must be kept at arm's length, if we are going to protect our own well-being.

Alex's story about the care he and his family provide for their mother, who has schizophrenia, was incredibly moving. In many ways, their example demonstrates what Joy Hibbins explained is crucial in the care offered to those with severe and enduring mental illness: kindness. Alex and his siblings have effectively become their mother's medicine. Their gentle and caring approach is an example to us all about how to include, not isolate, those dealing with these conditions. And that doing so isn't just a way of coping with or tolerating their existence—it is to help them thrive, the way we are all entitled to do.

Through writing this book, I have filled in many of the gaps in my father's life. The medical records provided an almost too revealing—but necessary—explanation of his condition and his life. He is a much more complex person to me now. I think he's still that hero that I described, but his heroism is not imagined anymore. It's real. I've seen what he experienced, even read the words he spoke when he was in psychosis. I've understood more of his "madness," and that has allowed me to separate it from my own struggles. I've come to understand that perhaps genetically, my sadness is linked to him. But equally, it is within my power to mute those feelings in how I lead my life now.

I think in some ways, I've wanted my depression to be linked to him because I've had so little to go on, so few facts about him. It's felt like a deep connection that I've been holding on to for a very long time because I've never had anything else to remember him by. Writing this book has allowed me to let those feelings go. It has also given me fresh perspectives on how I see people in the world today. We have all walked past someone on the street acting strangely. Maybe they're shouting, maybe they're mumbling to themselves, maybe they seem dangerous. But when I see people like this, I see my dad. Without people like Liz and Pat in his life, or my mother, or the support of other health professionals, his illness could well have completely taken over and left him homeless and vulnerable. It shows me how much more we need to prioritize care and compassion when we choose the people who make decisions about our lives.

Diving into the science of schizophrenia and the genetics of mental illness has demystified, to a certain extent, the incredibly broad and therefore seemingly unmanageable reality of these conditions. When you deal with depression, it can feel all-consuming because such a huge cloud descends, and with it, confusion and a sense that it's all simply too overwhelming to deal with. These medical notes, these facts, have dissipated some of that cloud. The notes have also helped me to better understand my mother's own struggles. I feel better able to empathize with her now. Perhaps this will improve our relationship. Maybe reading this will help her understand me.

When I was filming the short news story on this topic nearly ten years ago, I returned to my father's grave. I had only been once before, years earlier, and couldn't remember exactly where he was in the cemetery. It's in a small village called Shere in the English countryside—in which, incidentally, the Christmas movie *The Holiday* was filmed. Think of it like that: a charming, sleepy, ancient little English village, with chocolate box houses and rolling open fields. But unlike the movie setting, this was springtime, and the trees were thickening with bright greens, daffodils lined the paths, and all kinds of birds sang at me as I closed the small wooden gate into the cemetery. I walked around with the producer and cameraman, our shoes darkening from the dewy grass, scanning names on the gravestones. Beloved mothers, cherished grandfathers, loyal friends, some dead for hundreds of years, others for a few short months, all of them remembered at one time even if some were forgotten now. Eventually, we found Beric James Longman—my grandfather Jimmy—and the date of his death in 1979 carved into the stone. I looked hopefully at the graves either side of his. But then I could see the words continued on Jimmy's stone: JOHN JAMES LONGMAN, written just above the mossy base. And it dawned on me that my father had not been buried here, but cremated—a detail I hadn't absorbed until then. His ashes had been spread on his father's grave. After such a long absence of my father from my life, I think I was hoping for a physical presence in that cemetery. It's a presence I've missed my whole life. These two men, after whom I am named, both took their own lives. Seeing my name on their grave deepened those concerns of generational trauma. But now when I visit their grave, I can do so having separated their experiences from my own. I can take the good that my father gave me. I can feel proud that I share a name with him. And I can leave the rest in that silent cemetery.

If you're wondering about your own family's history of mental illness, the best advice I can offer is this: Ask them. Find out. Don't let these issues remain buried as half-remembered secrets, as my family has done. These secrets live inside you, where they can fester and corrupt. Your family history then becomes a stone to weigh you down, rather than a tool with which you can better understand who you are today. When I think of my own depression and the most accurate way to describe it, it is as a feeling of inevitable powerlessness. The feeling that my emotions and my doubts and my insecurities will all control me. When I am well, I am able to control *them*.

So, all I can say to you, if you are struggling right now, is this: Ask for help, and you will find kindness is all around you, even if it seems hidden right now. The sadness you're experiencing may feel like it runs in your blood. But the answers to feeling happy again are swirling in there, too. You may carry a problem. You also carry the solution.

ACKNOWLEDGMENTS

Describing this book as "part memoir, part science" has often been met with looks of polite confusion. People usually expect one or the other. And when they know me, and my history of scientific ineptitude, they wonder if I have indeed lost my mind. Luckily, Hyperion Avenue editorial director Jennifer Levesque did not have a copy of my school science results when she agreed to publish this book. Instead, she immediately saw its potential, and so I must thank her and my agents at UTA, Ryan Hayden, Pilar Queen, and Marc Paskin, for appreciating what I was trying to do from the very start. I am equally grateful to editor Alexis Washam, whose extraordinary talents smoothed out the many, many rough edges of the manuscript. Her collaboration was an enormous privilege, and her instinct for good storytelling a wonder to work alongside.

This book has its origins in a piece of television I made for the BBC in 2016 entitled *Did I Inherit Mental Illness?* It was commissioned by my then-editor Louisa Compton, who has not only a supremely sharp eye for TV but an enormous heart and soul, which guided the process throughout. Thanks also to producer Sarah Hatchard for her humor and sensitivity. Cathryn Lewis and Roland Zahn from King's College London opened their research to me for that piece, and it is their patience in dealing with a science novice that gave me the confidence to tell that story. Cathryn was also kind enough to proofread this book and help me fine-tune in myriad ways. Cathryn and Roland armed me with the knowledge to broaden my scope and conduct interviews with specialists in a variety of academic fields, all of whom I am extremely grateful to.

I spoke to many people with experiences of severe mental illness in this book. Michelle, Matthew, Theo, Kim, Olivia, Alaina, Alex, and

Eleanor all opened their hearts to me and allowed me into what are deeply personal moments in their lives. I hope I did their stories justice, and I hope you found their experiences enlightening.

Huge thanks to my father's care workers, Liz Morrison and Pat Leung—not only for providing such candid and colorful insights into my father, and thus this book, but for giving his son some of the answers he needed. Thanks also to his doctor, Anne Salkeld; Matt May at St. Guy's and St. Thomas', who I repeatedly pestered for help; Paul Rowledge and everyone at the Central and North West London NHS Foundation Trust; the General Medical Council; Social Work England; the Brookwood Hospital Archive; the Mind mental health charity; the Genomics Project; and the many beleaguered receptionists at a whole series of London GPs' offices who got messages from me out of the blue, hoping they might have answers about my father's mental health history.

Thank you to Worth School, and to all the people who took such great care of me as I grew up: Keith and Gilly Owers, Peter and Jo Hearn, Ben Dunhill, Nathan Brown, and Fathers Martin McGee and Christopher Jamison. Thanks too to my dad's first girlfriend, Lizzie, for being so kind and openhearted when it came to reliving memories that might have been painful. And thank you for introducing me to Sarah and Frank, and for their memories, too. Knowing he had these people in his life has sweetened my father's memory to no end.

Anderson Cooper has long been an inspiration and a guide, and I'm so honored to have had his help with this book. Rob Rinder's raw intellect is matched only by his emotional intelligence, and his magic was cast over these words. Melissa Bowden is not only one of my best friends but a writer of real beauty, and I feel so lucky to have had her input. Barbara Fedida has been a mentor and friend, and her wisdom helped this book along at multiple stages. Thanks also to China Collins and Matthew

Shaw, two extremely bright people whose reassurances kept me going when I reached (multiple) dead ends.

Thorough research has been integral to this book. Ginte Priudokaite's help has been invaluable, and I thank her for staying on top of my random WhatsApp messages, sent from far-flung places whenever I had what seemed like a useful thought come to me. Thanks also to Yeehuin Chin, Kimia Mahdavi, and Giovana Chanilo for their contributions. Special thanks to Leah Croll for making sure the science in this book made sense, and to Jen Ashton and Godfrey Pearlson. I am also lucky to have a father-in-law like Joseph Brannan—both for his scientific knowledge and for his sage-like presence in my life.

Thanks should also go to my ABC colleagues. Partnering with Bruno Roeber on some of the most thrilling assignments has been a great joy, his flair and wit enlivening every story. Clark Bentson is an ABC legend, and I'm so grateful for every moment on the road we've had together. Thanks to Katie den Daas—it makes a difference to have a boss who knows what sadness can feel like. And to Justin Dial, on whom I can always rely to make me laugh, and to give me sound advice. Thank you to Aicha El Hammar, Sohel Uddin, Angus Hines, Zoe Magee, Somayeh Malekian, Guy Davies, Mike Trew, Rashid Haddou, Joe Simonetti, Dimitrije Stejic, Susan Archer, Jamie Baker, Scott Munro, Nicky de Blois, Andy Laurence, Jimmy Gillings, Magnus Macedo, Ian Pannell, Maggie Rulli, and Marcus Moore, all of whom have been either turned down for dinner by me while on deployment or completely ignored as they walked past my office—all because I had my nose in this book. From Ukrainian hostels to the backs of Icelandic taxis and everywhere in between—thank you for giving me the time and space to get it done (and the occasional laptop charger). A special thanks to Scott for the photograph on the front cover, snapped on deployment in Kyiv. Thanks also to Amy King, art director at Hyperion

Avenue, who did such a fantastic job designing the book cover, and to Daneen Goodwin and Kaitie Leary for their expert marketing efforts.

I'm so happy to work alongside US colleagues Kate Hodgson, Jasmine Browne, Robert Zepeda, Molly Shaker, Seni Tienabeso, Kirit Radia, and many others who make me glad to do this job. There is so much talent at ABC, and David Muir, Diane Sawyer, and Deborah Roberts are among those who give it heart and soul. Their example has been a shining one for me, and I cherish their support. Before ABC was Sky News and the BBC. John Jelley gave me my first job in news, Jon Williams my first job at the BBC, Jonathan Munro my first reporting gig, and James Goldston my job at ABC News. Since this book would not have happened without this career, I owe them all huge thanks. And also to Rich Ross, whose mentorship has been a blessing, and to Mary Noonan for her quiet wisdom and friendship. Molly Hunter may work for "the other side," but she and Paul Ziad Nassar show how good journalism starts with being a good human. Fergal Keane, Quentin Sommerville, Clarissa Ward, Terry Moran, Lyse Doucet, Frank Gardner, and Caroline Hawley are among those who have been unwitting examples to me, and I'm lucky to know them.

I must also thank every person whose story I've ever told in this job. Every one of them has enriched me, and I hope I've treated them with the respect they deserve.

This book has been about family, and I leave most space in my heart for my grand-maman Gabrielle Claridge. I miss her love and warmth. My dad's mother Nancy Longman was an extraordinary example of fortitude. Both of them kept me safe. While my nuclear family seemed small and fragmented, I've always been grateful for my Scottish cousins. Karen and Jonathan Marks, Ewan and Eileen Buchanan, James and Chloe Buchanan, and the whole Scottish clan: Thank you.

Alex's family is the best thing to happen to me. Suzannah, Joe and

Georgie Brannan, Lucy and Dan Richards, Laura and Simon Povey . . . and Remi, Harrison, Quinn, and Max. And of course, Mabel and Milly! I feel so lucky to have you all.

My friends are my family. I cannot list them all here. But Melissa Bowden, Yasmin Revell, Natalie and Mark Breen, Vivianne Heath, Polly Brown, Harriet Fraser, Katherine Kimber, Katherine Stiff, Mark Gettleson, Stephanie Langley-Poole, Tina Daheley, Nicky Kelvin, Florence Schmitt, Emily Strand, and Seyi Martins-Allen have been there for me when I've been at my lowest. Thank you isn't enough. My godparents Lucien Klat and Jean-Marc Perez not only are full of love but have provided an extraordinary example of a committed gay relationship. Without much immediate family around me, Lucien and Jean-Marc provided the stability and unconditional love I've needed. My godmother Nayla Milne and her family have also been a stable and loving constant. I hope I can be the same guide for my own godchildren, Rumi Revell, India-Grace Schmitt, Frank Stubbs, and Athena Daheley-Smith.

Writing this book has allowed me to understand more fully what my mother Ann lived through. She provided me with memories that I know are difficult for her. Reliving some of my life has made me so grateful for all she has done for me and shielded me from.

And to Alex. Everything I do is for you.

If you or someone you know is struggling with their mental health, there are free resources available to help.

If you are in the US and are suicidal or in emotional distress, you can reach out to the Suicide & Crisis Lifeline by calling or texting 988 to speak with a trained crisis counselor. You can also visit the National Institute of Mental Health's website to find additional resources.

If you are in the UK and are having a difficult time or are worried about someone else, you can call Samaritans at 116 123. You can also contact Mind's support line at 0300 102 1234 for further support.

SELECTED SOURCES

Introduction

Filer, Nathan. *The Heartland: Finding and Losing Schizophrenia.* London: Faber & Faber, 2019.

Chapter 1

Callanan, Liam. *The Cloud Atlas.* New York: Dial Press, 2012.

Gray, Kurt, and Daniel Wegner. *The Mind Club: Who Thinks, What Feels, and Why It Matters.* New York: Viking, 2016.

Haig, Matt. *How to Stop Time.* New York: Penguin Books, 2017.

Didion, Joan. *The Year of Magical Thinking.* New York: Alfred A. Knopf, 2005.

Ashton, Jennifer. *Life after Suicide: Finding Comfort, Courage and Community after Unthinkable Loss.* New York: HarperCollins, 2019.

Chapter 2

#TeamEBONY. "Was This Maya Angelou's Final Interview?" *Ebony,* May 30, 2014. https://www.ebony.com/was-this-maya-angelous-final-interview-987/.

Chapter 3

Kolker, Robert. *Hidden Valley Road: Inside the Mind of an American Family.* New York: Doubleday, 2020.

World Health Organization. "Schizophrenia." January 10, 2022. https://www.who.int/news-room/fact-sheets/detail/schizophrenia.

Karlsgodt, Katherine H., Daqiang Sun, and Tyrone D. Cannon. "Structural and Functional Brain Abnormalities in Schizophrenia." *Current Directions in Psychological Science* 19, no. 4 (Aug. 2010): 226–31. https://doi.org/10.1177/0963721410377601.

Van Erp, Theo G. M., Esther Walton, Derrek P. Hibar, Lianne Schmaal, Wenhao Jiang, David C. Glahn, Godfrey D. Pearlson, Nailin Yao, Masaki Fukunaga, and Ryoto Hashimoto. "Cortical Brain Abnormalities in 4474 Individuals with Schizophrenia and 5098 Control Subjects via the Enhancing Neuro Imaging Genetics through Meta Analysis (ENIGMA) Consortium." *Biological Psychiatry* 84, no. 9 (Nov. 1, 2018): P644–54. https://www.biologicalpsychiatryjournal.com/article/S0006-3223(18)31517-8/fulltext.

Salgado-Pineda, P., A. Caclin, I. Baeza, C. Junqué, M. Bernardo, O. Blin, and P. Fonlupt. "Schizophrenia and Frontal Cortex: Where Does It Fail?" *Schizophrenia Research* 91, no. 1–3 (March 2007): 73–81. https://www.sciencedirect.com/science/article/abs/pii/S0920996407000345?via%3Dihub.

Schreber, Daniel, Ida Macalpone, Richard A. Hunter, and Rosemary Dinnage. *Memoirs of My Nervous Illness*. New York: NYRB Classics, 2000.

National Institute of Mental Health. "Schizophrenia." https://www.nimh.nih.gov/health/topics/schizophrenia.

Evans-Lacko, Sara, Claire Henderson, and Graham Thornicroft. "Public Knowledge, Attitudes, and Behaviour regarding People with Mental Illness in England 2009–2012." *The British Journal of Psychiatry* 202 (2013): s51–s57. https://www.cambridge.org/core/services/aop-cambridge-core/content/view/11CA0F5B4BB9C71048121C836FEB7B9E/S0007125000246084a.pdf/public_knowledge_attitudes_and_behaviour_regarding_people_with_mental_illness_in_england_20092012.pdf.

Parcesepe, Angela M., and Leopoldo J. Cabassa. "Public Stigma of Mental Illness in the United States: A Systematic Literature Review." *Administration and Policy in Mental Health and Mental Health Services Research* 40, no. 5 (Sept. 2013): 384–99. https://www.ncbi.nlm.nih.gov/pmc/articles/PMC3835659/#:~:text=In%20all%2C%20public%20stigma%20toward,2010%2C%20p.

National Centre for Social Research. Public Health England: British Social Attitudes Report. Attitudes to mental health problems and mental well-being. 2015. https://bsa.natcen.ac.uk/media/39109/phe-bsa-2015-attitudes-to-mental-health.pdf.

Durand-Zaleski, Isabelle, Jan Scott, Frédéric Rouillon, and Marion Leboyer. "A First National Survey of Knowledge, Attitudes and Behaviours toward Schizophrenia, Bipolar Disorders and Autism in France." *BMC Psychiatry* 12, no. 128 (Aug. 2012). https://bmcpsychiatry.biomedcentral.com/articles/10.1186/1471-244X-12-128.

Chapter 4

Rollins, Henry. *Get In the Van: On the Road with Black Flag*. Los Angeles: 2.13.61, 1994.

Substance Abuse and Mental Health Services Administration (SAMHSA). "2020 National Survey on Drug Use and Health (NSDUH) Releases." https://www.samhsa.gov/data/release/2020-national-survey-drug-use-and-health-nsduh-releases.

NHS England. "Adult Psychiatric Morbidity Survey: Survey of Mental Health and Wellbeing, England, 2014." Sept. 29, 2016. https://digital.nhs.uk/data-and-information/publications/statistical/adult-psychiatric-morbidity-survey/adult-psychiatric-morbidity-survey-survey-of-mental-health-and-wellbeing-england-2014.

Duffy, Marie. "'It Will Be Sunny One Day'—Stephen Fry's Inspirational Letter to Someone Struggling with Their Mental Health." *Medium*, February 23, 2018. https://medium.com/mental-health-arena/stephen-fry-f2fc17921cba.

Cherry, Kendra. "An Overview of Sigmund Freud's Theories." *Verywell Mind*. Accessed November 2022. https://www.verywellmind.com/sigmund-freud-his-life-work-and-theories-2795860#:~:text=Personality%3A%20Freud%20proposed%20that%20personality,regulates%20how%20the%20ego%20operates.

Whitaker-Azmitia, Patricia Mack. "The Discovery of Serotonin and Its Role in Neuroscience." *Neuropsychopharmacol* 21, no. 1 (1999): 2–8. https://doi.org/10.1016/S0893-133X(99)00031-7.

Hemingway, Ernest. *The Sun Also Rises*. London: Pan Books, 1926.

Chapter 5

Mackesy, Charlie. *The Boy, the Mole, the Fox and the Horse*. London: Ebury Press, 2019.

Oppenheim, Janet. *"Shattered Nerves": Doctors, Patients, and Depression in Victorian England*. New York and Oxford: Oxford University Press, 1991.

Young, Sarah. "Who Were the Queen's 'Hidden' Cousins Nerissa and Katherine Bowes-Lyon?" *The Independent,* September 16, 2022. https://www.independent.co.uk/life-style/royal-family/queen-cousins-nerissa-katherine-bowes-lyon-crown-netflix-b2168724.html#.

Hellinger, Bert. "Foreword." In *Family Constellations: A Practical Guide to Uncovering the Origins of Family Conflict,* by Joy Manné. Berkeley, CA: North Atlantic Books, 2009.

Hilker, Rikke, Dorte Helenius, Birgitte Fagerlund, Axel Skytthe,

Kaare Christensen, Thomas M. Werge, Merete Nordentoft, and Birte Glenthøj. "Heritability of Schizophrenia and Schizophrenia Spectrum Based on the Nationwide Danish Twin Register." *Biological Psychiatry* 83, no. 6 (March 2018): 492–98. https://pubmed.ncbi.nlm.nih.gov/28987712/.

MSU Twin Registry. "Why Twin Studies?" https://msutwinstudies.com/why-twin-studies#:~:text=Twin%20studies%20allow%20researchers%20to,influence%20on%20a%20specific%20trait.

Austin, Jehannine. "How to Protect Your Mental Health When Genetics Make You Vulnerable." National Society of Genetic Counselors. 2019. https://www.aboutgeneticcounselors.com/Resources-to-Help-You/Post/how-to-protect-your-mental-health-when-genetics-make-you-vulnerable.

Gauvain, Peter. *Alastair Campbell: Depression and Me*. London: BBC One, 2019.

Filer, Nathan. *The Heartland: Finding and Losing Schizophrenia*. London: Faber & Faber, 2019.

National Human Genome Research Institute. https://www.genome.gov.

Howard, David M., Mark J. Adams, Toni-Kim Clarke, Jonathan D. Hafferty, Jude Gibson, Masoud Shirali, Jonathan R. I. Coleman et al. "Genome-Wide Meta-Analysis of Depression Identifies 102 Independent Variants and Highlights the Importance of the Prefrontal Brain Regions." *Nature Neuroscience* 22, no. 3 (March 2019): 343–52. https://doi.org/10.1038/s41593-018-0326-7.

Gebbing, Maren, Thorsten Bergmann, Eric Schulz, and Anja Ehrhardt. "Gene Therapeutic Approaches to Inhibit Hepatitis B Virus Replication." *World Journal of Hepatology* 7, no. 2 (2015): 150–64. https://www.ncbi.nlm.nih.gov/pmc/articles/PMC4342598/.

Vaswani, Akansha. "Fighting for the Meaning of Madness: An Interview with Dr. John Read." *Mad in America,* May 8, 2019. https://www.madinamerica.com/2019/05/an-interview-with-dr-john-read/#:~:text=the%20World%20News-,Fighting%20for%20the%20Meaning%20of%20Madness%3A%20An%20Interview%20with%20Dr,John%20Read&text=On%20MIA%20Radio%20this%20week,mental%20health%20over%20the%20years.

Chapter 6

Freud, Sigmund. *Beyond the Pleasure Principle.* London: The Hogarth Press, 1920.

Cole, Daniel, and Lisa Millraney. "Sigmund Freud's Little Hans: Case Study & Implications." Study.com. Last updated November 21, 2023. https://study.com/academy/lesson/psychology-case-study-little-hans.html.

van der Kolk, Bessel. *The Body Keeps the Score: Brain, Mind, and Body in the Healing of Trauma.* New York: Viking, 2014.

Centers for Disease Control and Prevention. "Anxiety and Depression in Children." Last updated July 25, 2023. https://www.cdc.gov/childrensmentalhealth/depression.html.

Stonewall.org. "LGBT in Britain: Health (2018)." November 2018. https://www.stonewall.org.uk/resources/lgbt-britain-health-2018.

Bettelheim, Bruno. *The Uses of Enchantment: The Meaning and Importance of Fairy Tales.* New York: Alfred A. Knopf, 1976.

Nock, M. K., I. Hwang, N. A. Sampson, and R. C. Kessler. "Mental Disorders, Comorbidity and Suicidal Behavior: Results from the National Comorbidity Survey Replication." *Molecular Psychiatry* 15, no. 8 (Aug. 2010): 868–76. https://pubmed.ncbi.nlm.nih.gov/19337207/.

Kandel, Eric R. *In Search of Memory. The Emergence of a New Science of Mind.* New York: W. W. Norton & Company, 2006.

Squire, Larry R. "The Legacy of Patient H. M. for Neuroscience."

Neuron 61, no. 1 (Jan. 2009): 6–9. https://doi.org/10.1016/j.neuron.2008.12.023.

Chapter 7

Miller, Madeline. *Circe*. Boston: Little, Brown and Company. 2018.

Chapter 8

Carey, Nessa. *The Epigenetics Revolution: How Modern Biology Is Rewriting Our Understanding of Genetics, Disease and Inheritance*. New York: Columbia University Press, 2012.

Bellanti, Joseph A., and Russell A. Settipane. "Genetics, Epigenetics, and Allergic Disease: A Gun Loaded by Genetics and a Trigger Pulled by Epigenetics." *Allergy & Asthma Proceedings* 1, no. 40 (March 2019): 73–75. https://doi.org/10.2500/aap.2019.40.4206.

Lipton, Bruce H. *The Biology of Belief: Unleashing the Power of Consciousness, Matter and Miracles*. Santa Rosa, CA: Elite Books, 2005.

Yehuda, Rachel. "How Trauma and Resilience Cross Generations." *On Being with Krista Tippett*. Podcast audio. Last updated November 9, 2017. https://onbeing.org/programs/rachel-yehuda-how-trauma-and-resilience-cross-generations-nov2017/.

Hardman, Isabel. *The Natural Health Service: How Nature Can Mend Your Mind*. London: Atlantic Books, 2020.

Wolynn, Mark. *It Didn't Start with You: How Inherited Family Trauma Shapes Who We Are and How to End the Cycle*. New York: Penguin Life, 2016.

Roseboom, Tessa, Susanne de Rooij, and Rebecca Painter. "The Dutch Famine and Its Long-Term Consequences for Adult Health." *Early Human Development* 82, no. 8 (Aug. 2006): 485–91. https://doi.org/10.1016/j.earlhumdev.2006.07.001.

Lock, Margaret. "The Epigenome and Nature/Nurture Reunification:

A Challenge for Anthropology." *Medical Anthropology* 32, no. 4 (2013): 291–308. https://doi.org/10.1080/01459740.2012.746973.

Ridley, Matthew, Gautam Rao, Frank Schilbach, and Vikram Patel. "Poverty, Depression, and Anxiety: Causal Evidence and Mechanisms." *Science* 370, no. 6522 (Dec. 2020). https://doi.org/10.1126/science.aay0214.

Chapter 9

Miller, Madeline. *The Song of Achilles*. New York: Ecco, 2011.

Chapter 10

Nakazawa, Donna Jackson. *Childhood Disrupted: How Your Biography Becomes Your Biology, and How You Can Heal*. New York: Atria Books, 2015.

Bullmore, Edward. *The Inflamed Mind: A Radical New Approach to Depression*. London: Picador, 2018.

American Cancer Society. "Cytokines and Their Side Effects." Last modified December 27, 2019. https://www.cancer.org/cancer/managing-cancer/treatment-types/immunotherapy/cytokines.html.

Ebert, Andreas, and Karl-Jürgen Bär. "Emil Kraepelin: A Pioneer of Scientific Understanding of Psychiatry and Psychopharmacology." *Indian Journal of Psychiatry* 52, no. 2 (April 2010): 191–92. https://doi.org/ 10.4103/0019-5545.64591.

van Kesteren, C. F. M. G., H. Gremmels, L. D. de Witte, E. M. Hol, A. R. Van Gool, P. G. Falkai, R. S. Kahn, and I. E. C. Sommer. "Immune Involvement in the Pathogenesis of Schizophrenia: A Meta-Analysis on Postmortem Brain Studies." *Translational Psychiatry* 7, no. 3 (March 28, 2017): e1075. https://doi.org/10.1038/tp.2017.4.

Miller, Brian J., and David R. Goldsmith. "Towards an Immunophenotype of Schizophrenia: Progress, Potential Mechanisms, and Future Directions." *Neuropsychopharmacology* 42, no. 1 (Jan. 2017): 299–317. https://doi.org/10.1038/npp.2016.211.

Spector, Tim. *The Diet Myth: The Real Science behind What We Eat*. London: W&N, 2015.

Comer, Ashley L., Micaël Carrier, Marie-Ève Tremblay, and Alberto Cruz-Martín. "The Inflamed Brain in Schizophrenia: The Convergence of Genetic and Environmental Risk Factors That Lead to Uncontrolled Neuroinflammation." *Frontiers in Cellular Neuroscience* 14 (2020): 274. https://www.ncbi.nlm.nih.gov/pmc/articles/PMC7518314/.

Brown, Alan S. "The Environment and Susceptibility to Schizophrenia." *Progress in Neurobiology* 93, no. 1 (Jan. 2011): 23–58. https://doi.org/10.1016/j.pneurobio.2010.09.003.

Gupta, S., P. S. Masand, D. Kaplan, A. Bhandary, and S. Hendricks. "The Relationship between Schizophrenia and Irritable Bowel Syndrome (IBS)." *Schizophrenia Research* 23, no. 3 (Feb. 1997): 265–68. https://doi.org/10.1016/s0920-9964(96)00099-0. https://pubmed.ncbi.nlm.nih.gov/9075306/.

The Sinclair Lab, Harvard Medical School. "Research." https://sinclair.hms.harvard.edu/research.

Sinclair, David. *Lifespan with Dr. David Sinclair*. Podcast. https://www.lifespanpodcast.com/.

Byrne, Dom. "How Deep Brain Stimulation Is Helping People with Severe Depression." *Nature*, April 21, 2023. https://www.nature.com/articles/d41586-023-01375-5.

Mayberg, Helen. "Examining Depression through the Lens of the Brain." TEDxEmory, Atlanta, GA. Video. May 27, 2015. https://www.youtube.com/watch?v=KwHFHV9Jfd8&themeRefresh=1.

Chapter 11

Dickens, Charles. *The Pickwick Papers*. London: Chapman and Hall, 1836.

Treatment Advocacy Center. "Serious Mental Illness and Homelessness." https://www.treatmentadvocacycenter.org/reports_publications/serious-mental-illness-and-homelessness/ Accessed July 27, 2024.

San Francisco local government: Mental Health Population Summary https://www.sf.gov/sites/default/files/2023-03/Mental%20Health%20SF%20Population%20Summary.pdf

Chapter 12

Boccia, Maddalena, Laura Piccardi, and Paola Guariglia. "The Meditative Mind: A Comprehensive Meta-Analysis of MRI Studies." *BioMed Research International* (June 2015). https://doi.org/10.1155/2015/419808.

Tomasino, Barbara, Alberto Chiesa, and Franco Fabbro. "Disentangling the Neural Mechanisms Involved in Hinduism—and Buddhism—Related Meditations." *Brain and Cognition* 90 (Oct 2014): 32–40. https://doi.org/10.1016/j.bandc.2014.03.013.

Luders, Eileen, Arthur W. Toga, Natasha Lepore, and Christian Gaser. "The Underlying Anatomical Correlates of Long-Term Meditation: Larger Hippocampal and Frontal Volumes of Gray Matter." *NeuroImage* 45, no. 3 (April 2009): 672–78. https://doi.org/10.1016/j.neuroimage.2008.12.061.

Chapter 13

Keane, Fergal. "Letter to Daniel." PBS.org. February. 1996. https://www.pbs.org/wgbh/pages/frontline/shows/rwanda/todaniel/.

Helliwell, John, Richard Layard, Jeffrey D. Sachs, Jan-Emmanuel De Neve, Lara B. Aknin, Shun Wang, and Sharon Paculor. *World Happiness Report 2022.* New York: Sustainable Development

Solutions Network, 2022. https://worldhappiness.report/ed/2022/.
de Vries, Lianne P., Margot P. van de Weijer, and Meike Bartels. "The Human Physiology of Well-Being: A Systematic Review on the Association between Neurotransmitters, Hormones, Inflammatory Markers, the Microbiome and Well-Being." *Neuroscience and Biobehavioral Reviews* 139 (Aug. 2022):104733. https://doi.org/10.1016/j.neubiorev.2022.104733.
van de Weijer, Margot P., Dirk H. M. Pelt, Lianne P. de Vries, Bart M. L. Baselmans, and Meike Bartels. "A Re-evaluation of Candidate Gene Studies for Well-Being in Light of Genome-Wide Evidence." *Journal of Happiness Studies* 23 (May 2022): 3031–53. https://doi.org/10.1007/s10902-022-00538-x.
Cembrowski, Mark S., Lihua Wang, Andrew L. Lemire, Monique Copeland, Salvatore F. DiLisio, Jody Clements, and Nelson Spruston. "The Subiculum Is a Patchwork of Discrete Subregions." *eLife* 7 (Oct. 2018): e37701. https://doi.org/10.7554/eLife.37701.
De Neve, J.-E., N. A. Christakis, J. H. Fowler, and B. S. Frey. "Genes, Economics, and Happiness." *Journal of Neuroscience, Psychology, and Economics* 5, no. 4 (2012): 193–211. https://doi.org/10.1037/a0030292.
Mukherjee, Siddhartha. *The Gene: An Intimate History*. New York: Scribner, 2016.
Mukherjee, Siddhartha. *The Song of the Cell: An Exploration of Medicine and the New Human*. New York: Scribner, 2022.
Grabowska, Wioleta, Ewa Sikora, and Anna Bielak-Zmijewska. "Sirtuins, a Promising Target in Slowing down the Ageing Process." *Biogerontology* 18, no. 4 (Aug. 2017): 447–76. https://doi.org/10.1007/s10522-017-9685-9.